"SUPERB. *HOT MONOGAMY* WILL IMPROVE THE SEXUAL HEALTH OF THE COUNTRY.... AN EXTREMELY VALUABLE, PRACTICAL AND MUCH-NEEDED RESOURCE WHICH BASES SEXUAL ENRICHMENT ON MUTUAL CARING AND RESPECT." —Wendy Maltz, M.S.W.,
author of *The Sexual Healing Journey*

"My work with thousands of men has convinced me that a majority of American males want a great deal more out of sex. They want more excitement, more intimacy, and above all—more passion. Finally, there's a solution for them and for the millions of women who want the same thing. *Hot Monogamy* is a no-nonsense book that delivers on its promise. Read the book, do the exercises, and watch out for the fireworks!" —Marvin Allen, therapist and
author of *In the Company of Men*

"*Hot Monogamy*'s sensitive, down-to-earth suggestions can help turn up the temperature in your romance. The book's thought-provoking exercises and questionnaires are especially valuable for starting discussions that might lead anywhere." —Michael Castleman, author of
Sexual Solutions and *Playboy* columnist

"A WINNER." —*Page Turner*

DR. PATRICIA LOVE, a marriage and family therapist in Austin, Texas, is executive director of the Austin Family Institute and president of the International Association for Marriage and Family Counselors. She and JO ROBINSON collaborated on a previous book, *The Emotional Incest Syndrome*, and have appeared on such network TV shows as *Oprah Winfrey*, *Donahue*, and the *Today* show. Ms. Robinson lives in Portland, Oregon.

DR. PATRICIA LOVE & JO ROBINSON

H O T
MONOGAMY

Essential
Steps to More
Passionate,
Intimate
Lovemaking

A PLUME BOOK

PLUME
Published by the Penguin Group
Penguin Books USA Inc., 375 Hudson Street, New York, New York 10014, U.S.A.
Penguin Books Ltd, 27 Wrights Lane, London W8 5TZ, England
Penguin Books Australia Ltd, Ringwood, Victoria, Australia
Penguin Books Canada Ltd, 10 Alcorn Avenue, Toronto, Ontario, Canada M4V 3B2
Penguin Books (N.Z.) Ltd, 182–190 Wairau Road, Auckland 10, New Zealand

Penguin Books Ltd, Registered Offices: Harmondsworth, Middlesex, England

Published by Plume, an imprint of Dutton Signet,
a division of Penguin Books USA Inc.
Previously published in a Dutton edition.

First Plume Printing, January, 1995
10 9 8 7

 REGISTERED TRADEMARK—MARCA REGISTRADA

The Library of Congress has catalogued the Dutton edition as follows:
Love, Patricia.
Hot monogamy : essential steps to more passionate, intimate
lovemaking / Patricia Love and Jo Robinson.
p.   cm.
ISBN 0-525-93649-1
0-452-27366-8 (pbk.)
1. Man-woman relationships.   2. Communication in sex.
I. Robinson, Jo.   II. Title.
HQ801.L6518   1994
613.9'6—dc20
93–31491
CIP

Printed in the United States of America
Original hardcover design by Steven N. Stathakis

BOOKS ARE AVAILABLE AT QUANTITY DISCOUNTS WHEN USED TO PROMOTE PRODUCTS
OR SERVICES. FOR INFORMATION PLEASE WRITE TO PREMIUM MARKETING DIVISION,
PENGUIN BOOKS USA INC., 375 HUDSON STREET, NEW YORK, NEW YORK 10014

CONTENTS

ACKNOWLEDGMENTS

My interest in exploring the connection between passion and intimacy was sparked in graduate school by my mentor, Dr. Ed Jacobs, a professor at West Virginia University. Long before others in the field, Dr. Jacobs believed that therapists needed to be skilled at resolving sexual difficulties as well as emotional ones. Through Dr. Jacobs' training I was able to blend sex therapy with more traditional couples therapy from the very beginning of my career.

My skill at helping couples resolve their emotional problems was enhanced through my association with Dr. Harville Hendrix, creator of Imago Relationship Therapy. One of Harville's strengths is his ability to combine theory with practice, creating a program to help couples move beyond conflict to profound relationship growth.

Jo and I would also like to acknowledge celebrated sex therapists Helen Singer Kaplan, whose work and writing inspired the title of this book, and William Masters and Virginia Johnson, who changed the course of modern sex therapy.

Our editor, Arnold Dolin, was a careful shepherd of this project, showing attention to detail that is becoming increasingly rare in the publishing world. We benefited as well from the perceptive comments of Frances Robinson.

Finally, we would like to thank the hundreds of individuals and couples who participated in the research that made this book possible.

HOT
MONOGAMY

FOREWORD

A wise person once said you should not commit a single word to paper until you're fifty years old. I might have laughed at those words years ago, but now that I've turned fifty, I'm more of a mind to agree—at least when it comes to this particular book. I don't believe I could have written it one day earlier. It has taken me all my years of professional training, plus fifteen years spent working in the trenches with more than twelve hundred couples, plus the wisdom gained from a failed marriage, to begin to unravel all the complexities of creating passion and intimacy in a long-term relationship.

My main impetus for writing this book came from my frustration at seeing more and more couples coming to me for therapy too late in the game. What had started out as ordinary sex differences had turned into overwhelming sex problems, and most couples had all but given up on the relationship. Years' worth of frustration and resentment had to be scaled away before the couple could get to the heart of their problems. When one or both members of a couple tried to find the missing excitement by having affairs, the resulting pain in their relationship was often immense. If only they could have gotten the support and advice they needed early on, they could have spared themselves years of anguish.

I began to see a pressing need for a program of *preventative* sex therapy, one that would give couples the insights and skills they needed to create loving, lasting sexual relationships. It was painfully evident to me that this kind of support was missing from the general culture. The popular media gave people the unrealistic notion that the way to have wonderful sex is to hop in bed with the right person. The fact that great sex requires communication, cooperation, maturity, and empathy was nowhere to be seen, and a program to create those insights and skills was woefully lacking.

Also missing from general discourse was all the exciting insights into sexuality that researchers have gained in recent decades. Although AIDS prevention was getting well-deserved coverage, new findings about sexual desire remained hidden away in the sex journals. For example, very few couples that I saw knew about the changes in desire that often accompany childbirth and nursing. They didn't know the reason for the fundamental differences between the male and female sex drive. They didn't know how the aging process alters sexuality or how a woman's menstrual cycle can raise or lower her libido. Even more important, most of them didn't realize that the burst of sexual passion that accompanies a new relationship is a time-limited phenomenon and that couples who want to sustain passion and intimacy consciously have to create it. Couples simply assumed that if they weren't consistently aroused by each other, something was wrong with them: They were falling out of love; they were no longer attractive; they weren't cut out for monogamy; they were married to the wrong people.

I began to grow very excited about the prospect of sharing all that I knew about passion and intimacy with couples who were not yet in crisis. I wanted to do more than help them avoid sexual problems; I wanted to help them realize their sexual potential, that heady realm of intense sexual passion and emotional closeness that all people long for. I wanted to eradicate the notion that monogamy must always result in monotony and that hot sex is reserved for the young or those newly in love. My goal was to develop a program that was comprehensive, theoretically sound, and thoroughly field-tested—one that would allow couples to create intimate, exciting love relationships in the privacy of their own homes.

As I developed the outlines of the Hot Monogamy program, I was careful to design exercises that addressed a couple's emotional as well as sexual needs because these two elements of a relationship are so intertwined. I created other exercises to help couples explore the related areas of romance, sensuality, body image, technique, and sexual variety, combining all those various facets into an organic whole, reflecting the richness and complexity of a primary love relationship.

Meanwhile, I made a concerted effort to ensure that the program met the needs of a broad range of couples. To this end, I supplemented my own clinical experience with an extensive search of the professional literature plus a two-year series of interviews and focus groups, ultimately surveying or interviewing more than a thousand people.

Jo Robinson, a best-selling freelance writer and my collaborator on my previous book, *The Emotional Incest Syndrome,* has been involved in the project from the very beginning. We learned in our earlier collaboration that her skills as a researcher, a writer, and an interviewer dovetail perfectly with my training and clinical experience. Although the book is written in my voice because of my role as a therapist, Jo's insights are interspersed throughout as well.

I believe that the program that has emerged from all this effort is the most effective of its kind, resolving key relationship issues in and out of the bedroom. It is also a customized program, allowing you and your partner to pinpoint your specific weaknesses and draw on your unique strengths. As you will see, unlike the authors of other popular books, I won't be giving you general advice on how to "drive all women crazy in bed" or telling you "how to satisfy any man." Instead I'll be helping you acquire the skills you need to become better acquainted with the nuances of your own sexuality and to learn how to bring more pleasure to your one-of-a-kind mate.

Note that I do not specifically address homosexual relationships in this book because I am not an expert in gay and lesbian sexuality. However, I believe that the program will also help gay and lesbian couples keep passion alive in their long-term relationships.

It is my hope that this book will be a resource you will refer to time and again, and that you will come to regard me as a trustworthy guide in what I promise you will be an exciting, rewarding adventure.

1

THE LONGING FOR HOT MONOGAMY

It was the beginning of a candid two-hour discussion about sex. Six women, five of them married and one of them in a long-term relationship, were participating in one of my research projects and had given me permission to tape the conversation. I began with a general question: "What, if anything, is missing from your sex life?" Gayle, a tennis pro in her mid-thirties, spoke first: "What I miss is the 'high' I felt when Stuart and I were first dating. I wanted him so badly that my goal for the week was to be with him, to see him. But about a year after we were married, familiarity set in, and the excitement went away. I'd do anything to get that back."

"You could always have an affair," joked the attractive woman sitting to her left. Everyone laughed.

"But I don't want another man," Gayle said. "No other man is like Stuart. He's everything I want. I just wish we could meet all over again and feel that intensity."

I'd heard this refrain hundreds of times before. Men and women alike want the security, safety, and comfort of a committed

5

love relationship, but they long for the passion that seems to come only from a new relationship or an affair. They want the best of both worlds. What they are searching for is what may appear to be a contradiction in terms: Hot Monogamy.

Unfortunately most couples can sustain passion and intimacy for only a short time. Once the honeymoon phase is over, the love-making becomes less exciting, less frequent—the kind of lovemaking that is often described as "married sex." Many people resign themselves to mediocre sex lives or look for the missing thrills in romance novels, sexual fantasies, or pornography. Others try to find passion in the arms of new lovers. Approximately half of all married men and 40 percent of all married women have had at least one affair. But while sex with the proper stranger is guaranteed to awaken the sexual appetite, it can also destroy a marriage.

I am currently working with a couple, Barbara and Rudy, who came to me in a last-ditch effort to avoid a divorce. It took them several sessions to give me a full account of their last few years together, a tumultuous time filled with fights and affairs. One of the few facts they agreed upon was that Barbara began to lose interest in sex shortly after the birth of their second child. Rudy was afraid that Barbara no longer found him sexually attractive, but Barbara insisted that her low sex drive was caused by stress and a lack of sleep. When money pressures forced Barbara to go back to her job as a dental assistant, their lovemaking became even less frequent, and when they did make love, there was little passion. "It was all mechanical," Rudy said to Barbara accusingly. "You would lie there and not make a sound."

Barbara's lack of interest in sex made Rudy feel unloved and rejected, feelings he couldn't talk about at the time because they were too painful to him. He tried to get his message across indirectly. He bought Barbara sexy lingerie and tried to make her jealous by talking about all the attractive women at the store where he worked, but those time-honored tactics didn't work. "The bras and teddies ended up at the back of her drawer," Rudy said bitterly. Eventually he resorted to criticism, taunting Barbara about her inadequacy as a lover, but she responded to his cutting remarks by dropping her level of passion another ten degrees. In despair Rudy began sleeping on the couch.

This went on for several months. Then, in frustration, Rudy began to have an affair with a woman named Julie who worked with him. Julie turned out to be what he called a "fantasy lover." Her sex drive was just as strong as his, and she delighted in seducing him in creative and exciting ways. Rudy secretly retrieved the lingerie from the back of Barbara's drawer and gave them to his lover.

The missing lingerie tipped Barbara off to his affair. Once the affair was out in the open, Rudy and Barbara began to have terrible fights, the most bitter, painful ones they had ever experienced. Barbara accused him of being a sex addict and destroying the family; Rudy boasted about the hot sex he was having with Julie. When the fighting threatened to turn physical, Rudy decided to move in with Julie. He didn't want to leave his two little girls, but he wasn't willing to stay in a hostile, celibate marriage.

Several months after Rudy moved out, Barbara began having an affair with a married man, the father of one of her daughter's friends, which instantly revived her interest in sex. "See, it wasn't me after all!" she announced to Rudy triumphantly in a late-night phone call.

Meanwhile, as Barbara's affair intensified, Rudy's affair was grinding to a halt. He was still enjoying the sex, but he and Julie were beginning to have a lot of emotional problems. He discovered that sex without intimacy was no more satisfying to him than a marriage without sex. He found himself becoming interested in reconciling with Barbara and was able to convince her to come in for therapy by using their children as leverage. Barbara's parents had divorced when she was three, the same age as their younger daughter, and she had grown up not knowing her biological father. Rudy knew that she didn't want her children to repeat the painful legacy.

During those first few sessions with Barbara and Rudy, I was acutely aware of their pain. Both of them had gone through long periods of intense anger, jealousy, guilt, and rejection. They were two fine people who had started out in their marriage with love and good faith but hadn't had the knowledge or the skills to hold it together. Instead of seeking help early on, they had blindly followed a path that led them farther and farther away from each other. It took many months of therapy before they were able to let go of their anger and focus on resolving their underlying issues.

To a large degree, working with couples like Barbara and Rudy convinced me of the need for some form of early intervention. If they had gotten good advice at the first hint of trouble, they could have found ways to revive their sexual passion. This was a lesson I had learned in my personal life as well. Years ago, I, too, had started out a relationship with high hopes and inadequate insights and skills. At first my lover and I spent hours making love, and I was as sexually motivated as he was. But after a short time my interest in sex began to wane. I didn't know why, but without desire, sex became a chore, like cooking dinner or cleaning the house. What confused both of us was that even when I had little interest in sex, I was easily orgasmic. After each orgasm I'd say to myself, "That felt good. I'm going to remember this and not be so resistant next time." But a few nights later I would find myself pulling away once again.

Before long we were locked in a battle of wills, each night facing the same inescapable question: "Will we or won't we?" He'd show his desire to make love in a variety of ways. When he was feeling hopeful, he'd ask, "Are you in the mood?" Other times I would see a certain glum look on his face and know he was feeling sexually deprived.

As soon as he signaled his interest, I withdrew into an internal monologue: "All you want is sex. How can you expect me to be turned on when we're feeling so distant? When is it my turn? When do you meet *my* needs?" I never said these things out loud because we had an unwritten rule that we did not voice our complaints. Unfortunately my one-sided dialogue only fueled my resistance.

Like most of the people I work with in therapy, I struggled to make sense of my lack of desire. I argued that I would be more interested in making love if we just spent more time together, if we weren't so busy, if we started earlier in the night, if he pressured me less. . . . Eventually he grew tired of my preconditions, and so did I. I sensed there was a more fundamental reason for my low sex drive, but I was afraid to look for it. I feared that if I dug any deeper, I'd discover that I didn't love him, that he wasn't the "right" man for me. Or worse yet, I would discover there was something wrong with me.

I still remember the night that I was so embittered by our struggles that I turned my face to the wall and said to my partner, "I don't care if I ever do it again." He didn't answer. He clung silently to his edge of the bed, feeling sexually frustrated, rejected, and angry; I clung to my edge of the bed, feeling defensive, guilty, and hopeless. It wasn't long after that that we dissolved our relationship.

As I write these words, I feel overwhelmed by sadness because so much of our pain was unnecessary. We were intelligent, well-meaning people, but we were held back by our lack of relationship skills and our ignorance about our sexuality. If someone had been able to convey to us the information and guidance contained in this book, I believe we could have found the road back to love.

Although I had no idea at the time, the problems we were facing were extremely common. In the vast majority of relationships, the sexual intensity begins to fade after a relatively short time. That initial surge of attraction is an evolutionary strategy designed to keep two people focused on each other as they begin the hard work of creating a relationship and starting a family. It needs to be replaced by a more sophisticated, consciously created, but even more fulfilling form of passion and intimacy.

The fact that my partner's sex drive was higher than mine is also a commonplace situation. As you will learn in a later chapter, a man's sex drive is often more intense than a woman's. Unfortunately we did not know this at the time, and there was no one to turn to for the advice and support we needed to cope with our differences in desire. The facts that we couldn't talk openly about sex and that we had minimal intimacy skills made it impossible for us to find a workable solution.

Through my subsequent professional training and clinical practice I have discovered ways to help couples override all these difficulties. These are the insights I will share with you in this book.

Whether you are locked in a battle, as my partner and I were years ago, or have a satisfying relationship that you want to infuse with more passion, this book is for you. As long as you have a mutual desire to enhance your relationship, it will lead you step by step to the intense, exciting sexual relationship you've always longed for.

THE PROGRAM FOR HOT MONOGAMY

One of the first things you should know about this book is that it's a comprehensive program, not just a series of observations or helpful hints. People can go to a lecture or read a book about love relationships and come away with a lot of good information. But without a structure to help them translate their insights into new behaviors, they often lapse into old habits. When I work with couples individually and in workshops, I give them homework assignments so they can create lasting change. Exercises are also an integral part of this book. At the end of each chapter you will find a series of activities that I have developed after spending thousands of hours working with couples, guiding them, listening to them, and then refining the procedures. In the process of reading the text and doing these exercises you will gradually enter a more exciting realm of passion and intimacy.

Another essential aspect of this program is that it is multifaceted. Unlike some other experts, I won't dwell on one narrow area of your love relationship, such as sexual technique or communication skills. Instead I will help you explore the totality of your sexual relationship, encouraging you to break new ground in the following nine separate areas:

1. *Communication About Sex:* the ease with which you talk about your sexual relationship
2. *Sexual Desire:* how much physical desire you experience on a regular basis
3. *Intimacy:* your ability to share your thoughts and feelings with your partner on an ongoing basis
4. *Technique:* your skill at arousing yourself and your partner

5. *Sexual Variety:* your willingness to add creativity and novelty to your lovemaking

6. *Romance:* your desire to show love for your partner in concrete ways

7. *Body Image:* your inner image of your outer self

8. *Sensuality:* your willingness to relax and involve all your senses in your lovemaking

9. *Passion:* your ability to combine intense feelings of arousal with love for your partner

These are not arbitrary categories. They are the nine areas I have found to be most problematic for couples. I settled on them after reviewing my own clinical practice, consulting with more than seventy-five therapists, and surveying an additional five hundred couples. I have further tested and refined these categories in workshops and lectures.

As you look at this list, you may quickly spot some problem areas in your relationship. For example, as is the case with many couples I see, your lovemaking may be missing an element of sensuality or you may long for more romance. *What you may not realize is that each of the nine areas plays a significant role in your ability to experience passion and intimacy.* I see couples coming to this realization every day. After going through this program in a workshop, a man wrote me to tell me how surprised he had been to learn that his wife's low body image was interfering with their lovemaking. "At first I wondered why you even included body image as one of the nine categories," he wrote. "I'm more or less comfortable with my body, and I assumed my wife was, too. Well, I was wrong. It's been really helpful for me to learn this. I thought she had lost interest in sex because she had lost interest in me. Now I know it has more to do with her inability to accept her weight. For the first time we have been able to talk about that part of our sexuality. It's made a great deal of difference."

Something else that may not be readily apparent to you is the degree to which the nine categories of this program are interrelated. As you focus on any given category, you will be making progress in other areas as well. For example, as you make an effort to become more romantic, your partner may automatically feel more sexual desire. Or, while taking the risk to try out a new love-making technique, the two of you may suddenly experience a deeper level of emotional intimacy. You will not always be able to predict where the process will lead you. Prepare to be surprised.

I have seen evidence of the synergistic nature of the program in my own life. My husband's Christmas present to me last year was a professional massage table, coupled with a pledge to give me a weekly massage. I love massages and was looking forward to the sensuality of that experience. However, neither one of us was pre-pared for how intimate and *sexual* the massages would be. One massage in particular led to one of the most profound lovemaking sessions we have ever had. Even though my husband was not fo-cusing on my erogenous zones, the fact that he was so eager to please me and that I was so relaxed and open to his touch turned an ordinary massage into extended foreplay. We moved seamlessly into lovemaking, reaching a level of passion and intimacy that brought both of us to tears. One of my goals in creating this pro-gram is to help couples experience more moments of ecstasy like this.

To begin the program, you will be taking the Sexual Style Sur-vey featured in the next chapter. This survey will determine where you and your partner currently stand in each of the nine areas of the program. When you plot your scores on a graph, you will have a clear picture of the skills, attitudes, and behaviors each of you brings to your relationship. Potential areas of growth will be clearly defined, and your strengths will stand out in bold relief. These in-sights will help you customize the program, focusing your energy where you have the most to gain.

The remaining nine chapters of the book will explore the nine categories of the survey in detail, one area per chapter. I will be inviting you into my therapy sessions and workshops, giving you insight into some of the problems I see with regularity. Since few of us talk openly about our sexual difficulties, this may be your first glimpse into the intimate lives of other couples. I will then give you support and advice for resolving these issues as they manifest them-selves in your particular relationship. In some of the nine areas of the program you may be resolving long-standing problems; in others you may be expanding on areas of strength. As you will see, there is no upper limit to passion and intimacy.

In each of the nine chapters I will be sharing with you the latest research in the field. I have included this material because it has proven helpful to so many couples. At times I have been able to resolve a sexual problem simply by providing reliable, practical information. For example, one woman took me aside during a break in a recent workshop to confide to me that her orgasms weren't normal. "I've never talked to anyone about this," she said, "but my orgasms last only a few seconds. I mean, I enjoy them, but they're no big deal. I feel like I'm missing out." I reassured her that it is the rare orgasm that lasts longer than five or ten seconds. However, I told her it was possible to increase the intensity of her orgasms by doing a simple exercise, which I described to her in detail. (You will find these instructions in a later chapter.) She was so grateful for this information that tears came to her eyes.

SUPPORT FOR LONG-TERM MONOGAMY

As you can tell by the title of this book, I have designed this program for people in committed monogamous relationships. My intent is not to build a case for monogamy but to support those who have already chosen monogamy as a lifestyle. But it doesn't hurt to be reminded why fidelity is such an intelligent choice today. AIDS, of course, is a very good reason for mutual monogamy. As HIV spreads throughout the population, love affairs now can have life-threatening consequences. Having multiple sex partners also puts you at risk for a host of other sexually transmitted diseases, including chlamydia, genital herpes, hepatitis B, genital warts, syphilis, and gonorrhea. One out of every five adults now has some form of sexually transmitted disease, and that number is expected to rise in the coming years. If you have been in a mutually monogamous relationship since 1978 and have not participated in other high-risk behaviors such as multiple blood transfusions and intravenous drug use, you do not have to worry about the risk of AIDS through intercourse or oral sex. (The same holds true if you have an *exclusively* monogamous relationship that began after 1978 and have tested negative for the HIV virus.) Couples who do not meet these criteria should practice safe sex, which includes using a new latex condom every time you have sex, using a spermicide that contains nonoxynol-9, and using a condom or latex dental dam during oral sex. (For safe sex supplies see The Rubber Tree in Appendix B.)

Monogamy not only reduces the risk of contracting diseases but can also bestow some important health *benefits*. We have long known that people in supportive love relationships live longer and have fewer health problems. We are now learning that committed couples reap subtler health benefits as well. Dr. Winnifred B. Cutler, a pioneer in the field, has discovered that monogamous weekly intercourse promotes fertility and physiological well-being in women. She also notes that premenopausal and menopausal women who have regular sex have higher levels of estrogen, which helps prevent heart disease, preserves bone mass, minimizes hot flashes, and lowers the risk of depression. A man with a regular sex partner also stands to gain. His testosterone cycle tends to become synchronized with his partner's estrogen cycle, rising when she ovulates and then peaking again seven days later. Higher testosterone levels in men are associated with firmer erections and an increase in sexual activity. Meanwhile, an increase in sexual activity stimulates a further rise in testosterone. And the beat goes on.

The emotional benefits of long-term monogamy are too profound to explain in a few paragraphs. Couples who have grown to love and trust each other over the years form an unparalleled support system. Their shared history, their steadfast commitment, and their appreciation of each other create a vast reservoir of peace and contentment. It's a comfort so deep you rarely hear people talking about it.

For these reasons and more, people yearn to be in a lasting love relationship. Even after a bitter divorce, most people quickly marry again, a growing national pastime called serial monogamy. There's no denying that a new relationship can quickly revive sexual passion. But when the drug of romantic love wears off, sex loses its zing. Before long hauntingly familiar problems reemerge. Once again you have to compete for attention with Monday night football, put up with the smell of a new perm, or try to understand why your partner borrows from Visa to pay American Express. One man told me in exasperation, "I keep marrying the same woman over and over." Years ago a comedian offered some hard-earned advice for slowing down the marriage/divorce cycle. He said, "To save yourself some trouble, the next time you feel like getting married just find yourself a mean person and give 'im a house." Texas folklore offers even better advice: "You might as well dance with the one what brung you."

Mastering the sexual dance is another excellent reason for staying with your present partner. Your bodies are complex and ever-changing, and it can take years to learn each other's rhythms. When you choose monogamy you have the space and time to develop your expertise. You can direct your energy away from the time-consuming, gut-wrenching task of finding a new partner and learn how to experience maximum pleasure with one person.

This investment of time and energy pays high dividends in later years. As our bodies age, many of us require more physical stimulation and a higher level of love and acceptance from our partners to be fully sexual. Couples who stay together have the opportunity to experience what I call Vintage Sex, a potent, intimate sexuality that is fueled by love and emotional maturity, not by youth, newness, or physical beauty.

STRETCHING INTO THE PROGRAM

In my personal life and in my work with couples I have learned that creating passion and intimacy in a long-term relationship is not an endeavor for the immature or faint of heart. People looking for a quick fix to a flagging sex drive will find it more readily in an affair or a string of short-term relationships. Creating lasting passion with one person requires dedication, a willingness to compromise, and some tolerance for emotional discomfort. Many of the exercises in this program are fun and easy, and you will be drawn to them right away. But others will challenge you to work on problems you might rather avoid. More often than you would like, the ball will end up in your court when all along you thought your partner was to blame. For lasting change to occur, both of you will have to take a hard look at your own behavior.

Occasionally, this means acknowledging that your partner has been right all along. For example, if your partner has been pleading with you to be more sensitive, to spend more time together, to share more of your feelings, to be more romantic, or to loosen up and have more fun in bed, he or she is probably right. It is likely that you do need to change in those very ways—not just to please your partner but to allow more passion and intimacy into your own life. In my therapy practice I have become convinced that "the couple has the solution." By this I mean that two individuals in a long-term love relationship become extremely skilled at pinpointing how the other person needs to change. What they're *not* very good at is making those observations in such a way that the partner can act on them. My clients pay me good money to paraphrase what their partners have been telling them for years. One of the benefits of this program is that it will help you express your needs and desires in such a way that your partner will finally hear you.

At some point in the program you may feel some resistance to meeting your partner's needs. There's a core of self-centeredness in all of us. I remember one woman who said to me, "I don't want to have sex unless *I* want to. It may be my partner's genuine need, but it's *my* body." People who have been happily married for many years will tell you that their relationship would not have survived if they had not been willing to focus on their partners' needs a significant portion of the time. This is maturity. This is love.

I want to assure you that the rewards of the program will be well worth the effort. It can turn your life around. A sixty-year-old woman called me after a recent workshop to tell me that she had fallen in love with her mate of thirty-five years all over again. A young couple who attended my last workshop came to me early Sunday morning to say that doing one of the exercises I had assigned the night before had given them a dramatic breakthrough. "Now I believe in miracles," said the woman. This program holds the same promise for you.

I want to give you a brief preview of some of the major themes that lie ahead. In the chapter on sexual desire I will explore the mysteries of sexual attraction. You will learn about high-testosterone and low-testosterone women and the cycles of a man's desire. You will begin to explore the role that sexual desire plays in your own relationship and find ways to resolve conflicts over how often you make love.

In the chapter on sexual technique I will describe a skill essential to Hot Monogamy: educating your partner in the kind of lovemaking techniques you like best. Even if you've been married to the same partner for decades, you are likely to discover new ways to heighten your mutual pleasure.

In the chapter on sexual variety I will be offering a broad menu of sexual activities to add more novelty to your lovemaking. Your task will be to select the ones that are most exciting to you, gradually expanding the erotic boundaries of your relationship. In the process you will learn how to entice your partner into satisfying more of your hidden desires and find out how to overcome some of your own lingering inhibitions.

In the intimacy chapter you will be introduced to a simple communication exercise that can have profound consequences. As you practice the exercise, you will become more acquainted with your partner's inner world and learn to feel more comfortable with your many differences. Paradoxically, as you become more accepting of your separateness, you will be able to experience a much deeper sense of connection.

Finally, in the last chapter of the book I will show how the nine separate elements of your sexuality join together to create sexual passion, that potent combination of sexual desire and emotional intimacy. When you have reached this stage of the program, you will notice a dramatic improvement in your lovemaking. You will be talking about your sexual issues with a candor and comfort level you may not have believed was possible. You will have increased your knowledge of your sexuality, deepened your level of intimacy, learned to feel more accepting of your bodies, and begun to explore new sexual terrain. As you begin to accumulate all these insights and skills, you will be enjoying your first taste of the lifelong rewards of Hot Monogamy.

2

MAPPING YOUR SEXUAL RELATIONSHIP

When I ask couples how they would like to improve their lovemaking, they often speak in broad generalities, such as:

"We don't have as much fun as we used to."
"I wish there were some way to bring back the magic."
"We've just gotten too busy."
"The way we make love is cozy, but it's not hot."
"We seem to be growing farther apart."

Before they can experience more passion and intimacy, they need to move beyond these generalizations and view their love relationship in more detail. They need to understand *why* their lovemaking isn't "hot." They need to determine exactly what they can do to make a sexual encounter seem more magical. They need to identify the particular communication problems that are keeping them emotionally distant, and they need to figure out why they are no longer setting aside enough time for lovemaking.

18

To help couples see their relationship in this sharper focus, I developed the Sexual Style Survey featured in this chapter (see pages 21–35). This self-assessment survey has gone through numerous revisions and been tested in its present form by more than five hundred people. I have learned that it is an excellent tool to measure how couples fare in the nine key areas of this program: sexual communication, desire, emotional intimacy, sexual technique, variety, romance, body image, sensuality, and passion.

When you take the survey and plot your results on a line graph, you will have a visual record of the qualities each of you brings to the relationship, giving you the information you need to begin making positive changes. You will be able to pinpoint your strengths and weaknesses with more precision and identify the major differences between you.

You will also have a new awareness of your individual roles in the relationship. All too often people focus on their partners' behavior, not their own. A classic example comes to mind. A woman brought her husband to one of my workshops because she wanted him to be a more romantic partner. She was very mindful of his faults: He wasn't affectionate enough; he didn't surprise her with gifts; he didn't pay close attention when she was talking. When she took the Sexual Style Survey and added her own score in the romance category, she suddenly realized that she had been neglecting her husband in many of the same ways he had been neglecting her. The survey was a reality check, bringing her face-to-face with her own behavior.

The survey will also give you a window into the intimate world of your partner, letting you see longings and inhibitions you may not have known were there. For example, the same woman was surprised to discover that her husband scored high in the sexual desire category. This confused her because in recent years she had done most of the initiating. When she questioned his results, he revealed to her that he had stopped initiating sex for fear of not being able to maintain an erection. Until taking the survey she hadn't realized that he harbored this fear.

Finally, the survey is designed to help you focus your energy on the portions of the program that offer you the most potential for growth. As you begin each new category of the program, I recommend that you refer back to this chapter and review your survey results in that category. If there is a considerable gap between your scores or if both of you scored low in an area, you will know to focus more of your energy on that chapter. The peaks and valleys on your graph will serve as a topographical map, helping you wend your way through the program.

As you will see, the survey is composed of sixty-three positive statements about intimacy and sexuality. There are two identical surveys, one for each of you. I urge you to take the survey without consulting each other so that it accurately reflects your individual sentiments. As you read each statement, decide how well it describes your attitudes, feelings, or behavior in the past few months. The survey measures your own contribution to the relationship, not your feelings about your partner's contributions. *The more honestly you rate yourself, the more information you will have about how to improve your relationship.*

I encourage you to write notes in the margin of your survey whenever you feel the need to qualify a response. (Examples: "This may be due to work stress." "This is a recent change." Or "This was more true in my previous marriage.") These comments will help clarify your thinking and perhaps convey useful information to your partner.

It's important for you to take the survey now rather than skip ahead to the next chapter. Having your results in front of you will bring you added insight as you read each of the following chapters.

When you have taken the survey, discuss it with your partner. Exercise 1 at the end of this chapter will give you some discussion guidelines. However, if you think that talking about the survey will create tension between you or if you launch into a discussion and conflicts arise, set the survey aside until both of you have read Chapters 3 through 5, which will help you learn how to talk more safely and comfortably about your sexual relationship.

SEXUAL STYLE SURVEY—PARTNER 1

DIRECTIONS: Circle a number on the scale from 0 to 6 after each statement. The number indicates *how often* or *how well* the statement applies to you. Answer the questions in terms of the past few months.

NEVER	SOMETIMES (OR SOMEWHAT)	ALWAYS

0   1   2   3   4   5   6

1. I find it easy to block out mental distractions during lovemaking.
   0   1   2   3   4   5   6

2. I experience sexual desire on a daily basis.
   0   1   2   3   4   5   6

3. I help create a romantic setting for our lovemaking.
   0   1   2   3   4   5   6

4. I feel confident in my ability to arouse my partner.
   0   1   2   3   4   5   6

5. I introduce new lovemaking techniques into our relationship.
   0   1   2   3   4   5   6

6. I am a physically desirable person.
   0   1   2   3   4   5   6

7. I make an effort to feel emotionally close to my partner while making love.
   0   1   2   3   4   5   6

8. I share my thoughts with my partner throughout the day.
   0   1   2   3   4   5   6

9. I talk openly with my partner about my sexual needs and preferences.
   0   1   2   3   4   5   6

10. I caress my partner all over his/her body.
    0   1   2   3   4   5   6

11. I set aside enough time in my life to make lovemaking a relaxed, sensuous experience.
    0   1   2   3   4   5   6

12. I experience a growing sexual interest or tension when I haven't had sex for a number of days.
    0   1   2   3   4   5   6

13. I express feelings of love for my partner during lovemaking.
    0   1   2   3   4   5   6

14. I pay attention to my partner's sexual needs and desires during lovemaking.
    0   1   2   3   4   5   6

15. I surprise my partner by making love in new ways.
    0   1   2   3   4   5   6

16. I'm comfortable with the appearance of my genitals.
    0   1   2   3   4   5   6

17. I am physically affectionate throughout the day.
    0   1   2   3   4   5   6

18. I share my feelings with my partner.
    0   1   2   3   4   5   6

19. I talk to my partner respectfully about my unmet sexual needs.
    0   1   2   3   4   5   6

20. I initiate lovemaking because of sexual desire.
    0   1   2   3   4   5   6

21. I make our lovemaking a sensual experience.
    0   1   2   3   4   5   6

22. I like to have sex more than twice a week.
    0   1   2   3   4   5   6

23. I bring an element of courtship to our lovemaking.
    0   1   2   3   4   5   6

24. I make sure my partner understands what I want sexually.
    0   1   2   3   4   5   6

25. I seek out information about new lovemaking techniques.
    0   1   2   3   4   5   6

26. I feel comfortable having my partner see me in the nude.
    0   1   2   3   4   5   6

27. One of my goals is to feel united with my partner during lovemaking.
    0   1   2   3   4   5   6

28. When I am talking, I am careful not to overwhelm my partner with too many words or too much information.
    0   1   2   3   4   5   6

29. I have a comfortable way of letting my partner know when I would like to make love.
    0   1   2   3   4   5   6

30. I use romantic gestures (gifts, surprises, special favors, etc.) to show my love for my partner.
    0   1   2   3   4   5   6

31. I relax and luxuriate in our lovemaking.
    0   1   2   3   4   5   6

32. I experience sexual desire without being physically stimulated.
    0   1   2   3   4   5   6

33. I put loving effort into the celebration of our anniversary or other significant events in our relationship.
    0   1   2   3   4   5   6

34. I am a creative or adventurous lover.
    0   1   2   3   4   5   6

35. I bring my partner to orgasm in a variety of ways.
    0   1   2   3   4   5   6

36. When we are making love, I am comfortable with the appearance of my body.
    0   1   2   3   4   5   6

37. I am a passionate lover.
    0   1   2   3   4   5   6

38. I maintain an open line of communication with my partner.
    0   1   2   3   4   5   6

39. I let my partner know what I don't like about our lovemaking.
    0   1   2   3   4   5   6

40. I make an effort to learn about significant changes in my partner's sexual needs and desires.
    0   1   2   3   4   5   6

41. I take pleasure in all my senses during lovemaking.
    0   1   2   3   4   5   6

42. Sex is a priority to me personally.
    0   1   2   3   4   5   6

43. I experience spiritual connection with my partner during lovemaking.
    0   1   2   3   4   5   6
44. I tell my partner about the lovemaking techniques I like best.
    0   1   2   3   4   5   6
45. When I am bored with our lovemaking, I initiate changes in our routine.
    0   1   2   3   4   5   6
46. I have a positive body image.
    0   1   2   3   4   5   6
47. During lovemaking I freely surrender to sexual passion.
    0   1   2   3   4   5   6
48. I initiate intimate conversations with my partner.
    0   1   2   3   4   5   6
49. As we make love, I let my partner know which techniques and positions are most pleasurable to me.
    0   1   2   3   4   5   6
50. I keep our lovemaking from becoming routine.
    0   1   2   3   4   5   6
51. I am free from self-consciousness about my body during lovemaking.
    0   1   2   3   4   5   6
52. I am confident in my ability to bring my partner to orgasm.
    0   1   2   3   4   5   6
53. I listen attentively when my partner talks to me.
    0   1   2   3   4   5   6
54. I tell my partner what I enjoy about our lovemaking.
    0   1   2   3   4   5   6
55. I am a sensuous lover.
    0   1   2   3   4   5   6
56. I have spontaneous sexual thoughts, images, or daydreams.
    0   1   2   3   4   5   6
57. I daydream or fantasize about romantic moments or events.
    0   1   2   3   4   5   6
58. I look my partner in the eyes while we are making love.
    0   1   2   3   4   5   6

59. I vary the speed and pressure of my lovemaking techniques to heighten my partner's arousal.

   0   1   2   3   4   5   6

60. I feel comfortable with my body weight and degree of physical fitness.

   0   1   2   3   4   5   6

61. I give my partner the kind of physical affection he/she likes best.

   0   1   2   3   4   5   6

62. When I listen to my partner, I make a conscious effort to understand his or her point of view.

   0   1   2   3   4   5   6

63. I tell my partner about changes in my sexual needs and desires.

   0   1   2   3   4   5   6

TOTALING UP YOUR SCORES: PARTNER 1

DIRECTIONS: Beside each number below record the number you circled under each of the like-numbered statements on the previous pages. Then add up the numbers in each section, and plot the nine separate totals on the appropriate lines on the graph on page 27. Draw a line connecting your scores.

PHYSICAL DESIRE	TECHNIQUE	VARIETY
2. ____	4. ____	5. ____
12. ____	14. ____	15. ____
20. ____	40. ____	25. ____
22. ____	44. ____	34. ____
32. ____	49. ____	35. ____
42. ____	52. ____	45. ____
56. ____	59. ____	50. ____
Total: ____	Total: ____	Total: ____

PASSION	**TALKING ABOUT SEX**	**BODY IMAGE**
7. _____	9. _____	6. _____
13. _____	19. _____	16. _____
27. _____	24. _____	26. _____
37. _____	29. _____	36. _____
43. _____	39. _____	46. _____
47. _____	54. _____	51. _____
58. _____	63. _____	60. _____
Total: _____	Total: _____	Total: _____

SENSUALITY	**ROMANCE**	**VERBAL INTIMACY**
1. _____	3. _____	8. _____
10. _____	17. _____	18. _____
11. _____	23. _____	28. _____
21. _____	30. _____	38. _____
31. _____	33. _____	48. _____
41. _____	57. _____	53. _____
55. _____	61. _____	62. _____
Total: _____	Total: _____	Total: _____

SEXUAL STYLE GRAPH—PARTNER 1

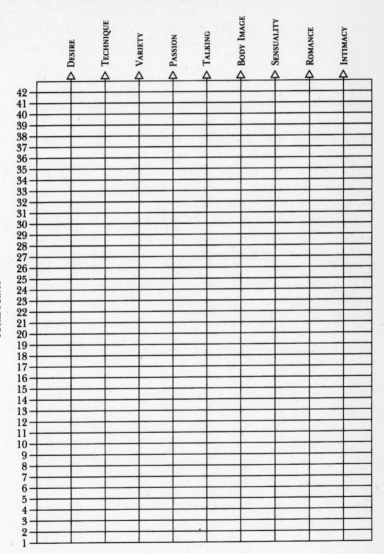

SEXUAL STYLE SURVEY—PARTNER 2

DIRECTIONS: Circle a number on the scale from 0 to 6 after each statement. The number indicates *how often* or *how well* the statement applies to you. Answer the questions in terms of the past few months.

NEVER		SOMETIMES (OR SOMEWHAT)				ALWAYS
0	1	2	3	4	5	6

1. I find it easy to block out mental distractions during lovemaking.
   0 1 2 3 4 5 6
2. I experience sexual desire on a daily basis.
   0 1 2 3 4 5 6
3. I help create a romantic setting for our lovemaking.
   0 1 2 3 4 5 6
4. I feel confident in my ability to arouse my partner.
   0 1 2 3 4 5 6
5. I introduce new lovemaking techniques into our relationship.
   0 1 2 3 4 5 6
6. I am a physically desirable person.
   0 1 2 3 4 5 6
7. I make an effort to feel emotionally close to my partner while making love.
   0 1 2 3 4 5 6
8. I share my thoughts with my partner throughout the day.
   0 1 2 3 4 5 6
9. I talk openly with my partner about my sexual needs and preferences.
   0 1 2 3 4 5 6
10. I caress my partner all over his/her body.
    0 1 2 3 4 5 6
11. I set aside enough time in my life to make lovemaking a relaxed, sensuous experience.
    0 1 2 3 4 5 6

12. I experience a growing sexual interest or tension when I haven't had sex for a number of days.

    0   1   2   3   4   5   6

13. I express feelings of love for my partner during lovemaking.

    0   1   2   3   4   5   6

14. I pay attention to my partner's sexual needs and desires during lovemaking.

    0   1   2   3   4   5   6

15. I surprise my partner by making love in new ways.

    0   1   2   3   4   5   6

16. I'm comfortable with the appearance of my genitals.

    0   1   2   3   4   5   6

17. I am physically affectionate throughout the day.

    0   1   2   3   4   5   6

18. I share my feelings with my partner.

    0   1   2   3   4   5   6

19. I talk to my partner respectfully about my unmet sexual needs.

    0   1   2   3   4   5   6

20. I initiate lovemaking because of sexual desire.

    0   1   2   3   4   5   6

21. I make our lovemaking a sensual experience.

    0   1   2   3   4   5   6

22. I like to have sex more than twice a week.

    0   1   2   3   4   5   6

23. I bring an element of courtship to our lovemaking.

    0   1   2   3   4   5   6

24. I make sure my partner understands what I want sexually.

    0   1   2   3   4   5   6

25. I seek out information about new lovemaking techniques.

    0   1   2   3   4   5   6

26. I feel comfortable having my partner see me in the nude.

    0   1   2   3   4   5   6

27. One of my goals is to feel united with my partner during lovemaking.

    0   1   2   3   4   5   6

28. When I am talking, I am careful not to overwhelm my partner with too many words or too much information.
    0 1 2 3 4 5 6
29. I have a comfortable way of letting my partner know when I would like to make love.
    0 1 2 3 4 5 6
30. I use romantic gestures (gifts, surprises, special favors, etc.) to show my love for my partner.
    0 1 2 3 4 5 6
31. I relax and luxuriate in our lovemaking.
    0 1 2 3 4 5 6
32. I experience sexual desire without being physically stimulated.
    0 1 2 3 4 5 6
33. I put loving effort into the celebration of our anniversary or other significant events in our relationship.
    0 1 2 3 4 5 6
34. I am a creative or adventurous lover.
    0 1 2 3 4 5 6
35. I bring my partner to orgasm in a variety of ways.
    0 1 2 3 4 5 6
36. When we are making love, I am comfortable with the appearance of my body.
    0 1 2 3 4 5 6
37. I am a passionate lover.
    0 1 2 3 4 5 6
38. I maintain an open line of communication with my partner.
    0 1 2 3 4 5 6
39. I let my partner know what I don't like about our lovemaking.
    0 1 2 3 4 5 6
40. I make an effort to learn about significant changes in my partner's sexual needs and desires.
    0 1 2 3 4 5 6
41. I take pleasure in all my senses during lovemaking.
    0 1 2 3 4 5 6
42. Sex is a priority to me personally.
    0 1 2 3 4 5 6

43. I experience spiritual connection with my partner during lovemaking.
    0   1   2   3   4   5   6
44. I tell my partner about the lovemaking techniques I like best.
    0   1   2   3   4   5   6
45. When I am bored with our lovemaking, I initiate changes in our routine.
    0   1   2   3   4   5   6
46. I have a positive body image.
    0   1   2   3   4   5   6
47. During lovemaking I freely surrender to sexual passion.
    0   1   2   3   4   5   6
48. I initiate intimate conversations with my partner.
    0   1   2   3   4   5   6
49. As we make love, I let my partner know which techniques and positions are most pleasurable to me.
    0   1   2   3   4   5   6
50. I keep our lovemaking from becoming routine.
    0   1   2   3   4   5   6
51. I am free from self-consciousness about my body during lovemaking.
    0   1   2   3   4   5   6
52. I am confident in my ability to bring my partner to orgasm.
    0   1   2   3   4   5   6
53. I listen attentively when my partner talks to me.
    0   1   2   3   4   5   6
54. I tell my partner what I enjoy about our lovemaking.
    0   1   2   3   4   5   6
55. I am a sensuous lover.
    0   1   2   3   4   5   6
56. I have spontaneous sexual thoughts, images, or daydreams.
    0   1   2   3   4   5   6
57. I daydream or fantasize about romantic moments or events.
    0   1   2   3   4   5   6
58. I look my partner in the eyes while we are making love.
    0   1   2   3   4   5   6

59. I vary the speed and pressure of my lovemaking techniques to heighten my partner's arousal.

    0　1　2　3　4　5　6

60. I feel comfortable with my body weight and degree of physical fitness.

    0　1　2　3　4　5　6

61. I give my partner the kind of physical affection he/she likes best.

    0　1　2　3　4　5　6

62. When I listen to my partner, I make a conscious effort to understand his or her point of view.

    0　1　2　3　4　5　6

63. I tell my partner about changes in my sexual needs and desires.

    0　1　2　3　4　5　6

TOTALING UP YOUR SCORES: PARTNER 2

DIRECTIONS: Beside each number below record the number you circled under each of the like-numbered statements on the previous pages. Then add up the numbers in each section, and plot the nine separate totals on the appropriate lines on the graph on the following page. Draw a line connecting your scores.

PHYSICAL DESIRE	TECHNIQUE	VARIETY
2. _____	4. _____	5. _____
12. _____	14. _____	15. _____
20. _____	40. _____	25. _____
22. _____	44. _____	34. _____
32. _____	49. _____	35. _____
42. _____	52. _____	45. _____
56. _____	59. _____	50. _____
Total: _____	Total: _____	Total: _____

PASSION	TALKING ABOUT SEX	BODY IMAGE
7. _____	9. _____	6. _____
13. _____	19. _____	16. _____
27. _____	24. _____	26. _____
37. _____	29. _____	36. _____
43. _____	39. _____	46. _____
47. _____	54. _____	51. _____
58. _____	63. _____	60. _____
Total: _____	Total: _____	Total: _____

SENSUALITY	ROMANCE	VERBAL INTIMACY
1. _____	3. _____	8. _____
10. _____	17. _____	18. _____
11. _____	23. _____	28. _____
21. _____	30. _____	38. _____
31. _____	33. _____	48. _____
41. _____	57. _____	53. _____
55. _____	61. _____	62. _____
Total: _____	Total: _____	Total: _____

SEXUAL STYLE GRAPH—PARTNER 2

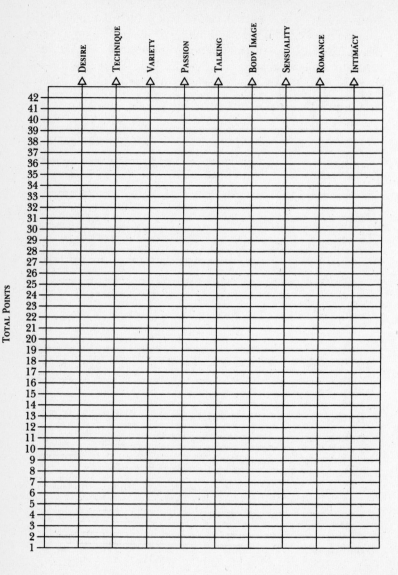

COUPLE'S SEXUAL STYLE

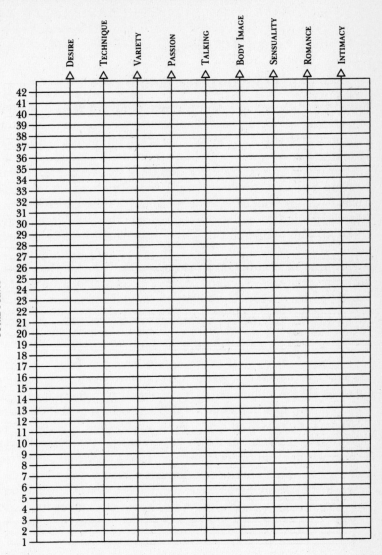

When you have completed your individual graphs, plot both of your results on the couple's graph. (Use a pencil and pen or two different colors of ink to keep your scores separate.) You may want to mark this page with a paper clip or bookmark because you will be referring back to it periodically as you read the book.

WHAT CAN YOU LEARN FROM YOUR SURVEY?

Each of the remaining chapters of the book will deepen your understanding of your survey results. However, you can gain some insights just by studying the couple's graph on the preceding page. If your graph is typical, both of your lines will zig and zag. Some of your scores may be quite low, and there may be noticeable gaps between you in a number of categories. Don't be disheartened. Virtually all the couples who have taken this survey, even the most happily married ones, have discovered that they have considerable room for improvement. This survey is designed to measure some sophisticated relationship skills. I encourage you to think of your survey results as the dot on a map that says: "You Are Here Now." How far you travel from this starting point will depend on how much new territory you are willing to explore and how determined you are to put your insights into practice. I encourage you to take the survey once again when you complete this book. Your scores are likely to show a marked improvement.

As you look at your survey results, you may be surprised by your partner's score in a given category. If so, you may find it helpful to reread the statements that pertain to that category and discuss your separate interpretations. You could be giving the statement different meanings. Another possible explanation is that you may be applying different standards to yourselves. For example, one woman was upset to discover that her scores were consistently low. Her husband took one look at her survey results and said she was being too hard on herself. He showed her how he would have ranked her, and it was higher in just about every category. If one of you is a harsher self-critic than the other, mentally adjust your scores.

Next, identify those areas, if any, where both of you scored above the midpoint. Any mutual peaks on your graph indicate an area of combined strength in your relationship. You may be able to draw on these strengths to offset areas of weakness. I have found this to be true in my own life. My partner and I both are comfortable with the appearance of our bodies; we're as comfortable nude as we are wearing clothes. This gives us a great deal of freedom when it comes to sexual technique, which helps us compensate for my low level of desire.

Now look for areas where both of you scored low. You may have to overcome some resistance to working in this area. For example, if both of you have low intimacy scores, you may be tempted to skip over the exercises in the intimacy chapter because they are likely to be difficult for both of you. You will need to make a conscious effort to work on that part of the program.

It is likely that the most conflict will arise in those areas that show a significant gap between your scores. For example, if you scored 35 in the desire category and your partner scored 10, you may have such different levels of desire that you face a nightly battle about whether or not to make love. Although you may be uncomfortable seeing your differences so clearly defined, taking the survey is the first step in finding some answers. This program is designed to take you step by step to a resolution.

Each couple's graph is as unique as a thumbprint, but after spending a number of years reviewing survey results, I have noted some common gender differences. When I look at a stack of anonymous surveys, I can correctly sort them into male and female categories much of the time. One of the clues to a person's gender is the slant of the line. Typically the line on a man's graph will zigzag up toward the left, indicating a relatively high level of sexual desire (the far left category) and some difficulty with verbal intimacy (the far right category). By contrast, the line on a woman's graph tends to zigzag up toward the right, indicating a somewhat lower level of sexual desire and greater verbal intimacy skills. This means that when a majority of heterosexual couples plot their scores on a common graph, their two lines will crisscross somewhere in the middle, forming an irregular X formation. A significant gap on the far left side of the graph indicates a marked difference in sexual desire, and a significant gap on the far right side indicates a marked difference in verbal intimacy skills. When a couple has this pronounced X formation, it's not uncommon for the woman to feel she's not getting enough love and attention and for the man to complain that he's sexually deprived. I hope to shed light on this common dilemma throughout the book.

Of course, this is not the only pattern I see. A significant number of couples are flipflopped, with the woman having a higher level of sexual desire and the man being more emotionally expressive. Other couples have lines that show no discernible slant. Although I will be talking about common gender differences throughout the book, I will also do my best to reflect the great variety I see among couples.

Starting with the next chapter, you will begin to explore the nine areas of your survey chapter by chapter. (Note that I discuss them in a different order from the way they appear on your graph.) You may be tempted at this point to turn immediately to chapters that initially appear to be of greatest interest to you, but I encourage you to read the chapters sequentially. All of them contain information that will prove important to your relationship, and the exercises are designed to follow one another in the order they appear in the book.

EXERCISE SECTION

EXERCISE 1: DISCUSSING THE SURVEY

COMMENTS: This exercise gives you some suggestions for making your discussion about your survey results more productive. It is important that you keep your comments positive. *If any tension or conflict arises, call time-out and discuss the survey at a later date.* (It should take only one person to call a time-out.)

Listen carefully to what your partner has to say. Your goal is to gain new insights. To make sure that you understand each other, you may want to paraphrase each other's remarks. If your partner reveals any self-doubts or vulnerabilities, show your appreciation.

DIRECTIONS:

1. If your partner has some scores that are lower or higher than you anticipated, talk about those areas. You may find it enlightening to refer back to the relevant survey statements and review your answers. As I said above, you may have interpreted the questions differently or may be applying different standards to your behavior.

2. Locate the areas where your scores indicate the most similarity. Are these areas of shared strength or weakness? Talk about how they affect your lovemaking.

3. Locate areas with a significant gap between your scores. Discuss these areas, paraphrasing each other to make sure you understand each other's point of view. This may be the most difficult part of your discussion. Call a time-out if conflict arises. Do not expect any solutions to emerge at this point in the program. What you are doing right now is gathering information.

3

WHY DON'T WE TALK ABOUT SEX?

Take some time now to review your scores on the couple's Sexual Style Survey under the category "Talking About Sex." I have placed this category in the center of the graph for a very good reason: More than any other factor, your ability to talk freely and honestly about sex is the key to a passionate sex life. Like many people, you may have a low score in this area, creating a dip in the middle of your graph. As you raise your score in this area, you'll find that it serves as a fulcrum to raise your score in every other category as well.

A number of important studies have underscored the importance of being able to talk about sex. In one, women who were able to talk openly about their sexual needs said they had sex more often and were more orgasmic than women who were verbally inhibited. A *Redbook* magazine survey of more than a hundred thousand married women, the largest of its kind, determined that the strongest indicator of sexual and marital satisfaction among the women was "the ability to express sexual feelings to their husbands. The more they talked, the better they rated their sex lives, their marriages, and their overall happiness." As you can see by the following table, 56 percent of the women who "always" talked about sex rated their sex lives as very good. Only 9 percent of the women who "never" talked about sex had enjoyable sex lives.

Wives Who Discuss Sex with Husband

	ALWAYS	OFTEN	OCCASIONALLY	NEVER
Percent in each category who rate sex lives as very good	56	43	21	9

Contrary to popular belief, talking about sex doesn't "destroy the magic"; it makes the magic come alive.

COUPLES WHO NEVER TALK ABOUT SEX

Regrettably, some couples never talk openly about their sexual relationship. Helen, thirty-six, told me that she and her husband didn't have one candid conversation about sex in the seven years of their marriage. Toward the end of the marriage she realized she wasn't having orgasms. "If you don't know what one is," she explained, "you don't know whether or not you've had one." By following the instructions in a self-help book, she was finally able to masturbate to orgasm. "All at once I knew what everyone was talking about," she said. She waited for the right opportunity to break the news to her partner. One Sunday afternoon, when they were driving down a country road, the mood between them was especially good. They had been shopping in an antiques store, and he had just bought her a Depression-era spice rack that she really wanted. She was driving, and he was admiring the spice rack. She took a deep breath and said to him, "I think we need to talk about our sexual relationship."

Her husband replied in a strained tone of voice, "What do you mean?"

She plunged ahead. "I'm not sure, but I think I haven't been having orgasms with you."

Her husband didn't say a word. Instead he picked up the spice rack and smashed it against the dashboard, splintering it into a hundred pieces.

These two people had been sharing their bodies in the most intimate way possible for seven years, but they hadn't been able to talk about the most basic aspects of their sexuality. One honest conversation could have dramatically improved their lovemaking and perhaps given them more incentive to stay together.

Why is it so difficult to talk about our sexual needs and desires? Considering the candor of our present society, it seems that we should be able to talk freely about sex—especially in the context of a committed love relationship. As we look around us, the message seems to be "Anything goes." On a recent visit to a West Coast city I saw just how candid our society has become. Walking across a central plaza during the height of the lunch hour, I chanced upon a display set up by the local organizers of Condom Awareness Week. The people staffing the booth were inviting people to fit brightly colored condoms over zucchini squash. The purpose of the event was to help stop the spread of AIDS by familiarizing people with the use of rubbers. The stunt was greeted with great humor. I watched a group of three well-dressed women joke with one another as they deliberated over exactly which zucchini to adorn with a rubber.

It's easy to forget how much more inhibited we were just a few decades ago. In the 1970's condoms would have been hidden in a remote corner of the drugstore. In fact, if you were single, you wouldn't have been able to purchase them in a number of states. Amazingly, it wasn't until 1965 that the Supreme Court struck down the last statute banning contraceptive use by *married* couples. We may be living in a time of relative sexual freedom, but most of us spent our formative years in a much more repressive era.

In one survey I asked people to write a few words about how their childhood experiences affected their adult sexuality. Here are some typical comments:

"I still feel embarrassed and shy about my body."

"My parents' attitude toward sex made me feel guilty about any interest, so now I rarely initiate sex."

"When I was about twelve years old, my mother punished me for masturbating. Forty years later I still feel a twinge of guilt each time I ejaculate."

"For a long time I thought a woman was getting her pleasure from the fact that I was having an orgasm. I didn't know she was supposed to have one, too."

"I didn't know women could have orgasms until I read about it in Playboy *magazine when I was twenty-one. No wonder I couldn't tell my boyfriends what I liked."*

"My parents taught me that sexuality was not a topic of discussion. It's no surprise that my wife and I don't talk about it either."

SELF-DEFEATING WAYS COUPLES TALK ABOUT SEX

While some people never talk about sex, many couples that I see are less inhibited. They can talk about sexual technique, joke about sex, and maybe even use graphic or erotic terms. But in my many years of clinical practice I have met only a handful of individuals who were talking about sex with as much candor, thoroughness, and goodwill as are necessary to sustain a passionate, intimate sex life. Most couples don't talk *about* sex; they talk *around* sex. They communicate through gestures, veiled comments, euphemisms, winks, sighs, gibes, jokes, put-downs, lies, and code words. At times the way they communicate is more harmful to the relationship than not talking at all.

Here are some of the typical ways that people talk around sex:

FILL IN THE BLANK: A great many people give their partners vague hints about their sexual needs but don't offer enough details. Their partners have to read their minds and fill in the blanks. For example, for three years all one man could say to his partner was "Be good to me, baby." She had no idea what he meant by those words, and she didn't have the nerve to ask. Long after the relationship was over, she figured out that he'd been asking her for oral sex. She said, "If only he'd told me what he wanted, I probably would have done it."

Another man gave his partner the following cryptic message numerous times throughout the course of their marriage: "I want you to want it." She interpreted these words as a request that she initiate sex more often, which she made an effort to do. But what he was really trying to tell her was that he wanted her to be a less inhibited, more passionate lover. Having "hot" sex was so important to him that he eventually had several affairs. She was devastated when she found out about the other women. Since they'd been making love three or four times a week, she thought she had more than satisfied his needs. His six-word sentence had failed to communicate what he wanted and how much it meant to him. Their relationship didn't survive the affairs.

Sara and Jamie, a couple I saw in private sessions, laughed as they related the following conversation. One evening Sara said to Jamie, "I want to talk before we have sex." Jamie obligingly spent half an hour telling her how much he appreciated her and what a fine person she was. They went to bed, he initiated sex, and Sara lashed out at him, "I told you I wanted to talk before we had sex! I hate it when this happens!"

"What!" he exclaimed. "Are you deaf? We've been talking for the past thirty minutes."

"Yes," she replied, "but I wanted to talk about what we're going to do with our current financial situation. How can we have sex when that's hanging over our heads?" Like many people, she had only given vague hints about what she required to "get in the mood."

THE SEXUAL SETUP: The sexual setup is a form of teasing, a cat and mouse game that can deaden a sexual relationship. One way to set up your partner is to say that you're interested in sex when you're not available. Jennifer called her husband at work and teased him over the phone: "If you were home right now, you could have me." When her husband came home later, she was no longer interested.

"I was hot this afternoon," she told him, "but I'm not anymore."

Pat said to Melissa: "If you didn't have that law exam tomorrow morning, I'd make passionate love to you." Melissa had been wanting to make love for days and now has to decide whether to take Pat up on the offer or be rested for the important test. She felt set up.

A sexual setup is a subtle way to provoke one's partner, and it's often a symptom of conflict elsewhere in the relationship. Said one woman: "My husband never failed to make advances when I was in the throes of PMS. He could tell I wasn't interested in sex from fifty feet away." The sexual setup is one of the many ways that sex can turn into a battleground.

Some people use the sexual setup not to torment their partners but to prove their sexual potency. Julio, a seasoned therapist in one of my training groups, confessed that he had a habit of asking his partner for sex when he was too irritable or tired to have any real interest. He eventually realized he was initiating sex simply to go on record as being the "virile male," ever-ready for sex.

THE PRECONDITION: Have you ever spent any time around kids who are trying to avoid going to bed? They come up with a half dozen vital rituals to perform before it's time to turn out the lights. Teeth have to be brushed; songs have to be sung; stories have to be read; stuffed animals have to be strategically arranged on the bed. The weary parents wonder if they will ever satisfy their children's demands.

Similarly, many people wonder if their partners are ever going to consent to having sex because there are so many preconditions that stand in the way. Look through this list and see if any of these excuses sound familiar to you:

"We can have sex, provided:
"I had eight hours' sleep the night before."
"The kids are asleep."
"We're not at your mother's."
"My menstrual period is nowhere in sight."
"I'm not fertile."

"I'm fertile."
"The room is dark, warm (or cool), neat, and clean."
"We don't make noise."
"Monday night football is over."
"We've both showered."
"It's the weekend."
"You've been nice to me for the past forty-eight hours."
"You do it my way."
"I'm not feeling fat or bloated."
"It's been X number of days since we last had sex."
"It's morning."
"It's evening."

Some preconditions are genuine and don't hide any ambivalence or unwillingness to have sex. For example, some people are very sensitive to body odors and don't enjoy lovemaking unless both partners are freshly showered. This is a legitimate precondition and one that can be satisfied with little difficulty. But when people set up a series of hurdles, there is usually a hidden agenda.

THE IMPERSONAL SEXUAL OVERTURE: Many people talk about sex in an impersonal manner. Instead of showing love and desire for their partners, they simply make it known that they're "in the mood." Consequently, their partners feel as though they have little to do with the phenomenon. Here are some typical, impersonal sexual overtures:

"I've been horny all day."
"I need to screw."
"Boy, that movie gave me a hard-on."
"Come on to bed."
"You ready yet?"
"Put down that book."
"Wow, just looking at this picture makes me hot."

This is not to say that some people don't enjoy hearing their partners talk about sex in explicit, crass, or raunchy terms. But when sexual communication is routinely depersonalized, the partner can feel used, negated, or taken for granted—as if they were just a convenient vehicle for sexual release.

We all long to feel loved, cherished, admired, and desired. Imagine for a moment that your partner is eager to make love to you. He or she is slowly admiring your body, feeling aroused by the sight of you, getting excited by the anticipation of touching you, recalling moments when you've been together. Your partner says to you, "I want to make love to you so much it hurts." A feeling of connection is created between you that heightens the eroticism.

Depersonalized sexual comments carry none of this deeper meaning. All they convey is horniness. As one woman said, "If you always want 'it,' when do you want *me*?"

TABOO TOPICS: Many people talk freely about some areas of their sex life but declare entire areas off-limits. They veer away from certain topics because they are afraid of hurting their partners' feelings, or they feel ashamed or embarrassed about some aspect of their own sexuality.

Here are some examples of taboo topics couples have reported to me:

An inability to reach orgasm
The need for more clitoral stimulation
Partner's hygiene
Erection difficulties
The risk of HIV infection
Sexually transmitted diseases in general
Birth control
The use of condoms
The need for a change in sexual positions
Oral sex
Masturbation
The use of vibrators
Desire to have the lights on or off
Sexual fantasies
The need for more variety

Faking orgasm
The need for more stimulation
Pain during intercourse
Unpleasant body odors
Vaginal dryness
Low sexual desire
Stress caused by a lack of sex
The desire for anal sex
The use of pornography or erotica
Lack of initiation by partner
The need to self-stimulate during lovemaking

No matter what the reason for the silence, when a significant concern goes unspoken, it builds a wall between lovers, lowering their level of passion. Couples need to raise their levels of trust gradually so they can talk about all areas of their sexuality.

THE VOCALIST: Talking too little about sex is the number one problem of most couples. However, some people talk about sex too freely—at least during moments of ecstasy. There are moments in life that defy words and command our undivided attention. That's why we are silent during a ballet or a concert. Can you imagine going to see *Swan Lake* with a person who insists on giving a running commentary: "The ballerina is down. She's wounded. No, she's dying . . ."?

Many people feel just that way during lovemaking. When they are being swept away by passion, the last thing they want is a question or a verbal instruction. An innocent question like "Am I doing it right?" can feel like a dash of cold water. Many people would rather do the talking ahead of time. During sex they want to communicate through short statements, body movements, facial expressions, sighs, and moans.

THE PROJECTOR: Projection occurs when you have a thought or feeling and believe that it belongs to your partner. It's as if you were a movie projector and your partner were a blank screen. Projection runs rampant in love relationships. Here's a simple example. A man and woman are driving down the road, and the woman says to the man, "I'll bet you're hungry." She is the one who wants to stop and eat, but she doesn't say so directly. Instead she *projects* her hunger onto her companion.

Here's a typical example from the sexual arena. A client of mine said that when her husband was sexually aroused, he would say to her, "I bet you want my cock in you." He was turned on and assumed she was, too. He didn't bother to ask. My client hated to be approached this way. For one thing she didn't like the word "cock." For another, if she wasn't feeling aroused, she either had to reject her partner or lie about how she felt. This made her feel trapped.

A similar example is the man who gestures down to the growing bulge under the sheets and says, "I've got a surprise for you!" Whether or not his partner finds his erection a welcome surprise at that particular moment remains to be seen.

People can also project their sexual *uninterest* onto each other. An example is a woman who's not feeling any interest in making love but who says to her husband, "You've got to get up early tomorrow, so you'd better get some sleep." *She's* the one not feeling any passion, but she wants to make it appear as if her husband were putting on the brakes.

It is common for people to project their sexual *anxieties* onto their partners. Carl, one of my clients, felt inadequate because he couldn't last longer than five minutes without reaching orgasm. When his wife came in for a joint session, she was surprised to hear what he was worried about. She said, "You've always lasted long enough for me. It's never seemed too short." For eleven years he had been projecting his feelings of inadequacy onto her.

Similarly, countless women project their discomfort about taking a long time to reach orgasm onto their partners. They assume their partners are growing impatient, so they become self-conscious, give up, or fake orgasm. A woman in one of my workshops said, "My poor husband has to work for twenty minutes to bring me to orgasm." Her husband immediately spoke up: "Who said fast is better? I enjoy every minute of it."

That isn't to say that some people aren't annoyed because their partners reach orgasm too quickly or too slowly. But many people fail to check out their projections; they assume that their mental pictures are their partners' reality.

POLARIZATION: Couples who argue about sex from entrenched positions, neither one of them budging an inch, are said to be polarized. For example, the more Peter makes a case for oral sex, the more Karen resists. They become more inflexible with each interaction. When couples are polarized, their communication about sex is predictable and nonproductive.

This was true for one of the couples I was seeing last year. The man kept pressuring for more frequent sex; the woman kept resisting. During the course of therapy they happened to spend two weeks apart, and each of them made an interesting discovery. The man realized he thought about sex less often than usual, and the woman was surprised to find herself feeling more sexual desire. Because they were apart from each other, they didn't have to defend their usual positions, and that allowed them to get in touch with their true levels of desire. Polarization had magnified the differences between them.

THE SILENT TREATMENT: In order to keep from upsetting their partners, many people keep their unhappiness about their sex lives to themselves. They assume that if they don't talk about what's bothering them, the relationship will remain safe. But leaving too many words unsaid can also jeopardize a relationship. Many, many relationships have failed because people were unable to talk about their sexual needs and desires and looked for passion in the arms of a new lover.

I have a recent example from my practice. Beth and Paul came to me for counseling after Beth discovered that Paul had been having sex with prostitutes. Paul had been unhappy with their sex life for years, but he'd never said anything about it to Beth. He told me during one session, "Every time we made love I wanted her to be more passionate, but she didn't seem capable of it. Besides, I didn't want to hurt her. She's very sensitive." Instead of revealing his discontent, he tried to satisfy his needs elsewhere. His reliance on prostitutes and the fact that he risked exposing Beth to AIDS created a rift in their relationship that took months of therapy to bridge.

HE SAID; SHE SAID—OUR GENDER AGENDAS: More than many couples realize, their ability to talk freely about sex is complicated by gender differences. One common difference between the sexes is that men tend to place a higher value on autonomy, and women a higher value on intimacy. In other words, men as a group are more motivated to establish their independence, and women as a group are more motivated to seek interconnection. These hidden gender agendas have sabotaged many a discussion about sex.

Imagine a typical man and woman talking about how they make love. The man may have a hidden objective of trying to prove his independence and mastery while the woman is feeling the need to create feelings of closeness and connection. When she asks for more kissing and touching, he sees this as a criticism of past performance. When she asks him to talk about *his* unmet sexual needs, he sees this as an invasion of privacy. To protect his independence, he withdraws emotionally, and the woman interprets this as proof that he doesn't love her. In reality, they are merely following their gender agendas.

I encountered a classic example of gender differences during a recent therapy session. A female client told me that a week earlier she had learned about a new lovemaking technique from her sister. She called her husband at work to tell him about it. She assumed he would be grateful for the information. Her husband listened to her suggestion for a moment, then said in a hostile tone of voice, "So, you don't like what you've been getting, huh?" He viewed her attempts to share information not as a loving act but as a challenge to his sexual prowess.

Male gender conditioning can make it just as difficult for a man to communicate his lack of interest in sex. A young man said to me, "It is hard for me to say no to my wife. I think I should have sex anytime she's interested because men are supposed to want it. I've finally learned to say, 'I don't feel like it right now.' But I still feel guilty saying it because I'm not supposed to." Like many of us, he grew up believing that "Nice girls don't say yes, and 'real men' don't say no."

On the other side of the gender gap, a woman's socialization can also interfere with the lovemaking. I have heard a number of men complain that women seem to think that the only valid form of communication is *verbal* communication. One man argued passionately: "Sex *is* the most intimate way for me to communicate. It shows caring. It shows my desire to please. It shows my love on the most profound level. To add words to lovemaking can dilute it, even degrade it. My wife doesn't understand that. She insists that I say it in words."

Just as many men need to be more verbally communicative about sex, many women need to appreciate the depth of passion that can be expressed through eye contact, touch, and body language.

CRITICISM AND SARCASM: With so many barriers to clear communication about sex, many people find that their frustrations build up until they leak out in the form of criticism. Criticism is a hurtful way to express one's needs, and it rarely, if ever, brings satisfaction. When people use criticism or sarcasm to convey their sexual needs, it's doubly damaging. Most people are very sensitive about their sexuality, and a critical remark can cut to the quick. Here are some critical, sarcastic ways some people talk about sex:

> She says: "I'd like to make love tonight."
> He says: "Great. I've been ready for a month."

> He "initiates" sex with this line: "Well, I guess we're not going to have sex tonight either."

> He says: "Let's have sex tonight."
> She says: "Well, what's gotten into you?"

> He says: "We haven't had sex for six days."
> She replies: "That's not true. We had sex two nights ago."
> He says: "Well, it must not have been any good because I blanked it out of my mind."

When people communicate their sexual needs through criticism, they are wounding each other in a very vulnerable area. Trust and intimacy will not develop when people are under attack, even when the attack is disguised as a joke or a "harmless remark."

HITTING BELOW THE BELT: Some couples go beyond mere criticism; they punish each other with verbal abuse. Here is a sample of actual statements couples have made to each other:

> *"Nobody would want you with a body like that."*
> *"Those mechanical sounds you make during sex are so fake they make me sick."*
> *"I can't stand to touch you."*
> *"I don't care if we ever have sex again."*
> *"I hate the way you smell."*
> *"I wouldn't have you if you were the last man on earth."*
> *"You're a lousy fuck."*
> *"What's the matter? Can't you get it up?"*
> *"Can't you last any longer than that?"*
> *"You are a pervert."*
> *"Is that all I get?"*
> *"You've gotten so fat I can't stand to look at you any more."*

A lasting, loving sexual relationship has no room for verbal abuse.

GENERALIZING: Generalizing occurs when people criticize each other and imply that the problem happens all the time. The words "never," "always," "all," and "any" are a tip-off that someone is resorting to a generalization.

> *"You're never affectionate."*
> *"You men are all alike."*
> *"You never show any interest in sex."*
> *"You always fall asleep right after we make love."*
> *"You never tell me what you're thinking."*

When people express their needs through blanket criticisms such as these, their partners feel like keeping score and then getting even.

What we want from our partners is not a broad accusation of what we're doing wrong but a positive statement of what they want or need from us. Think about how you would respond to the following two dramatically different approaches.

Generalization: "You never want sex. When am I going to see any action around here?"

Positive statement of need: "I'd really like to make love to you tonight. I've been thinking about you all day long."

The vast majority of us, no matter what our age or history, are inhibited when it comes to talking about sex. We may think we are being candid about our sexual wishes and needs, but we sabotage ourselves with self-defeating habits or share only a fraction of what's on our minds.

My many years of experience have taught me that one of the best ways for you to improve your relationship is to begin *to express your sexual needs and wishes in more positive and specific terms,* a skill that I call *sexual fluency.* When you become sexually fluent, you no longer have to guess at what your partner wants or defend yourself against critical comments. A greater sense of safety and intimacy develops between you, which greatly increases your chances of experiencing the kind of sexual pleasure you long for.

To help couples become more sexually fluent, I have developed the following series of graduated exercises. Through these simple exercises most couples can overcome their communication barriers in a matter of weeks. Even if you and your partner already feel comfortable discussing sexual issues, I guarantee you will explore new ground.

EXERCISE SECTION

EXERCISE 1: IDENTIFYING HOW YOU CAN IMPROVE COMMUNICATION

COMMENTS: This first exercise will help you identify ways you can communicate more safely and more effectively about sex. This is a simple exercise. Do it separately.

DIRECTIONS:

1. Below you will find some specific ways to communicate safely and respectfully about sex. Check all statements that apply to you.

To improve our communication about sex, I could:

a. State my needs more honestly.
b. State my needs more fully.
c. Talk about sex more often.
d. State what I want in positive, respectful terms.
e. Listen more carefully to what my partner has to say.
f. Ask my partner more questions about his/her needs and desires.
g. Be more receptive of what my partner says about my sexual technique.
h. Be more willing to grant my partner's wishes.
i. Refrain from criticism.
j. Praise my partner more often.
k. Talk about my resistance or hesitancy to communicate about sex.

Other: _____

2. Pick one improvement from the above list, and implement it sometime this week.
3. Make additional changes in coming weeks. (You might want

to reread this list weekly to refresh your memory about ways you wish to change.)

4. If you notice that your partner is making a conscious effort to communicate more positively or openly about sex, show your appreciation.

EXERCISE 2: TRANSFORMING CRITICISMS INTO REQUESTS

COMMENTS: Safety is an essential precondition for Hot Monogamy. Your sexual self is the most intimate, personal, private part of your being, and you are not likely to reveal a sexual longing or unmet need unless you are certain your partner is not going to get mad at you, criticize you, shame you, ignore you, or abandon you.

This exercise is designed to help you turn criticisms into positive statements of need. It's a variation of an exercise created by Harville Hendrix.

Behind every one of your criticisms of your partner is a hidden wish. What you need to do is determine what desire lies hidden within your criticism, then state what you want in specific, positive terms. In short, you need to transform your criticisms into requests. Here are some examples:

CRITICISM: *"All you want is sex."*
HIDDEN DESIRE: *"I want you to be more affectionate to me."*
POSITIVE STATEMENT OF DESIRE: *"I love it when you come up and kiss me during the day."*

CRITICISM: *"You never initiate sex."*
HIDDEN DESIRE: *"I would like you to show more interest in making love to me."*
POSITIVE STATEMENT OF DESIRE: *"I really like it when you initiate sex. It makes me feel more loved and desirable."*

CRITICISM: *"You never give me enough foreplay."*
HIDDEN DESIRE: *"I would like to be more aroused before we begin intercourse."*

POSITIVE STATEMENT OF DESIRE: *"Tonight I'd love it if we could have oral sex before intercourse."*

Note: Do this exercise separately. Do not share your criticisms with your partner. Communicate only your positive requests.

DIRECTIONS: Write down two criticisms you have of your partner's lovemaking. (Do this on a separate sheet of paper to ensure confidentiality.) Figure out what desire is hidden in the criticism, and write that down. Finally, think of a positive, specific way to state your desire; write this down as well.

CRITICISM 1: _____

_____

DESIRE HIDDEN WITHIN THE CRITICISM: _____

_____

POSITIVE STATEMENT OF DESIRE: _____

_____

CRITICISM 2: _____

_____

DESIRE HIDDEN WITHIN THE CRITICISM: _____

_____

POSITIVE STATEMENT OF DESIRE: _____

_____

At an appropriate time in the near future, share one of your desires with your partner. It is up to your partner to decide whether or not to satisfy that desire. Effective communication does not guarantee compliance.

EXERCISE 3: DEVELOPING A COMMON LOVE LANGUAGE

COMMENTS: If you're going to talk about sex, you have to use words. But which words? There are four sets of terms that people customarily use to communicate about sex: *clinical terms* ("sexual intercourse"), *dirty talk* ("fucking"), *slang terms* ("doing it"), and *romantic terms* ("making love"). As you see, there is a world of difference between these words. It's quite common for one person to be offended by the sexual terms used by the other. It is also common for couples to fail to explore the aphrodisiac quality of words.

In this exercise you will be creating a list of words that you find acceptable and/or exciting. Do this exercise alone or together. If you do it separately, set aside some time to share your results.

DIRECTIONS: Following is a list of clinical terms. (The list is not exhaustive.) Following each term, write down the vernacular terms you prefer. Make any comments that might prove helpful to your partner. (For example: "I like the word 'cunt,' but only when I'm really aroused. Otherwise I find it vulgar.") You may want to create two sets of terms, one to inform, the other to excite.

Once both of you have filled out your lists, exchange them. Talk about your reactions. The goal is to come up with terms that you both find acceptable and/or exciting.

If you like, indicate your reaction to your partner's terms with the following symbols:

"X"—words I don't like.

"OK"—words that are neutral or okay.

"!"—words I find erotic or hot.

LIST FOR PARTNER 1

FEMALE ANATOMY

Clinical term: **vulva**

Preferred terms: _____

Clinical term: **vagina**
Preferred terms: _____
_____

labia _____
_____

clitoris _____
_____

G spot _____
_____

breasts _____
_____

nipples _____
_____

buttocks _____
_____

anus _____
_____

pubic hair _____
_____

MALE ANATOMY
penis _____
_____

testicles _____
_____

scrotum _____
_____

nipples _____
_____

buttocks _____

_____

erection _____

_____

ejaculate _____

_____

anus _____

_____

pubic hair _____

_____

SEXUAL ACTIVITIES
intercourse _____

fellatio _____

cunnilingus _____

oral sex (in general) _____

masturbation _____

LIST FOR PARTNER 2

FEMALE ANATOMY
Clinical term: **vulva**
Preferred terms: _____

_____

Clinical term: **vagina**
Preferred terms: _____

_____

labia _____

_____

clitoris _____
_____

G spot _____
_____

breasts _____
_____

nipples _____
_____

buttocks _____
_____

anus _____
_____

pubic hair _____
_____

MALE ANATOMY
penis _____
_____

testicles _____
_____

scrotum _____
_____

nipples _____
_____

buttocks _____
_____

erection _____
_____

ejaculate _____
_____

anus _____

_____

pubic hair _____

_____

SEXUAL ACTIVITIES
intercourse _____

fellatio _____

cunnilingus _____

oral sex (in general) _____

masturbation _____

EXERCISE 4: GIVING ALTERNATIVE SUGGESTIONS

COMMENTS: Many people are hesitant to tell their partners to stop
a particular lovemaking technique they don't like, especially if their
partners have been doing it for a long time. They're afraid of hurting their partners' feelings. A respectful and effective way to communicate this information is to give your partner an alternative
starting with the words "Instead of . . ." Examples:

> *"Instead of using saliva on your fingers, I'd like you to use some
> lubricant."*
> *"Instead of sucking on the head of my penis, I'd like you to lick
> it."*
> *"Instead of putting your tongue deep in my mouth, I'd like you
> to dart it in and out."*
> *"Instead of blowing in my ear, I'd like you to whisper loving
> words."*
> *"Instead of pinching my nipples, I'd like you to suck on them."*

DIRECTIONS: Think of something you'd like to change about your
partner's lovemaking techniques. In the near future find an op-

portunity to give your partner an alternative suggestion. You can do this while making love or when you are enjoying a quiet moment together.

EXERCISE 5: BECOMING MORE SEXUALLY FLUENT

COMMENTS: Below you will find a list of incomplete sentences that you can use to start a discussion of your sexual relationship. They are arranged in approximate order of difficulty. (This will vary from person to person.) Pick a topic that you both can discuss comfortably right now. Work your way down the list over the next few weeks. Keep the discussion positive. If negative comments seep in, stop the conversation and come back to it at a later date.

DIRECTIONS: Take turns completing the following sentences. Listen carefully to what your partner has to say. Don't interrupt. Ask questions if you don't understand.

1. The first thing that I found sexually attractive about you was . . .
2. One of our best sexual experiences was . . .
3. My favorite time to make love is . . .
4. A sexual activity I'd like to try is . . .
5. In terms of sex I wish I were better at . . .
6. What I'd like more of in our lovemaking is . . .
7. What I'd like less of in our lovemaking is . . .
8. Something I find difficult to discuss is . . .
9. Something that concerns me about our sexual relationship is . . .
10. What I would like to know about you and sex is . . .

EXERCISE 6: SHARING YOUR SEXUAL VISION

COMMENTS: Most couples haven't taken the time to describe to each other what they consider ideal lovemaking experiences. They have beautiful images in their minds, but they haven't shared them. This is your opportunity to learn more about each other's unexpressed needs and longings.

DIRECTIONS: On separate pieces of paper, write down what you consider a deeply satisfying lovemaking session. (You may have a number of different fantasies to choose from.) In your description, consider the following questions:

> What is the physical setting?
> What is the mood between you and your partner before making love?
> Who initiates the lovemaking?
> How is it done?
> How does the partner respond to the initiation?
> How do you pleasure each other? (Be as detailed as you like. You may want to turn this into an erotic short story.)
> How do you wind down from the lovemaking?
> What is the mood between you and your partner following the lovemaking?

Once you have created this fantasy session, share it with your partner. How do your fantasies differ from your usual sexual encounters?

Look for common themes in your separate fantasies.

Pick a portion of your partner's fantasy you would be willing to enact.

Negotiate time, place, and details.

EXERCISE 7: CREATING A SEXUAL CONTRACT

COMMENTS: Having an agreed-upon sexual contract can increase the feelings of safety and commitment between you.

DIRECTIONS: Below is a model contract. Discuss each item. Decide which ones are important to both of you. Eliminate any statements that neither of you likes or you can't agree upon. Add any statements that have significance for you. The goal is to list all the conditions both of you require to feel comfortable and safe in your sexual relationship.

MODEL SEXUAL CONTRACT

1. We commit to being willing and interested sex partners.

2. We tell each other what we enjoy about each other's lovemaking.

3. We let each other know when we desire sex in a clear, positive, mutually agreed-upon manner.

4. We state our requests for a change in our sex practices in positive and specific terms.

5. We respect each other's sexual limits.

6. We keep information about our sex life private unless we have prior permission to share with others.

7. We let each other know when our sexual needs are not being met within the relationship and make a commitment to resolve the problem, either as a couple or with the help of a sex or marital therapist.

8. We honor all prior agreements, such as decisions to be monogamous, practice safe sex, and share birth control responsibilities.

9. We fill in any gaps in our understanding of each other's sexuality by asking questions.

10. We agree to change our sexual practices to accommodate any changes that occur because of aging, illness, or significant life events.

11. We agree to work together as a sexual team.

Other _____

4

WHEN I'M HOT AND YOU'RE NOT

Resolving
Differences
in Desire

The taxi was inching its way from Kennedy Airport to my hotel in Manhattan. My taxi driver was a talkative sort, as am I, and before long we were involved in a conversation. At one point he asked me why I had come to New York, and I said I was visiting my book editor. "An author," he said matter-of-factly. "I get you people all the time. What's your book?"

"A book on sexuality for couples. It's called *Hot Monogamy*," I replied.

"Good idea," he said. "You get kids. You get busy. All of a sudden sex is out of the picture."

We talked about traffic, politics, and the weather for a while; then he said he wanted some advice. "You're a shrink, right?" he asked, peering at me in his rearview mirror.

I nodded.

"Well," he said, "I want you to know that I love my wife. We've been married sixteen years, and I've never fooled around. I'm not that kind of guy. But the truth is, I'm not always happy, you know, with the lovemaking part. The problem is, I'm always the one wanting her, you know, doing the initiating. I think she's sexy. I wish she felt the same way about me."

"That makes sense," I said, slipping into my therapist's demeanor. "Everyone wants to feel desirable."

He continued: "One day I asked her why she didn't initiate. She said, 'I just don't think about it.' I said, 'Well, *think* about it.' I thought about buying a book on how to drive women crazy. I thought, maybe I'm doing it wrong. But she said I've always satisfied her, if you know what I mean. Then I tried laying off it for ten days. I thought she'd get the hint. You know, I don't think she even noticed. What's it gonna take to get her interested?"

My taxi driver was describing a phenomenon that sex therapists call desire discrepancy, which simply means that one partner has a higher sex drive than the other. It's a very common problem. Years ago a majority of couples went to a sex therapist because the man had erection difficulties or premature ejaculation or the woman had difficulty reaching orgasm. Now, for most couples seeking help, nothing is "broken"; it's just that one of them's hot when the other is not.

If you and your partner have a noticeable difference in scores on the desire section of the Sexual Style Survey, this may be an all-too-familiar situation in your household. But even if you have similar scores, you are likely to have some questions about sexual desire. It's the topic that generates the most interest by far in my lectures and workshops.

To begin with, I want to give you a working definition of the term "sexual desire." A typical lovemaking session can be artificially divided into three overlapping stages. *Desire*, the first stage, can be defined as a "spontaneous interest in engaging in a sexual experience." One minute you are reading the newspaper; the next minute you are daydreaming about sex. The trigger might be a sexy ad, a glimpse of your partially clothed partner, or a random thought. For some reason, you are in the mood for love. If you entice your partner to follow you to the bedroom and you receive sufficient stimulation, you will arrive at the second stage, *arousal.* Now you are not only liking the idea of sex but becoming physically aroused. If you are a man, your penis is becoming erect. If you are a woman, your genitals are becoming engorged and the walls of your vagina are lubricating. Both of you are breathing faster, and your skin is beginning to flush. If your arousal continues to build, you will eventually arrive at the next stage of lovemaking, *orgasm*, which is a rush of pleasurable feelings—sometimes mild, sometimes intense—caused by muscle contractions forcing the blood to flow away from the pelvic area.

I'm currently working with a couple, Pamela and Dan, who, like many couples, have problems with that first stage, desire. Pamela would be content to have sex three or four times a month. She is easily orgasmic—in fact, she is one of a minority of women who can climax without direct clitoral stimulation—yet she rarely desires sex. One reason for her lack of interest is that it takes her, like many low-desire people, a long time to become aroused. She gave me this candid account: "For the first fifteen or twenty minutes of lovemaking I could happily stop at any point. I have hardly any sensation. It's only when my orgasm is imminent that I begin to feel horny. Then, all of a sudden, I'm thinking, 'Don't stop! Don't stop!' But I crave sex for only about two minutes out of twenty. The rest of the time I could take it or leave it."

Her husband lives with a far different reality. Dan would like to make love every night and thinks about sex dozens of times a day. He gets turned on by seeing attractive women at work and by spontaneous daydreams. Pamela jokes that all it takes to give him an erection is a gentle breeze. Dan loves having sex, and as soon as he and Pamela start the preliminaries, his body is flooded with pleasurable sensations. Scant minutes after he's had an orgasm, he's wondering how soon it will be before they do it again. The only thing he knows for certain is that it won't be soon enough. "Dan feels as if I've put him on a restrictive diet," says Pamela, "and he doesn't like it one bit."

When the couple first came to me, both of them regarded Pamela as the one with "the problem." Considering our society's preoccupation with sex, this is not surprising. Today we expect people to have an unwavering interest in sex from adolescence to senescence. But if Pamela and Dan had been living a hundred years ago, society would have viewed their situation differently. Pamela would have been lauded for her "noble character," while Dan would have been given stern advice on how to curb his "immoral lust."

Although society's view of sexuality may change, there appears to be an underlying biological constant. Studies of human sexuality in cultures around the world have shown that most men think about sex more often, are more easily aroused, want sex more frequently, desire more partners, and masturbate more often than most women. Even in these days when people scrutinize gender differences for any hint of bias, experts still maintain that biologically men are the more highly sexed gender. Noted sex therapist Helen Singer Kaplan, speaking from decades of clinical experience, has said that "all the differences between male and female sexuality are due to the strength of the male sex drive, which seems much higher than the female's. All other differences follow from that."

When there is only a moderate difference in desire between a man and a woman, they may find it easy to bridge the gap. One person has sex somewhat less often than desirable, and the other person makes an effort to "get in the mood." Problems arise when there is a marked difference between a man and a woman or when they find it difficult to compromise.

When this is true, I have found it helps a great deal for the couple to gain more insight into their separate points of view. In one of my first sessions with Pamela and Dan, I asked Dan if he was willing to tell Pamela how he felt when he was filled with sexual energy. "What does your body feel like?" I prompted. "What thoughts go through your head?"

Dan turned to Pamela and said, "I can honestly tell you that there is rarely a moment in my life when I have no sexual desire. All I need is the slightest bit of encouragement—a woman walking down the hall—and there it is. When we were first married, those feelings were overpowering. Sex was the only thing worth doing. Now that I'm over forty, I don't think about sex every minute of the day. I can focus on other things for the first time in my life. But it's always there on the back burner, bubbling away. Do you understand?"

Pamela didn't. At least not from her own experience. She told him there were brief periods in her life when she had been highly interested in sex, primarily when she was in her twenties, and she had found those times very enjoyable. But most of the time she has had little spontaneous interest. "Now I rarely think about sex," she said to Dan. "To be honest, I think if it weren't for pressure from you, I could go for a week without having one sexy thought. You initiate sex when your level of desire builds up; I initiate sex when my level of guilt builds up."

"That's so hard to understand," said Dan, shaking his head. "If you enjoy sex and you always reach orgasm, I don't understand why you don't want it more often. It doesn't compute."

Indeed, it *doesn't* compute, not when you run the data through the typical male computer. But on my part I had little trouble understanding Pamela's lack of desire because I have had a low sex drive most of my life. Many people don't realize that there are millions of women like Pamela and me who find that the needle on our sex meters points to zero most of the time. We need an infusion of energy to get it to move. We may enjoy sex, and we may be orgasmic, but we don't experience a pressing *physical* need to make love. Some studies suggest that a third of all women rarely have enough spontaneous interest in sex to initiate lovemaking.

I want to make it clear that although there are many low-desire women, there are even more women with ample sexual desire who experience sexual urges on a regular basis. In fact, a common complaint for many women is that their busy schedules keep them from making love as often as they would like. Even so, it is likely that their male partners are even more interested in sex. In the majority of heterosexual relationships, the man has a higher sex drive than the woman. Some degree of desire discrepancy seems to be the human condition.

As I was explaining this fact of life to a male client recently, he asked me plaintively, "Aren't there any horny women out there?" Yes, I assured him, there are. A significant number of women experience an especially strong desire for sex. Liz, one of my new clients, fits this category. In her freshman year at college she had a lover who wanted sex three or four times a day. She says with a grin, "I had no trouble keeping up." Now, twenty years later, her appetite is just as keen. In fact, her interest in sex as a forty-three-year-old woman resembles that of a young man. "My sex drive is always with me," she says. "I have to suppress it, or it gets in the way. I walk around with an unspecified sexual interest. It's almost like I pick up sexual auras from other people. I don't know how else to describe it. It's always there."

When a woman with a high sex drive for her gender is paired with a typical man, the lovemaking can be especially passionate. If you and your partner fit this description, consider yourselves lucky; to have two people with high levels of desire is the exception, not the rule. Ironically, many women with high sex drives either are single or are married to men with *low* sex drives.

When a woman has a higher sex drive than her male partner, the difference between them can be especially troubling. Liz is struggling with this issue. She would like to make love once a day, while her husband, Tom, feels a sexual urge about once a week. Liz has resigned herself to sleeping in the back bedroom because she finds it difficult to be in the same bed with Tom and not become aroused. When they do sleep in the same bed, she waits for Tom to make the first move. "He is so easily intimidated," she says. "I'm afraid my high sex drive will blow him out of the water." She is not only frustrated by the lack of sex but worried about emasculating her husband. Sadly, physical affection is missing from their marriage as well. "The only time Tom will reach for my hand is in public," Liz says. "Maybe that's because he knows it can't go any farther than that.

WHAT CAUSES SEXUAL DESIRE?

I have found that all couples, whether or not they have conflicting sex drives, gain some valuable insights when they learn more about the science of desire. It's one of those instances when a little information goes a long way. I dearly wish that this body of knowledge had been available to me years ago.

Until the 1970's most of the discussion about sexual desire focused on psychological factors such as marriage problems or repressed upbringings. These factors do indeed influence desire. It's difficult to have a healthy appetite for sex if you were shamed for your sexual curiosity as a child or if you and your partner are feuding. Gender conditioning can also play a significant role. Our society has long given men more permission to explore their sexuality than women, and this may partly explain the greater interest men have in sex. As society slowly lifts its restrictions on female sexuality, we are seeing more and more women who are forthright about their sexual desire.

Still, psychological and social factors do not fully explain the differences between male and female sexuality. Even though today's young women have Madonna for a role model and were raised by the Woodstock generation, studies show that they still experience less sexual desire than young men.

Only when we examine the role played by sex hormones do we get the complete picture. Through sophisticated measuring devices developed in the 1960's, researchers are now able to measure the nanograms (billionths of a gram) of hormones circulating throughout our bodies. What they have learned is that men and women have the same half dozen sex hormones, only in differing amounts. Testosterone, which has long been regarded as the "male" hormone, fuels the sex drive in both genders. The fact that men have from ten to twenty times more testosterone than women is one of the primary reasons they experience more desire.

Dr. Barbara Sherwin, professor of psychology, obstetrics, and gynecology at McGill University, has given us many of our insights into testosterone and women. As part of her research, Sherwin has given various hormonal preparations to women who have low levels of hormones as the result of removal of their ovaries. In one experiment she divided forty-four of these women into three separate groups. The women in the first group were given estrogen, which is commonly given to women who have been through natural or surgical menopause. The women in the second group were injected with a mixture of estrogen *and* testosterone. The women in the third group were given placebos. Sherwin monitored the sexual activities of all three groups. The women who were given estrogen and placebos experienced little change in their sexuality. By contrast, the women who were given the testosterone additive had a dramatically higher level of desire and arousal (see graphs).

Few studies produce such dramatic results. In fact, Sherwin received a few phone calls from disgruntled husbands who complained that their wives had become too hot to handle. "Everyone laughs about this," she says, "but when a man is over fifty, he may not be interested in increased sexual frequency." Most of the women elected to stay with the program. Sherwin comments, "Besides restoring desire, testosterone can give women an enhanced sense of well-being. Estrogen can elevate a woman's mood as well." When a woman is given both estrogen and testosterone, it appears to be a powerful tonic indeed.

What about the testosterone that naturally occurs in a woman's body? What effect does it have on her sexuality? To find out, Dr. Patricia-Shreiner Engel, Director of Psychological Services of the Department of Obstetrics and Gynecology at Mount Sinai Hospital, New York, studied the relationship between testosterone and sexual arousal in a group of thirty healthy young women. First, she measured the testosterone levels of all the women, discovering some significant differences among them. She labeled the women with the highest levels of naturally occurring testosterone the "high-T" group and the women with the lowest levels the "low-T" group. Then she monitored the sexual activity of all the women for a period of weeks. She discovered that the women in the high-T group had the highest levels of sexual arousal and maintained their arousal for the longest period of time. Whether testosterone comes from an injection or occurs naturally in a woman's body, it seems to have a significant effect on her sex drive.

Schreiner-Engel also noted some intriguing personality differences between the high-T and the low-T women. The high-T women were assertive, inquisitive patients who asked a lot of questions and were drawn to high-powered, demanding careers. By contrast, the low-T women were less inquisitive and had more traditional jobs. Paradoxically, although the high-T women had strong interest in sex, they had more difficulty with love relationships than the low-T women. In fact, only two of the high-T women had stable, satisfying love relationships. Testosterone, which pro-

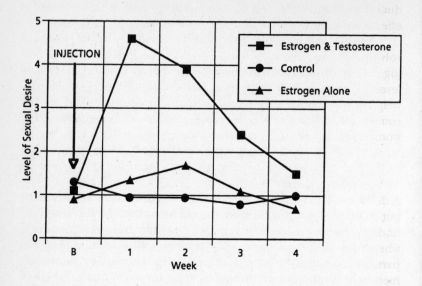

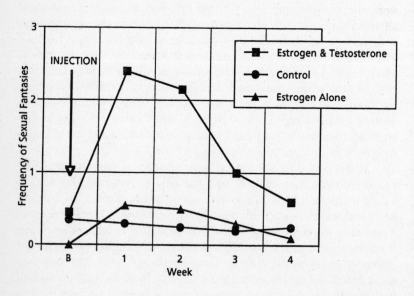

duces both aggression and sexual desire in men, may have a similar effect on women.

Another study of testosterone and sexual desire, this one involving fifty-two menopausal women, came up with equally intriguing results. The researchers discovered that the women with higher levels of testosterone not only were more sexually active but weighed an average of eighteen pounds less and had higher incomes. It's obvious that testosterone has far-reaching effects on women that we are just beginning to understand.

FLUCTUATING LEVELS OF SEXUAL DESIRE

A desire for sex not only varies considerably from woman to woman, but it can also vary within a woman from day to day. Some women find they are more interested in sex during ovulation, which is when their bodies produce the most testosterone. Other women, particularly high-T women, feel more sexy just before or during menstruation. (This monthly surge of desire is so typical of high-T women that it may prove to be a good indicator of a woman's overall testosterone level. Women with lower levels tend to have flat responses throughout the menstrual cycle.) Other women appear to be more interested in sex during the first half of the menstrual cycle, and that may be caused by the sense of well-being that typically accompanies the monthly rise in estrogen.

In addition to these periodic ups and downs, women tend to have longer cycles of desire that correspond to the hormonal changes that occur with pregnancy, lactation, and menopause. A friend of mine confided to me that she had an unusually strong sex drive during her last pregnancy. "I would attack my husband," she told me. "He didn't know what had come over me, but he wasn't complaining." As soon as her baby was born, her desire plummeted. "The only way I can explain it is that all of a sudden I felt totally full. One minute I was incredibly sexy, and the next minute I didn't care if I ever had sex again. There was no urge left in me whatsoever." When her baby was four months old, her husband finally got up the nerve to ask what was wrong. Said my friend: "He was feeling horny, confused, and neglected."

What this couple didn't know is that women often experience a dramatic drop in sexual interest when they are nursing, which may be caused by either a rise in prolactin (the hormone that stimulates milk production) or a decline in testosterone. This temporary loss of interest in sex may function as a natural form of family planning, creating more space between children. But it can also create unwanted distance between husbands and wives. Many of the couples I see can trace the beginning of their sexual problems to the birth of a baby. It's easy to see how this might happen. When a new baby arrives, a woman has to cope with the relentless demands of motherhood, a lack of sleep, and a sudden drop in sexual desire. If she and her husband do not know that hormones may be causing the loss of desire, they may think they are falling out of love.

It is widely assumed that a woman's level of sexual desire increases during midlife. This is true for some women but not all. In fact, most women have a *diminished* sex drive when their ovaries stop producing testosterone. One study followed a group of women through their menopause years. Once their menses had stopped, the women had fewer sexual thoughts and fantasies and less vaginal lubrication and were less satisfied with their partners as lovers. They also reported a lower frequency of intercourse.

TESTOSTERONE, MEN, AND SEXUAL DESIRE

For a long time it was thought that only women experience this ebb and flow of hormones, but men have internal tides as well. A man's testosterone level can *double* in the morning hours, a circadian rhythm that tends to decrease with age. Peaks and valleys of longer duration have been documented. For example, a group of men submerged in a nuclear submarine for months at a time had periods of increased beard growth accompanied by noticeable mood swings from euphoria to mild depression. Researchers attributed these changes to a previously unobserved four- to six-week testosterone cycle.

Life events—even relatively minor events, such as winning or losing at sports—can also affect a man's testosterone level. In one study six college tennis players were monitored over the course of a varsity season. The winners of a match had a rise in testosterone levels, while the losers experienced a decline. Curiously, the same testosterone surge has been observed in men who win sedentary chess matches.

But do these testosterone spikes translate into a greater interest in sex? We don't know for sure. But it appears that a man's *average* level of testosterone does affect his desire. A study of a group of young men revealed that the men with the higher baseline levels of testosterone had more sexual activity (including masturbation) than men with lower levels. Another long-term study concluded that men with the highest levels of hormones displayed the most sexual behavior.

Does a temporary dip in a man's testosterone level reduce his interest in sex? Probably not. Most men have more than enough testosterone to sustain their interest in sex even when they are on the low end of a cycle. For most men it is only the steady drop in testosterone occurring with age that results in a noticeable decline in sexual activity. Only 1 percent of men between the ages of twenty and forty have a significant testosterone deficiency. This rises to 5 percent in men between forty and sixty-five and to 20 percent for men over sixty-five.

The story appears to be different for women. Researchers believe that the testosterone level of many women dips below a critical threshold at regular intervals throughout the month, diminishing or eliminating their interest in sex. Other women have such low levels that they never desire sex, even when their hormones are at peak levels.

I have found that this brief introduction to the biology of desire clears up much of the confusion some couples experience. One man said, "You tend to believe that your partner has the same interest in sex that you do. If she doesn't want to make love, you assume she doesn't love you or doesn't find you attractive. It's a relief to know there's another explanation." A woman in her early sixties came to a similar conclusion: "I now see my husband's age might have a lot to do with his decreasing interest in sex. He's got less testosterone. I thought he no longer found me desirable." A woman said to me during a break in a workshop, "I've never had much of a sex drive. After listening to you, I feel normal for the first time in my life. It's a tremendous relief."

But information and insight are rarely enough. Most couples want to minimize their differences, not just understand them. One man said bluntly, "Great. Now I know why my wife isn't interested in sex. But I still want her to change."

One question I am always asked is if it's possible to raise one's level of desire with testosterone supplements. The answer is a qualified yes—as long as the person happens to be a man with abnormally low levels of sex hormones. For some time now physicians have been giving testosterone injections to older men or men with abnormally low levels of the hormone. Now that testosterone can be administered through a transdermal patch, the process has become more pleasant. However, unanswered questions about the relationship between testosterone and prostate cancer have kept the practice from being more widespread.

What about prescribing testosterone for the millions of women with low sexual desire? When the dramatic results of Barbara Sherwin's studies on testosterone and women hit the presses, she was besieged with requests for more information. What drug was she administering? What dosage? What were the side effects?

Despite this initial flurry of excitement, doctors have been slow to prescribe testosterone for women. A physician at a recent conference on sexual desire disorders said he spent five hours on the phone before he found an endocrinologist who would even listen to his request to give testosterone to one of his female patients.

Why this reluctance? Some physicians may not be well informed about the role that testosterone plays in female sexuality. Others don't seem to consider a woman's lack of interest in sex a serious problem. Many women have had physical exams all their adult lives without once being asked about their sexuality. One woman told me she complained to her doctor about low desire, and he said to her, "Don't worry. Be grateful that you can fake arousal. Your husband can't."

Possible side effects may be keeping other physicians from prescribing the hormone. Excessive amounts of testosterone can cause increased facial hair, a lowering of the voice, acne, and changes in the menstrual cycle. Even though the women in Barbara Sherwin's study had only mild and reversible side effects, many physicians are still concerned about the virilizing effects of testosterone—and the distinct possibility of lawsuits.

My advice for someone with an unusually low level of sexual desire is to get a comprehensive physical exam. A physician can rule out some physical causes of low desire, such as depression, the side effects of prescription drugs, excessive drinking, and certain chronic diseases. If blood tests indicate a hormone deficiency, the patient may be referred to an endocrinologist for further testing and treatment. (Women may have to interview a number of specialists before they find one who has experience administering testosterone to women.)

OVERCOMING POLARIZATION

What about the majority of couples who have normal hormonal levels or do not want to take sex hormones? What can they do to even out their differences in desire? Years ago I tried to cope with the nightly battle with my partner in a wide variety of self-defeating ways, including feigning interest, making excuses, shaming him, picking a fight, faking orgasm, and avoiding sex altogether. If I had known more about the biology of desire, I would have felt less inadequate about my own sexuality and had more empathy for my partner. This would have helped us deal with the situation more constructively.

However, in order to find a workable solution, I believe we would also have had to know more about the *psychology* of desire, in particular the confusing dynamic of polarization. When my partner and I were first together, he wanted sex only slightly more often than I did. As time went on, his desire seemed to increase and mine to decrease. Eventually we resembled the characters in the movie *Annie Hall*, he thinking we were having sex "hardly ever" and I believing we were having it "all the time." We had become polarized around the issue of sexual frequency, which seemed to exaggerate our physical differences.

Many people who come to me for sex therapy have fallen prey to polarization. An extreme example stands out in my mind. Several years ago I worked with a young woman named Janet who had a lively libido. She told me that during a college love affair she was so filled with desire she had to masturbate to take the edge off her appetite, even though she and her lover were having sex every day. After one particularly heated session in the backseat of a car, she was so aroused she had trouble walking back to the dorm. She said, "My knees kept buckling—just like in the romance novels."

When Janet graduated from college, she moved in with Frank, a man whose desire was even greater than hers. At first she found living with Frank a sensuous banquet. Whenever Janet wanted sex, it was available to her. But after a year she began to feel over-whelmed by Frank's relentless desire: "Sex was offered to me whether I wanted it or not, morning and night. I began to long for a break." At the end of three years she felt invaded by him. "It got to the point where I had zero desire. How could I when he was jumping my bones all the time? Get off me! I started pushing him away more and more often. Soon sex was the number one problem in our relationship. He felt he was never getting enough, and I felt I was under siege." She and her partner had become a study in polarization.

It may be easier to understand Janet's point of view when it's taken out of the sexual realm. Imagine what it would be like to have a partner who always serves you a meal an hour before you are hungry. At first you welcome the attention; it's flattering to have someone anticipate your needs. But after a few weeks you are likely to feel annoyed. Food is being offered to you whether you want it or not. You begin to push it away. If your partner persists in feeding you when you're not hungry, you may become resentful. You love food, you need food, you'd die without it—but you don't want your partner to determine when and how often you eat! You have be-come polarized by the issue of food.

The same dynamic applies to sex. If someone consistently ap-proaches you for sex before you experience any desire, you lose your sexual appetite. You may begin to feel like just a vehicle for the other person's sexual release. Soon you begin to set up more and more barriers to lovemaking: "Yes, honey, I'd be happy to make love—provided the room is warm enough, it's early enough in the evening, the dishes are washed, I've finished my work from the office, the dog has been taken for a walk. . . ." Regrettably you have lost sight of the fact that you, too, have a sex drive and that you used to enjoy sex very much.

Now let's examine this situation from the other side of the bed. The view looks dramatically different to you as a high-desire person. In the beginning of the relationship your partner is likely to be a highly motivated lover. The newness of your relationship plus the contagion of romantic love results in wonderful, passionate love-making. Then, after a few months or years or perhaps the birth of a baby, your partner begins to lose interest. Now it seems as if you are always the one initiating sex. To your dismay your partner also begins to find it hard to become highly aroused. This makes it hard for you to experience much passion because you are held back by your partner's inertia. (I recall a client's saying to me, "When my wife and I make love, I feel like she is a heavy load and I have to push her up the mountain in a wheelbarrow. I'm doing all the work.")

If, despite your best efforts, the situation doesn't improve, you may feel angry or rejected. You begin to worry that your partner doesn't love you anymore or is having an affair or doesn't find you physically attractive.

I gained more sympathy for the point of view of the high-desire partner when I listened to a group of men talk about what it was like to have their partners reject their advances time after time. Their pain and disappointment were palpable:

LENNY: When my wife shows no interest in sex, I feel empty, sad, discounted, left out, separate. . . .

TREVOR: I feel worthless. It has to do with my total being.

FRANK: I feel frustrated, angry, irritated.

MARK: I feel embarrassed.

JOHN: Rejected. It's castration.

TREVOR: Humiliation.

MARK: You know, the lack of response doesn't necessarily

start in bed. I can read about a mile and a half away when the no sign is up. I don't have to wait until I get in bed. I already know. So I feel depressed throughout the day.

DAN: There's a sign that says, "In case you wondered, the answer is no!" It gets posted on the door. [Group laughter]

STUART: I feel helpless. When I know my wife is going to turn me down, there's nothing I can do. That's an awful feeling.

DAN: I truly desire my wife. I would like her to desire me. Is that too much to ask?

In this particular group, whether the feelings of anger and rejection the men were experiencing were mild or intense seemed to depend to some degree on the length of the relationship. One of the men said that unlike the others, he wasn't upset when his girlfriend had no interest in sex. In fact, he took it as a challenge. He said, "That's when I get a grin on my face."

"Yeah?" said the man sitting next to him. "How long have you been living together?"

"Two years," he replied.

"Well, come talk to me after you've been married for thirteen years," he said grimly. "We'll see if you're still smiling."

Men are not the only ones to experience this frustration. High-desire women who have low-desire partners can feel just as unloved and hopeless. One of my female clients is deeply distressed about the lack of sex in her marriage. "I'm going to be forty in August," she told me. "I was alone in my hotel room on a recent business trip. I thought about how long it's been since my husband approached me for sex. I got to thinking, 'I'm never going to have sex again.' I got to thinking about the early days in our relationship when we did wild and crazy things. If I did that now, he'd say, 'Leave me alone. Don't bother me.' There's no excitement in my marriage. No passion. The more I thought about it, the more unhappy I became. I wound up crying for an hour and a half."

When two people are at odds about how often they make love, both individuals can suffer. At times the high-desire partner may feel rejected, disappointed, or deprived, while the low-desire partner may feel pressured, inadequate, or guilty. However, when couples make a concerted effort to understand each other's point of view, they often experience a dramatic turnaround.

Two of my clients, Karen and Arnold, both in their late thirties, went a long way toward resolving a five-year stalemate by gaining insight into their separate realities. Following my instructions, they took turns talking about their sexuality, being careful not to blame each other, make critical comments, or bring up stale issues. To the best of their ability, they simply described how they felt about their own levels of desire.

What touched Karen most was hearing Arnold describe how he felt when he had gone without sex for several days. It was so different from her experience. From her point of view a week without sex was a vacation. It allowed her to catch up on her sleep and do more reading. She joked to Arnold that her "reading drive" was stronger than her sex drive.

By contrast, Arnold revealed that sex was very important to him, not just for the welcome physical release but for emotional reasons as well. He talked to her about his strong need to touch and be touched. He said that sex seemed to be almost a healing form of contact for him. "If we haven't made love in a long time," he told her, "then I feel emotional pain. It's as if my psyche grows harder and smaller. I feel more isolated, not just from you, but from everyone around me." Karen had assumed that all he was experiencing was a simple sexual urge, "like an itch that needed to be scratched."

Before this conversation Arnold had never been able to articulate to himself—much less to her—the central role sex played in his life. In the weeks that followed, Karen found herself more willing to make love on a regular basis. "Most of the time our lovemaking lasts for only fifteen or twenty minutes," she said to me. "I'd been resisting too much, especially considering the fact that I enjoy sex just as much as he does once I get going. Now that I know what our lovemaking means to him, I'm more willing to say yes."

Not surprisingly, as Karen became less resistant, Arnold became less *insistent.* Two people can't play tug-of-war when one person drops the rope.

Another change that took place after their conversation was that Arnold became more reconciled to the notion that Karen would never match his level of desire and that there would be times when she agreed to make love just to satisfy his greater needs. At first this was very disappointing to him. I remember his saying in one of the early sessions, "I don't want to make love unless Karen wants to as well. It takes away my pleasure if it's all for me. I want her to be turned on, too!" But he began to see it was unrealistic to expect her to be as aroused as he was every time they made love. Now he is able to view her willing participation for what it truly is: an act of love. "It's easy to want to make love when you've got a lot of sexual desire," he admitted to her at our last session. "I know there are times when you do it just to please me. I thank you for that."

An exercise at the end of this chapter will enable you and your partner to have a similar discussion about the role that sexual desire plays in your relationship. (See Exercise 1, p. 88.) Even if you have similar levels of desire, you are bound to gain new insights into your partner's reality.

In addition, I want to share with you the following practical suggestions, gleaned from my work with hundreds of couples struggling with differences in desire. Read through them to see which ones would help make your sexual relationship more harmonious and enjoyable.

SUGGESTIONS FOR THE PARTNER WITH GREATER DESIRE

1. *Be more direct in asking for sex.* Ironically, many people with high desire are passive about meeting their needs. They hint about their sexual readiness and then expect their partners to take over. Practice being more straightforward. You might say to your partner, "I'm feeling really sexy tonight. I'd like to make love to you," or "I would really appreciate it if we had sex tonight. I'm really turned

on by you.'' Clear, positive communication may evoke a more positive response.

2. *Initiate sex out of love and desire, not out of habit.* It is common for people with high desire to initiate lovemaking out of habit, asking for sex even when they're not feeling aroused. They've become locked in a role and lost sight of their actual level of desire. Make sure you are not polarizing the situation by asking for sex when you're not all that interested.

3. *Become an expert in creating desire in your partner.* Because your partner has lower desire than you do, your skill as a lover becomes especially important. The more adept you become at arousing your partner, the more often you will have a highly excited partner.

4. *Accept the fact that your partner may need extra stimulation to become fully aroused.* Many people with low desire find that being caressed or kissed is not enough to take them to high levels of arousal. They may need additional stimulation in the form of sexual fantasies, erotica, or a vibrator. The more graciously you can accept this reality, the more harmonious and satisfying your sexual relationship will be.

5. *Don't deliberately heighten your level of desire.* If a difference in desire is a significant problem between you, cut back on activities that stimulate your desire. When you indulge in sexual fantasies, read pornography, or watch steamy movies, you will only exaggerate your differences in desire.

6. *Honor your partner's sexual preconditions.* Your partner is likely to have a number of preconditions that makes him or her more willing to make love. Satisfy those conditions whenever possible. For example, if your partner is more receptive to lovemaking at night, honor this request. It may not make much difference to you when you make love, but your partner will be more responsive.

7. *Consider satisfying some of your purely physical needs through masturbation.* Masturbation is normal and natural. The vast majority of people do indeed "do it"—yes, even those who are happily married. If you are highly aroused and your partner is not in the mood, self-stimulation is one way to reduce your sense of urgency. Masturbation will not satisfy your need for love, affection, and intimacy, but it will take the edge off your appetite. Then, the next time you

make love, you can concentrate on the emotional connection, not just on your pent-up physical needs.

8. *Redirect some of your sexual energy.* In the larger sense of the word, "libido" means "life energy," not just "sexual desire." When your life is full and exciting, your energy has a number of outlets besides sex. If sex has become an obsession, you may find that channeling your energy in other directions will even out some of the differences between you.

9. *Do not confuse lust with love.* Try not to take your partner's lower interest in sex too personally. It may be the result of a number of factors, including the aging process, fatigue, a history of sexual abuse, a repressed upbringing, or a low level of hormones. If you are worried that your partner's lack of desire is caused by a lack of love, you will see confirmation of this in all areas of your relationship, not just your lovemaking.

SUGGESTIONS FOR THE PARTNER WITH LOWER DESIRE

1. *Accept more responsibility for your own arousal.* Don't expect your partner to do all the work. What turns you on? Reading erotica? Wearing sexy clothes? Hugging and kissing? Having an intimate talk? Getting dressed up and going out for the evening? Because you have less spontaneous desire, you must learn how to create it. Initiate those activities *you* find erotic. Give your partner a treat from time to time by coming to bed already turned on.

2. *Pay attention to subtle sexual cues.* Unlike your partner, you may never experience a strong surge of sexual desire. You may have to amplify each pulse of pleasure. When you feel even the slightest pulse of desire, follow through on it. If you wait for a tidal wave of passion to wash over you, you may wait a long, long time. Also, see if you can detect any cycles of desire. Are you more receptive at a certain time of day? In a certain place? In a particular situation or position? During a predictable time of the month? Note these times, and take advantage of them.

3. *Be clear and* reasonable *about your preconditions.* Define the conditions that make you most eager for lovemaking, and let your

partner know about them. For example, you may be a more willing partner if you've had a relaxing massage or a long soak in the tub. Be reasonable about your requests. (Be aware that if you have a long list of preconditions, you may be covering up some unresolved issues.)

4. *If you masturbate, do so less often.* Paradoxically, many people with low sex drives release some of the little sexual energy they have through masturbation. In light of all the complexities of a sexual relationship, this is understandable. At times you want to satisfy a physical urge without confronting all the complicated issues between you and your partner. But if you have a sincere wish to even out the differences between you, reserve more of your sexual energy for your partner.

5. *If you choose not to have sex, say so—and don't feel guilty.* If you make an effort to meet your partner's sexual needs much of the time, you don't have to feel guilty those times you say no. But when you say no, also say when. In other words, let your partner know when you will be available. Then no won't seem forever.

6. *Balance your life.* Low sexual desire can be a reflection of a lack of excitement in your life in general. If few of your daily activities "turn you on," it's not surprising that your sexuality is muted as well. Get involved. Get physical. Create a life that is full and interesting. If you have a good reason to wake up each morning, your libido may wake up as well.

7. *Make room in your life for sex.* Many people with low desire enjoy sex a great deal once they're aroused. The problem is that their low libidos don't provide them with much motivation to initiate sex. You may deliberately have to schedule time for lovemaking. Your partner is motivated by spontaneous desire; you may have to rely on mental incentive.

8. *Celebrate your mental desire.* You can be a wonderful sex partner even if you have low sexual desire. Your willingness to satisfy your partner's needs and to create more sexual desire in yourself is a cause for celebration. Rejoice in your positive attitude and be assured that the two of you can create a long-lasting, mutually satisfying sexual relationship.

In the rest of the book you will be examining sexual desire from a number of different angles. For example, by experimenting with one of the lovemaking techniques suggested in Chapter 7, one or both of you may experience a renewed surge of sexual interest. Or by doing the mirroring exercise in the upcoming chapter, you may reach a deeper level of emotional intimacy, which often leads to more sexual passion. Sexual desire is a fascinating, complex phenomenon, and you are likely to gain new insights into it through the course of this program.

EXERCISE SECTION

EXERCISE 1: THE VIEW FROM THE OTHER SIDE OF THE BED

COMMENTS: The goal of this first exercise is to help you become more aware of your partner's level of sexual desire. The more freely and objectively you share your experiences, the more insights you gain.

DIRECTIONS: Take turns answering questions from the list below. When it's your turn to talk, choose your words carefully. It's important that you describe your own experience and refrain from blaming or criticizing your partner. When your partner is talking, listen carefully. Do not defend yourself. Merely gather information.

If conflict arises, call time out. Try the exercise once again when you have read through Chapter 5 and practiced the Mirroring exercise on page 115.

POSSIBLE TOPICS:

How often a day (week) do you feel aroused?
How do you feel when we haven't made love for several days (weeks)?
What role does sex play in your life?
Are there any predictable times of the day, week, or month when you experience sexual desire?
How do you feel when I'm not interested in making love?

How do you feel when I'm interested in making love and you are not?

How do you feel when we start out making love when you're not aroused?

How do you feel when you have to suppress your sexual arousal because I'm not interested?

When do you feel most aroused?

EXERCISE 2: CHANGING BEHAVIORS

COMMENTS: In this chapter you've had a chance to read a list of suggestions about how to cope with differences in desire. This exercise asks you to make a commitment to follow through with some of those suggestions.

DIRECTIONS:

1. Turn back to pages 84–87 and read the suggestions to partners with high and low sexual desire.

2. Put a check mark by each suggestion that you believe would improve your relationship. (The changes should apply to your behavior alone.) Ask your partner to do the same.

3. Decide which of the marked suggestions you are willing to do now. Indicate with a star. Ask your partner to do the same.

4. Discuss the changes you will be making.

5. When your partner follows through on one of the suggestions, acknowledge his or her effort.

EXERCISE 3: FANNING DESIRE

COMMENTS: This exercise is designed to help the partner with lower desire amplify subtle feelings of sexual interest.

DIRECTIONS:

1. Over the next few weeks pay attention to any sexual thoughts or feelings you might have. See if they follow a pattern.

For example, you may notice that you spontaneously think of sex at a particular time of day, at a particular time of the month, when you're alone, when you're exercising, or when you're involved in a particular kind of book, movie, or TV program. Try to repeat or take advantage of those experiences that spark your interest in sex.

2. Think back to times in your life (if any) when you experienced a greater amount of sexual desire. Are there any common themes among those separate experiences? (For example, you may have felt more turned on while on vacation, when out of doors, after intimate discussions, early in a relationship, or when you were feeling especially relaxed or energetic.) Are there any ways to re-create those situations?

3. Choose an evening in the next two weeks to come to bed already sexually aroused. Before climbing into bed, indulge in thoughts, activities, or behaviors that you find sexually stimulating. You might:

Stimulate yourself in the bath or shower (stop before reaching orgasm).
Read a book or magazine that excites you.
Watch a movie or video that excites you.
Close your eyes and focus on sexual imagery.
Dress in a manner that you (not your partner) find seductive.
Talk with your partner in an arousing manner.
Request a sensual/sexual massage.

4. Sometime during the next few weeks, suggest a new sexual activity to your partner that you find arousing. (Read Chapter 7 for suggestions.)

QUESTION AND ANSWER SECTION

The people who have attended my workshops have had so many questions about sexual desire that I thought it would be helpful to provide a question and answer section on this subject here.

QUESTION: My partner seems to have an *excessive* level of desire. He wants sex every night and masturbates two or three times a day. He thinks and talks about sex all the time. I feel overwhelmed by him. What can I do?

ANSWER: For some people sex is not just a high priority in their lives; it's an obsession. Their sexual desires are stronger than they are.

Typically, people who display compulsive sexual behavior were raised in dysfunctional families or were victims of sexual abuse. Patrick Carnes, a national authority on the subject, lists ten indicators of compulsive sexual behavior in his book *Don't Call It Love*.

1. A pattern of out-of-control behavior
2. Severe consequences caused by sexual behavior
3. Inability to stop despite adverse consequences
4. Persistent pursuit of self-destructive or high-risk behavior
5. Ongoing desire or effort to limit sexual behavior
6. Sexual obsession and fantasy as a primary coping strategy
7. Increasing amounts of sexual experience because the current level of activity is no longer sufficient
8. Severe mood changes around sexual activity
9. Inordinate amounts of time spent in obtaining sex, being sexual, or recovering from sexual experience
10. Neglect of important social, occupational, or recreational activities because of sexual behavior

If your partner exhibits one or more of these behaviors, I suggest he or she see a therapist who specializes in this area.

QUESTION: I have a very low sexual desire. I often wonder if I was sexually abused and repressed all memories of it.

ANSWER: It is common for victims of sexual abuse to remember the incident or incidents involved but not to realize that the situation was harmful to them. A small percentage of abuse survivors remember only brief moments or feelings associated with the trauma.

In her book *The Sexual Healing Journey*, psychotherapist Wendy

Maltz, a pioneer in the field of sexual healing, offers the following checklist to help you identify sexual problems commonly caused by sexual abuse:

1. I avoid, fear, or lack interest in sex.
2. I approach sex as an obligation.
3. I experience negative feelings such as anger, disgust, or guilt with touch.
4. I have difficulty becoming aroused or feeling sensation.
5. I feel emotionally distant or not present during sex.
6. I experience intrusive or disturbing sexual thoughts and images.
7. I engage in compulsive or inappropriate sexual behaviors.
8. I have difficulty establishing or maintaining an intimate relationship.
9. I experience vaginal pain or orgasmic difficulties.
10. I have erectile or ejaculatory difficulties.

Maltz's book contains a more extensive survey on the sexual symptoms of sexual abuse and details a comprehensive program of healing, helping survivors regain a feeling of safety with sexual intimacy.

If you suspect you were abused, there is additional help available. There are self-help books, tapes, newsletters, support groups, therapy groups, and conferences on the subject. I want to assure you that there is sexuality beyond abuse. I have seen many people create wonderful sexual relationships despite a history of rape or incest. You owe it to yourself and your partner to recover your sexual and emotional health.

QUESTION: My girlfriend doesn't just have low sexual desire but seems afraid of sex. She'll do anything to avoid it. When she finally agrees to make love, she grits her teeth and waits for it to be over. Then she hurries to take a shower. Sex seems as pleasurable to her as going to the dentist. Is there any help for us?
ANSWER: When a person has sexual urges, fantasies, or activities (including masturbation) less than twice a month, they meet the

criteria for Hypoactive Sexual Desire, or HSD. There are two general categories of HSD: normal HSD and phobic HSD. The person with normal HSD displays little interest in sex. He or she would rather read a book or watch TV than initiate lovemaking. By contrast, a person with phobic HSD has a strong *aversion* to sex. He or she may dread being sexual and may have panic attacks or nausea during lovemaking. Afterward he or she may equate the act of love with being raped or violated. It is common for such a person to want to shower or take a bath to cleanse himself or herself of the ordeal.

Sex therapists have made great strides in helping people with phobic HSD. By gradually exposing the person to sexual experiences, they are able to break the link between sex and fear. If you suspect your partner has phobic HSD, I strongly recommend that you and your partner make an appointment with a competent sex therapist. Therapists report a greater than 90 percent cure rate with this form of sexual dysfunction.

5

INTIMACY

What Is It?
How Do You Get It?
What Does It Have to Do with Sex?

Intimacy is a curious phenomenon. Most couples profess to want more of it, but few people can define what it is. Thomas and Mara, married for eleven years, came to me complaining of a lack of intimacy. This was the second marriage for both of them, and they were determined to make it work. For Mara the low point of their marriage had occurred two years earlier in the middle of a marriage enrichment seminar held at their church. Thomas was so frustrated by one of the communication exercises that he left the seminar. As he was leaving the room, he tossed his half-completed workbook to Mara and made his stand: "I'm not going to change. This is who I am. This is all there is, and you're not getting any more."

Mara was depressed for months afterward. She believed that her previous husband had built up walls between them, and once again she found herself married to someone who seemed incapable of intimacy. She was tired of being married and feeling lonely, but she didn't want to get divorced a second time. She felt trapped.

To her relief, in the year following the workshop, Thomas became less resistant to working on the marriage and eventually agreed to come to me for couple's therapy. In one of our sessions I asked Mara to give me an example of what "intimacy" meant to her. She thought for a moment, then laughed. "I guess I've never had a good definition for intimacy. It's just a label for something I know that I need. But what is it? I guess the message I send out to Thomas is: If you love me, you'll figure it out."

I turned to Thomas and asked him what intimacy meant to him. His answer was equally vague: "I got divorced thirteen years ago, and my first wife got custody of the kids. She moved a thousand miles away. Not being able to see the kids . . . I didn't want to be hurt again. I think I began to wall up my feelings."

Like many people, Thomas and Mara had trouble explaining what they meant by the word "intimacy." All Mara could say was that intimacy was something she wanted but didn't have; all Thomas could say was that intimacy was something he found hard to give. At that point I volunteered a very simple definition that has always worked for me: *Intimacy is communicating on a personal level.* Mara and Thomas thought for a moment and decided that the definition made sense to them. Mara said, "I guess that's what's missing in our relationship. I don't feel Thomas talks or listens to me—at least not about anything personal. I just don't feel we're intimately connected." She turned and spoke directly to her husband: "You answer my questions with one or two sentences and then let them drop. It's like a tenth of you is there. The rest of you is gone somewhere. I never know what you're thinking, and that creates this incredible distance between us."

Later in the session Mara remarked that there seemed to be a direct connection between their lack of intimacy and her unhappiness with their lovemaking. She said to Thomas, "When you've been silent and distant all day and then come to me at night and want to make love, I feel you're expressing a physical need, not love. I feel I'm having sex and you're having sex, but we're not having sex together. We're missing a basic connection. I want all of us to be involved in the lovemaking, not just our genitals."

From listening to hundreds of interactions like this, I've come to the conclusion that good verbal communication is one of the keys to a good sex life. When couples share their thoughts and emotions freely throughout the day, they create between them a high degree of trust and emotional connection, which gives them the freedom to explore their sexuality more fully.

Intimacy begets sexuality.

INTIMACY AND GENDER DIFFERENCES

Unfortunately many couples find it hard to create lasting intimacy. They find it relatively easy to feel close at the start of a relationship, but as time goes on, they spend less time talking about their inner thoughts and feelings and more time discussing the bills, housework, and mortgage rates.

While it is easy to see how the logistics of daily life can gradually intrude on a love relationship, there are other, less obvious reasons why husbands and wives drift apart. One of them is that men and women often have markedly different conversation styles, which subtly undermine their attempts to communicate.

Thanks to the work of linguist Deborah Tannen, author of *You Just Don't Understand,* we've gained more insight into these common language barriers. One of Tannen's observations is that men as a group excel at what she calls "report talk," the exchange of useful information, while women as a group excel at "rapport talk," conversation that creates an emotional bridge between people. She also notes that men talk more freely in social circles and the workplace, while women talk more freely in one-on-one situations and the home. This means that when a husband and wife are having a quiet dinner together, the wife may want to talk about her feelings and family affairs, while the husband may want to study the financial section of the newspaper. She sees the evening meal as a time to establish interpersonal links; he sees it as a time to arm himself with facts.

I see much evidence of these gender differences in my therapy practice. As a rule, my female clients find it easier than my male clients to talk about personal matters. The women are usually the first ones to bring up a relationship issue, and they talk about it for a longer time. One of the topics that women bring up a great deal is the lack of emotional intimacy. Occasionally a man will complain that his female partner is emotionally distant, but I have lost track of the number of times that women have made comments like these:

"He never listens to me."
"He won't tell me what he's thinking."
"The only emotion he shows is anger."
"I've never seen him cry."
"He keeps everything bottled up."
"He talks with his head, not his heart."

However, even though many women have complained to me about their male partners' seeming inability to communicate on a personal level, this doesn't mean that the women have mastered the art of verbal intimacy. A woman's gender conditioning may make it easier for her to express her thoughts and feelings, but it doesn't automatically give her better relationship skills.

I got an eye-opening look at the way that women can contribute to the communication gap when I asked a group of fourteen men to talk about problems they were having with intimacy. Not surprisingly, they focused on their partners' failings, not their own. Here's what three of the men had to say:

STEVE: My wife is the talker, and I'm not. I don't know about the rest of you, but I just get overwhelmed. We got up this morning, and in the first fifteen minutes Sally talked fourteen minutes on twelve different subjects. I get in this double bind of: Do I try to be attentive? If I do, I get overwhelmed trying to take in all that information. Or do I pretend I'm being attentive and just zone out? If I do, I get caught. She'll say, "What do you think about that?" And I haven't been listening.

MARIO: I've learned the art of "selective ignoring," even though it's a cynical thing to say. What you have to do is have your processor running in the background so

you can parrot back something and make it sound like
you're paying attention.

MARK: I do the same thing. It's a kind of filtering process.
My wife is talking and talking and talking. It's a kind of
background process. I keep one ear open for significant
words. I'll pick up a tone of voice or topic that alerts
me to pay more attention. But half the time I'm letting
it go in one ear and out the other.

As I sat there listening to the men, I had the sudden realization
that they were "faking" verbal intimacy, the same way that some
women fake orgasms. They were making an effort to nod and "uh-
huh" in all the right places, but they were too overwhelmed by the
sheer volume of words aimed in their direction to pay close
attention.

Much of the advice given to couples about good communication skills focuses on the responsibility of the listener: Be attentive,
don't interrupt, don't be critical, don't be defensive, etc. But the
speaker has responsibilities as well, and one of them is to choose his
or her words wisely. This is especially true in long-term relationships. People can't inundate their partners with their thoughts and
feelings any time of night or day and always expect to have good
listeners. Many of the women who have complained to me that their
partners were emotionally distant were unwittingly contributing to
the problem. In my office I've seen many women display one or
more of the following off-putting behaviors:

Frequent interruption of their partners
Talking too much
Talking too fast
Talking about too many topics in one conversation
Overreacting to what their partners have to say
Dwelling exclusively on relationship problems
Putting words in their partners' mouths
Being insensitive to their partners' need for peace and quiet

While it is true that many men need to be more verbally expressive, it is equally true that many women need to *withhold* more of their thoughts and feelings, saving them for a more appropriate time or place. In most love relationships, both individuals have a great deal to learn about verbal intimacy.

THE MIRRORING EXERCISE

Fortunately there is a simple technique I use that helps couples experience deeper levels of intimacy. One of its merits is that it counteracts the intimacy-blocking behaviors common to both men and women, effectively leveling the playing field between the sexes.

The technique, called the mirroring exercise, is a variation of an exercise used by therapist Harville Hendrix, author of *Getting the Love You Want*, with whom I have trained and been associated for more than ten years. Time and again I have seen this powerful technique transform relationships. The exercise is deceptively simple. One person, the sender, begins by stating a brief sentence or two. The other person, the receiver, restates the message in his or her own words. In essence the receiver becomes a mirror, reflecting back the content and the tone of the message. The receiver's role is not to interpret, diminish, or magnify the message but simply to reflect what was said.

Once the message has been reflected back, the receiver asks the sender if the message was correctly understood. If not, the sender clarifies the statement. This process continues until the message is "received as delivered." The sender is then free to deliver another chunk of information. The two stay in their roles until a complete train of thought has been communicated. Then the receiver becomes the sender and can either respond to the previous message or take the conversation in a new direction.

Here is a brief example, from one of my workshops, of two people "mirroring" each other:

Sender makes a brief statement: "I want us to communicate more, but I want it to be constructive, not destructive.

So many times we've tried, but we end up worse than
we started."

*Receiver paraphrases the statement, then asks if the message was
clearly understood:* "So, you would like us to communicate
more often, but you want it to be positive. When we've
talked in the past, sometimes we've made the situation
worse. Did I get it?"

*Sender indicates that the message was correctly received and then
adds a thought:* "Yes, I mean, it seems as if we always end
up at odds with each other or in some sort of contest
when we bring up certain subjects."

*Once again the receiver paraphrases the statement and then asks
for confirmation:* "There are certain topics that seem to
end up in a competition or with us yelling at each other.
Right?"

Sender makes a slight clarification: "Well, not always yelling.
But it's as if we're against each other, not working as a
team."

Receiver continues to paraphrase and ask for confirmation: "So
it's not that we're always yelling, but we're not working
as a team, more as if we're against each other. Did I get
it?"

Sender responds: "Yes."

*The receiver can ask if there's anything more the sender wants to
say:* "Is there more you want to say about this?"

Sender continues to clarify the statement: "Well, not right now.
I guess I just want to feel we're on the same side, not
always fighting each other. I don't want to feel like en-
emies anymore."

Receiver paraphrases: "You want to feel like a team, not
fighting each other. You want us to be on the same
side."

Sender: "You got it."

At this point in the exercise the two partners changed roles
and the receiver became the sender, turning the conversation into

a dialogue. (The exercise is explained in more detail in Exercise 4 at the end of this chapter.)

THE MANY REWARDS OF THE MIRRORING EXERCISE

Is this process tedious? Clearly. When you mirror each other, the conversation slows to a snail's pace. Is practicing the exercise worth the effort? Absolutely.

One of the reasons the exercise is so helpful is that it prevents many of the common intimacy-blocking behaviors I mentioned earlier, including dominating the conversation, interrupting, being overly critical, being too closemouthed, and failing to pay close attention. It also puts an end to the "shoot and reload" school of communication, in which one partner "fires" the first shot of words and "reloads" the mental gun while the other person is talking. You can't shoot and reload during the mirroring exercise because you have to listen too carefully to your partner.

The fact that you can't fire verbal bullets at each other during the exercise creates an all-important demilitarized zone. As long as you stick to the rules, you won't be able to wound each other psychologically by ignoring, discounting, shaming, interrupting, or contradicting each other. All you can do is paraphrase each other. Once you learn that you can rely on your partner's neutral response, you are likely to become more willing to talk about sensitive subjects, opening up whole avenues of discussion. Subjects that once touched off bitter arguments can now be discussed in safety.

Another benefit of the exercise is that it gives you the luxury of having your partner's undivided attention. It can be moving to know that your partner is paying attention to you and trying to understand what you're saying. Too often we listen to our partners with half an ear. Like the men in the discussion group, we "uh-huh" and nod at all the right places while we daydream about something else. When your partner paraphrases you accurately, you have proof that your message has gotten across. Many times in my therapy sessions I have seen people moved to tears by the simple fact that they have been heard and understood.

But the benefits of the mirroring exercise go beyond even this.

If you faithfully practice it over a period of weeks, you will begin to experience a fundamental shift in your perception of both your partner and yourself. Most of the transformation takes place on an unconscious level. When you are in the role of the receiver, you are confronted with the inescapable fact that your partner is different from you. On some level you've always known this, but like most people, you may have gone to great lengths to keep from absorbing this unpleasant truth. In my office I see partners try to coerce each other into adopting similar points of view by using an endless variety of maneuvers, including bullying, manipulating, shaming, and lecturing each other.

This mental coercion is not unique to love relationships. Many families are built on the premise that "we are all the same," the parents dictating to the children how to think, feel, and behave. Friendships, too, are often formed around shared opinions and values. Many of your closest friends are likely to have similar politics, values, and lifestyle.

One of the primary reasons we surround ourselves with like-minded people is that we don't want to experience our separateness. If someone else agrees with everything we say, we can fool ourselves into thinking we are not separate from them. And the reason we want to feel psychically joined with others is that when we're aware of our separateness, we are confronted with the fear of death.

This may not make sense on a conscious level, but the unconscious mind has its own logic. On an unconscious level we are under the mistaken impression that we cannot survive on our own. Actually, this is true for about the first decade of our lives because human beings require caretaking for a longer period of time than any other species. To ensure that we get this care, we are programmed to bond closely with our caretakers. This is why a two-year-old girl clings to her mother when she is left with a strange baby-sitter or a three-year-old boy breaks into tears when he loses sight of his mother in the shopping mall. "Without you, I will die," believes the unconscious mind, and for many years this is regarded as the absolute truth.

Regrettably this survival mechanism doesn't disappear when we are old enough to fend for ourselves. The primitive part of the brain that governs reflexes and primal emotions still operates on the belief that "If I am not intimately connected with someone else, I will die." This is why relationship issues can ofttimes feel so life-threatening. On an unconscious level to be abandoned by a lover is to come face-to-face with the fear of death.

There was a time when my own separation anxiety was so great that I became angry whenever my husband even complimented another woman. Unconsciously I was using my anger to cover up my fear that my partner found the other woman more interesting, more attractive, or more clever than me and that he was going to leave me for her. If he left me, a hidden part of me was convinced I was going to die. Is this bizarre? Yes. Is this common? Yes.

One of the profound consequences of the mirroring exercise is that the simple act of listening attentively to your partner compels you to confront your separateness. You cannot use anger or any other defensive maneuver to deny that you and your partner are separate beings. The exercise forces you to be a mirror, validating whatever your partner has to say—no matter how much those words accentuate your differences.

But the genius of the exercise is that it doesn't force you to confront this existential truth all at once. You absorb it in small increments. Each time you paraphrase your partner, you are acknowledging another small aspect of your partner's individuality. This gives the primitive part of your brain time to adjust to the reality of your separateness.

You will not be aware of this process as you practice the exercise. You are more likely to be thinking of what you don't like about the exercise: "This is tedious." "We're not getting anywhere." "Do we have to do this again?" "I hate not being able to answer you right away." "This feels contrived and awkward." But underneath your surface complaints your unconscious mind will be slowly registering the many differences between you and your partner, along with the comforting fact that you are still alive. Gradually your unconscious mind will be able to construct a more adult worldview:

"Yes, I am indeed separate from my partner. But I have yet to die. Perhaps I am mature enough to survive as an independent being after all."

When you are in the role of the sender, your unconscious mind makes an equally significant discovery. When you make a statement and hear it paraphrased accurately by your partner, you are acutely aware of your partner's presence. Mirroring is primary proof that someone else is out there, listening to you, understanding you, validating you. Maybe there *is* intelligent life in the universe after all! Furthermore, because your partner is willing to go through this tedious, time-consuming, frustrating exercise with you, you have tangible proof that your partner cares about you. On a deep, fundamental level you begin to sense that, yes, you are indeed separate from your partner, *but you are not alone.*

Thus the mirroring exercise gives you the confidence that you can survive as a separate entity at the same time that it reassures you that your partner cares about you. These seemingly contradictory insights result in a highly evolved state of mind called differentiation: the sense that I am separate from you but still able to connect. Differentiation is the final stage in the adult developmental process. A person who is differentiated fears neither abandonment nor engulfment. I know I can be me and still be in a relationship with you. You can't swallow me up, control me, or manipulate me because I have learned that I can survive without you. I have come to terms with my own separateness. You can leave me, and I won't die.

Paradoxically, this feeling of independence allows me to bond with you all the more deeply. Because I'm no longer terrified of being left alone or being engulfed, I don't have to put up so many defenses. I can safely and freely explore what it means to be intimate. It's not fear or need that binds me to you but conscious choice. I am a separate and distinct individual who *chooses* to be in a relationship with you.

There is no question in my mind that differentiation is the key to a deep and lasting love relationship, and the fastest way I know to become more differentiated is to practice the mirroring exercise.

AN INTIMATE CONVERSATION

When I first assign the mirroring exercise to couples, I suggest that they start by discussing simple, nonthreatening topics. Once they have mastered the mechanics of the exercise, they can move on to more sensitive topics. Ultimately they will be able to share the full range of their thoughts and feelings in safety and comfort.

To show you what such discussion is like, I have mapped out an intimate conversation between a couple, Jane and Fred. They start out by discussing trivial matters, but in just a few minutes they reach a deep level of intimacy. It is the rare couple who can talk this openly. The reason Jane and Fred are able to be so intimate is that over time they have created a high level of trust and respect. As you will see, through practice and repetition they have been able to dismiss the rigid structure of the mirroring exercise, but they have retained its essence. They have learned to listen attentively, validate each other's experience, and paraphrase each other when necessary, showing that they have mastered the art of intimate conversation.

Setting the scene: Jane has just gotten home from the movies, and she and Fred are getting ready for bed. Fred is taking off his shirt. Jane is plumping up her pillow and getting ready to climb into bed. Jane begins to talk, and Fred turns his head to look at her. He gives her his full attention. His face is relaxed and open.

JANE: Oh, I forgot to tell you. The Red Cross called this morning to remind you of your appointment tomorrow morning. It's at eight.

FRED: Thanks. I'd forgotten. Uh, I watched *Wall Street Week* while you were at the movies. It was about mutual funds. Not much new information, so you didn't miss anything. By the way, what did you think of the movie *Alice?*

So far Fred and Jane are discussing fairly trivial topics. However, just because Fred and Jane are listening attentively to each other, a feeling of safety and closeness is beginning to develop between them.

JANE: There was a part of the movie that really got me thinking. Do you remember the final scene where Alice is pushing her kids on the swing set? I know it's been a long time since you saw the movie.

FRED: Oh, yeah. I remember thinking it seemed an abrupt ending. Like Woody Allen had just pasted a two-minute conclusion onto what I thought was an excellent film.

JANE: Well, I had a strong reaction to that final scene. To me, the message at the end of the movie was that we should all get out of the rat race and make life simpler. It made me think how frantic my life feels and how burned out I feel at work. But if I take time off from my job, I'm afraid I'll be left behind, forgotten. I'll have to start all over again. I feel really trapped.

The conversation has now become more intimate. First Jane shares her feelings about the movie; then she reveals some intimate thoughts about herself. Fred has a sympathetic look on his face and is nodding in mute agreement. Without realizing it, he paraphrases Jane to make sure he understood what she was saying. Then he shares some of his own feelings.

FRED: Yeah. You want to simplify things, but it's not easy. I can see why you feel that way. We're both so wrapped up in our jobs. Everyone gets shortchanged: you, me, the kids. I get depressed thinking about it. But there doesn't seem to be an easy solution. I wish you could quit your job, too, so at least one of us could spend more time with the kids, but you'd lose your seniority. I don't have the answer either.

As Fred was talking, Jane listened closely to what he had to say. Her face showed sympathy, not fear or anger at the fact that Fred was revealing his own vulnerability. Her body language gave him permission to express his genuine feelings, not stay in the mold of the strong, silent male.

JANE: Sometimes the only thing that keeps me going is knowing that we're in this together. That we're both working hard not just to get ahead in the world but to try to find more time to spend with the kids, to carve out some time together, to simplify things.

You always say, "We can do it. We'll work things out." I rely on your optimism.

FRED: I'm glad to know that. I really love you, you know.

As Fred says this, he climbs into bed with Jane and puts an arm around her. He doesn't say, "I love you," reflexively, the way many people do. He looks into her eyes and says it with obvious emotion. Jane rests her head on Fred's shoulders. They lie quietly together for a few moments. As the psychological barriers between them dissolve through honest, intimate conversation, the physical ones disappear as well. When they begin to make love, their verbal intimacy extends into a profound level of sexual intimacy.

Think for a moment about all the ways that Fred and Jane could have kept this intimate interlude from developing:

1. Fred could have failed to give Jane his full attention when she started talking to him about the Red Cross appointment. If he'd acted annoyed, bored, or distracted, it's not likely that Jane would have been willing to volunteer her complex reaction to the movie.

2. Fred and Jane might have gotten involved in a discussion of the movie itself, bypassing the feelings Jane wanted to express. It's a lot safer to keep the conversation impersonal.

3. Fred might have invalidated Jane's reaction to the movie in any of a number of ways. He might have switched the conversation to his reaction, not hers, he might have made her feel foolish for reacting the way she did, he might have criticized her for being so emotional, he might have been angry at her for bringing up an unresolved problem, and on and on.

4. Fred, like many men, might have felt obliged to solve Jane's problems as soon as she uttered them, without revealing any feelings of his own. This would have placed a Band-Aid on the situation and circumvented any intimacy.

5. Finally, Jane, like many women, might have displayed anger or anxiety when Fred began revealing his own vulnerability, thereby sending out a contradictory message: "I want you to listen to me express my feelings, but I am threatened by yours."

Jane and Fred managed to avoid all these pitfalls. They did this because they had learned to:

1. Give each other their full attention.
2. Listen carefully for meaning.
3. Validate each other's reality.

Their excellent intimacy skills allowed them to experience the feelings of love and intimacy that all couples yearn for.

In the exercises that follow you will be able to hone some of your own relationship skills. First you will be identifying differences in your conversation styles. Then you will be writing down the conditions that make you most willing to engage in a personal conversation. Finally, you will be tackling the all-important mirroring exercise.

EXERCISE SECTION

EXERCISE 1: DEFINING VERBAL INTIMACY STYLES

COMMENTS: You are probably aware of some of the differences in the way you and your partner communicate. This exercise will help you clarify your observations.

DIRECTIONS FOR PARTNER 1:

1. Read the following statements, and circle the number that best describes you. (There is a separate checklist for each of you.)

NEVER	SELDOM	SOMETIMES	OFTEN
0	1	2	3

1. I absorb information quickly.
   0 1 2 3
2. I am talkative early in the morning.
   0 1 2 3

3. I pay attention to visual details.
   0   1   2   3
4. I give short, concise answers to most questions.
   0   1   2   3
5. I keep most of my thoughts to myself.
   0   1   2   3
6. Much of the time I am absorbed in my own ideas.
   0   1   2   3
7. It is easy for me to identify my feelings.
   0   1   2   3
8. I believe most of my thoughts are of interest to others.
   0   1   2   3
9. I rigorously defend my thoughts and opinions.
   0   1   2   3
10. I have difficulty expressing my thoughts.
    0   1   2   3
11. I base my decisions more on logic than emotions.
    0   1   2   3
12. I have difficulty expressing my feelings.
    0   1   2   3
13. I like to talk about intimate matters.
    0   1   2   3
14. I like to be the center of attention.
    0   1   2   3
15. I have a hard time knowing what I'm feeling.
    0   1   2   3
16. I feel overwhelmed when people jump from one idea to another.
    0   1   2   3
17. I am a fast talker.
    0   1   2   3
18. I quickly tire of a subject.
    0   1   2   3
19. I speak slowly, often pausing to think.
    0   1   2   3
20. I feel bored or anxious if my partner talks too slowly.
    0   1   2   3

2. Now go through the checklist a second time, this time putting a check mark by the numbers that best describe your partner. Note the similarities and differences.

DIRECTIONS FOR PARTNER 2:

1. Read the following statements, and circle the number that best describes you. (There is a separate checklist for each of you.)

NEVER	SELDOM	SOMETIMES	OFTEN
0	1	2	3

1. I absorb information quickly.
   0   1   2   3
2. I am talkative early in the morning.
   0   1   2   3
3. I pay attention to visual details.
   0   1   2   3
4. I give short, concise answers to most questions.
   0   1   2   3
5. I keep most of my thoughts to myself.
   0   1   2   3
6. Much of the time I am absorbed in my own ideas.
   0   1   2   3
7. It is easy for me to identify my feelings.
   0   1   2   3
8. I believe most of my thoughts are of interest to others.
   0   1   2   3
9. I rigorously defend my thoughts and opinions.
   0   1   2   3
10. I have difficulty expressing my thoughts.
   0   1   2   3
11. I base my decisions more on logic than emotions.
   0   1   2   3
12. I have difficulty expressing my feelings.
   0   1   2   3

13. I like to talk about intimate matters.
    0   1   2   3
14. I like to be the center of attention.
    0   1   2   3
15. I have a hard time knowing what I'm feeling.
    0   1   2   3
16. I feel overwhelmed when people jump from one idea to another.
    0   1   2   3
17. I am a fast talker.
    0   1   2   3
18. I quickly tire of a subject.
    0   1   2   3
19. I speak slowly, often pausing to think.
    0   1   2   3
20. I feel bored or anxious if my partner talks too slowly.
    0   1   2   3

2. Now go through the checklist a second time, this time putting a check mark by the numbers that best describe your partner. Note the similarities and differences.

BOTH PARTNERS: When you have completed your surveys, discuss ways you can better understand, respect, and accommodate each other's natural style of communication. As you talk, check to see whether or not you are manifesting the very traits you are talking about.

EXERCISE 2: RECONCILING DIFFERENT COMMUNICATION STYLES

COMMENTS: People often choose partners with very different communication styles. A fast talker marries a slow talker. A rational thinker falls in love with someone who is highly emotional. A person who enjoys concrete details marries a person who dwells in abstractions.

This exercise explores two of the most common mismatches in

communication styles and gives you some suggestions for resolving them.

DIRECTIONS: Read through the following tips, and see if they apply to you and your partner. If so, discuss relevant ones with your partner. Pay attention to your conversation styles as you are talking. State any changes you are willing to make to help accommodate your differences in communication styles.

TIPS FOR A FAST THINKER/SLOW THINKER PARTNERSHIP

▪ *If you are the fast thinker*, monitor the conversation to make sure your partner is keeping pace with you. If your partner is getting left behind, slow down your rate of delivery, stick to one topic for a longer time, or leave more air space for your partner to jump in. You may have to be silent for as long as one full minute (this will feel like an eternity) before your partner comes up with a reply. All these suggestions are difficult to execute, but intimacy won't develop if you continually dominate the conversation.

Also, refrain from (1) interrupting your partner, (2) putting words in your partner's mouth, (3) finishing your partner's sentences, (4) displaying irritability at your partner's slower pace, and (5) failing to listen attentively when your partner *does* talk. I have yet to work with an individual who complained about a partner's unwillingness or slowness to communicate who didn't manifest at least one of these intimacy-blocking behaviors.

▪ *If you are the slow thinker*, make your thought processes more transparent to your partner. Instead of remaining silent for long periods of time, train yourself to make helpful comments like the following:

> *"Wait a minute. I'm still thinking."*
> *"I'm not ignoring you; I'm trying to think of what to say."*
> *"Let's get back to topic X. I have some more thoughts on that one."*
> *"I'll let you know in thirty minutes. Is that all right?"*

> *"I'm not paying attention to you right now. I'm still reacting to what you said five minutes ago."*

Your partner will appreciate the feedback.

Some slow thinkers tend to stick to one subject for a long time, exploring its many nuances. If this is true of you, check to see if your partner is getting bored by your fascination with detail.

TIPS FOR A RATIONAL THINKER/ INTUITIVE THINKER PARTNERSHIP

▪ *If you are the rational thinker,* acknowledge the fact that a logical presentation and a good command of facts and figures are not the sole standards for determining whether an idea is right or wrong. As you know, a rational argument can be constructed on both sides of an issue.

If your partner is less skilled than you in your preferred mode of thinking, be sure that you aren't using your keen mind as a weapon. You may win debating points, but you will only succeed in driving the two of you farther apart.

To the best of your ability, supplement your rational presentation with feelings. Ask yourself, "How am I feeling right now?" Let your partner witness your inner reaction.

▪ *If you are the intuitive thinker,* there are times when it will help to buttress your opinions with facts and figures. This may seem like a waste of time to you, but you will gain credibility in your partner's eyes. For example, a friend of mind found herself drawn to Ross Perot as a presidential candidate. She had a positive response to him after watching him on TV. But she knew that her husband would not respect her opinion unless she was also able to talk rationally about Perot's politics, so she made the effort to learn more details about his policies.

To initiate a discussion on a feeling level with your more rational partner, pick your time wisely. You may discover that your partner is more emotionally available late at night, after making love, or during a leisurely Sunday morning breakfast. When your partner *does* reveal an emotion, make sure that you accept what he or she tells you, whatever it may be. Invalidating your partner's feelings is a surefire way to prevent further disclosures.

Exercise 3: Preconditions for Verbal Intimacy

COMMENTS: This exercise will help you define the conditions that make each of you most willing to have an intimate conversation.

DIRECTIONS: Complete the following sentences:

PARTNER 1:
As a general rule, the times of day or situations when I feel most available to talk to you are _____

_____

_____

I listen most attentively when you (examples: talk slowly, don't dwell on one subject too long, speak with animation, speak calmly, share your emotions, etc.) _____

_____

_____

It is difficult for me to pay attention when you (talk at length about work, jump from topic to topic, talk only about problems, etc.) —

_____

_____

_____

PARTNER 2:
As a general rule, the times of day or situations when I feel most available to talk to you are _____

_____

_____

I listen most attentively when you (examples: talk slowly, don't dwell on one subject too long, get to the point, speak with animation, speak calmly, share your emotions, etc.) _____

_____

_____

It is difficult for me to pay attention when you (talk at length about work, jump from topic to topic, talk only about problems, etc.) —

_____

_____

_____

EXERCISE 4: THE MIRRORING EXERCISE

COMMENTS: I strongly recommend that you practice this exercise.

DIRECTIONS: For best results, practice the mirroring exercise for ten or fifteen minutes at least three or four times a week. Start with simple, neutral exchanges of information. (Begin by completing the sentence fragments that follow the exercise.) When you are comfortable conversing on that level, you can begin to introduce more sensitive topics.

SENDER	RECEIVER
1. Makes a short two- or three-sentence statement.	2. Paraphrases or "mirrors" the statement without adding to or taking away from the content.
	3. Checks for accuracy: "Did I get it?" (Or some other phrase.)
4. Clarifies the original statement if necessary.	5. Mirrors and checks for accuracy until the sender indicates message has been correctly received.
6. Sender continues with the train of thought.	7. Receiver continues to mirror and check for accuracy.

This process continues until the sender delivers a complete train of thought. Then the partners switch roles, and the receiver becomes the sender and now has a chance to respond to the partner or take the conversation in a new direction.

You can begin practicing the mirroring exercise by taking turns completing the following sentence fragments:

If I could have any job in the world . . .
One experience I would like to have before I die is . . .
I think it would be really fun to . . .
When I wake up in the morning, I sometimes feel . . .
One of my fondest memories with you is . . .
I regret that I never . . .

TIPS FOR THE MIRRORING EXERCISE

1. *Keep your statements short.* Especially in the beginning, talk in short bites. This increases the probability you will be heard accurately. If your partner has difficulty mirroring you, shorten your message even further.

2. *Use a hand signal to show when you're overloaded.* Signal your partner when he or she is giving too much information at one time. You can use a two-handed T for "time-out," or raise a hand vertically in the traditional stop signal. Or you can say something like "Stop just a minute and let me get this." Use a calm, respectful voice whenever you interrupt your partner.

3. *Use the mirroring exercise to make positive comments.* Most couples use communication techniques such as this one to handle the tough issues, but I have found that some people have as much or more difficulty communicating messages of love. Use the mirroring exercise when you really want your partner to hear and absorb a positive comment. Likewise, when your partner compliments you and you're having trouble taking it in, go into the mirroring mode. You may be surprised by how much impact this can have.

4. *Take turns!* Don't perpetuate bad habits by allowing the more talkative or dominant member to spend more time as the sender. Take equal turns. (When you practice the mirroring exercise for a number of weeks, you are likely to find that the talkative partner

dominates the conversation less often and the more recalcitrant partner is more forthcoming. At first, however, you will have to make sure you take turns.)

5. *Expect strong feelings to come up with the mirroring exercise.* It is common for strong feelings to come up while mirroring. Stay with the process if this happens. If you are the receiver, mirror your partner's feelings by your tone of voice or your words. You might say something like "and that touches you deeply" or "and you're angry about that." Caution: Do not mirror feelings unless the sender has clearly expressed them. Your role is not to interpret but to reflect.

6. *Don't let your partner get you out of the process.* Just because your partner refuses to participate doesn't mean you have to stop. If you are the sender and your partner stops mirroring you, switch to the mirroring role. This takes a lot of maturity and ego strength, but it puts you in control of your own behavior and builds trust and safety in the relationship.

7. *Respect time limits and personal boundaries.* Some couples tend to overuse this process. They want to do it too often, or for extended periods, or in place of other activities, such as sex, playing, or relaxing. It is best to agree ahead of time when and how long you will do the exercise and to adhere to your plan.

8. *Use it.* The most common problem I have found with the mirroring exercise is that couples don't use it often enough. They tend to give up right before the breakthrough. If you truly want a deep level of emotional intimacy, practice this exercise faithfully for two or three months.

9. *If you get stuck, get some help.* Come to one of my workshops or work with a local therapist. Many therapists use some form of the exercise. (They may call it reflective listening or empathic listening.) Couples in a great deal of pain or conflict may need a third party to act as coach and referee. If you value your relationship, get the help that you need.

EXERCISE 5: TALKING ABOUT ENJOYABLE SUBJECTS

COMMENTS: Many people erroneously believe that intimacy means talking about "the relationship" or exploring painful topics. It's equally important to talk about activities and ideas that excite you. One particular kind of talk—what I call future talk—can be especially comforting. When you discuss activities you would enjoy doing in later years, you are building a positive future for the two of you.

DIRECTIONS: Pick one or more sentence fragments from the following list. Take turns completing them. Using the mirroring exercise, reflect back to each other what you hear.

This is not a problem-solving exercise. Resist the temptation to explore conflict or to try to reach a joint conclusion. The goal is to simply gain new information about each other and explore nonthreatening topics.

1. I still laugh when I think about the time that you and I . . .
2. A project that I would really like to do with you is . . .
3. Five years from now my wish is that you and I . . .
4. An ideal retirement situation for us would include . . .
5. At some time in our life, I would like us to . . .
6. I'd love to see you expand your talent in . . .
7. I've always appreciated your ability to . . .
8. What I miss about you when we're apart . . .
9. I'd like us to take a trip to . . .
10. A hobby I'd like to share with you is . . .

EXERCISE 6: EXPLORING MORE INTIMATE TOPICS

COMMENTS: Once you have mastered the mirroring exercise, you can discuss more sensitive topics. Come up with your own topics, or use the following sentence fragments as a springboard to take you into increasingly personal revelations.

Directions: Use the mirroring exercise to express your thoughts and feelings about important relationship issues, or choose any of the topics suggested below.

1. I get really anxious when . . .
2. I've never told you that I . . .
3. I don't think you've ever really understood the way I feel about . . .
4. The most intimate moment for me when we're making love is . . .
5. It still hurts me to think about . . .
6. If I ever lost you, I would feel . . .
7. Something I don't tell you often enough is . . .
8. I felt the deepest love for you when . . .
9. I feel angry when you . . .
10. If you were not in my life, I would miss . . .

Exercise 7: Exploring Hot Topics

Comments: If you practice the mirroring exercise several times a week for several months, you can gradually dispense with the harness of the exercise and return to a more spontaneous flow of conversation. But you may find it helpful to revert back to the formal exercise whenever you have a "hot topic" to discuss, one that causes a flare-up of emotions. When you paraphrase your partner's comments and ask for clarification, you can keep the discussion moving in a positive direction.

When the most sensitive issues are being discussed, I suggest that you go one step farther and schedule an "appointment" to talk about them. The sender can say something like this: "I have a sensitive issue to discuss. When would be a good time to talk?" Deliver this message in a calm, quiet, rational tone of voice. The receiver will suggest a time for discussion, trying to pick a time when she or he will be rested and relaxed.

I recommend setting the appointment at least ten minutes ahead even if you are available right away. This will give you time to prepare yourselves mentally. When the appointed time arrives, discuss the issue slowly and calmly, making sure you listen with full attention and paraphrase each other's comments. If these techniques fail and the discussion becomes heated, call a time-out until you regain your composure. Reschedule the conversation if tempers continue to flare.

It's possible to get through the most painful subjects if you faithfully adhere to the mirroring exercise. This simple exercise can save your relationship.

DIRECTIONS:

1. List two hot topics you would like to discuss with your partner sometime in the future.

PARTNER 1:

1. _____
2. _____

PARTNER 2:

1. _____
2. _____

2. Agree upon a time when you will use the mirroring exercise to talk about one of the topics listed above.

3. When the time arrives, sit down with your partner and establish a time limit for the discussion.

4. One person volunteers to be the sender and selects a topic to discuss.

5. The process begins with the sender making an opening statement—e.g., "I am so frustrated because you never initiate sex." The receiver reflects back this statement and those that follow until the sender is finished talking or the time is up.

6. You may switch roles if there is time, but do not go over the time limit unless both of you are comfortable with changing your agreement.

6

SEXUAL TECHNIQUE

Learning to Ask for
What You Want

One of the lectures I give during my weekend Hot Monogamy workshops is on sexual technique. I describe the various erogenous zones and talk about some basic lovemaking techniques. Then I give couples a list of suggestions to try out in the privacy of their hotel rooms. The activities range from sensual massage to some novel lovemaking positions. At a recent workshop, when the group reconvened the next morning, an outspoken gray-haired man raised his hand and said he wanted to comment on the previous night's "homework" assignment. "My wife and I discovered the G spot," he said. "We've been married forty-three years, but this is the first time we've even looked for it. We thought it was a media hoax."

"It's not," said his charming wife, blushing beet red.

I have found that most couples, regardless of age, need some encouragement to explore the full range of sexual and sensual pleasure that resides in their bodies. Even though married love is sanctioned by church and state, many couples are still reluctant to experiment. Surprisingly, a significant number of the people I see are relying on lovemaking techniques that predate Masters and Johnson, and their limited, outdated repertoire keeps them from experiencing their full erotic potential.

One reason that many people are slow to experiment is that on some level we all seem to want sex to be instinctual and "natural." We want to make love without talking about it or referring to the textbooks. We want to forget about technique—who does what to whom where—and lose ourselves in a rising tide of pleasurable sensations. In the words of the Nike commercial, we want to "Just Do It."

But the problem with just doing it is that the only techniques that come naturally to us are those that guarantee procreation. Without conscious technique, the only certainty in our lovemaking is that over time enough sperm will be deposited in the proximity of the woman's cervix to ensure the survival of the species. But today we expect a great deal more from our lovemaking than this. We want sex to be exciting, romantic, spiritual, mutually pleasurable—fulfilling enough to keep us satisfied and faithful. This more passionate, intimate, and enduring lovemaking requires sophisticated technique.

BIOLOGICAL BIAS

By necessity a lot of this technique has to be devoted to pleasuring women because, like it or not, the male of the species is better designed for sexual gratification. First of all the extra bounty of testosterone allotted to men makes it easier for them to be aroused. Nature has given men a further advantage by equipping their female partners with warm, self-lubricating, size-accommodating vaginas ideally suited for the stimulation of the penis. A few minutes of thrusting is sufficient to bring most men to orgasm. Although most men enjoy variety in their lovemaking and look for ways to heighten their pleasure, few men require more exotic techniques in order to climax. In fact, many lovemaking techniques for men are designed to *delay* the moment of orgasm.

Women are a different story. The millions of women who have

moderate or low sex drives often need some encouragement simply to get in the mood. In addition, all women, regardless of their level of desire, have to contend with the fact that a man's penis is not well equipped to stimulate the clitoris, the most sensitive part of a woman's body. In most lovemaking positions the clitoris receives only indirect stimulation, which for many women is not enough to produce orgasm. A recent survey of more than forty thousand married women revealed that almost half of them failed to reach orgasm either frequently or occasionally during intercourse. In short, unlike male orgasm, female orgasm is not guaranteed by biology.

This makes sense from an evolutionary point of view because in order for conception to occur, only the male has to climax. All a woman has to do to carry on her genes is to be receptive. But if both partners are to experience sexual satisfaction, then either the woman has to have the good fortune to be easily orgasmic or she and her mate have to be skilled in sexual technique.

SOCIETY'S CHANGING VIEW OF FEMALE SEXUALITY

Regrettably, until recent years Western society has frustrated rather than encouraged the sexual gratification of women. In our great-grandmothers' era, for example, it was widely believed that well-bred women engaged in intercourse only because of duty or a wish to bear children. In 1857 William Acton, a respected English physician, called the very idea that women would have sexual feelings a "vile aspersion." He remarked: "I should say that the majority of women (happily for society) are not very much troubled with sexual feeling of any kind. Love of home, of children, and of domestic duties are the only passion they feel." A woman who displayed passion during the sex act was thought to be encouraging the immodest nature of her husband. If she went so far as to have a "nervous spasm"—i.e., an orgasm—she defiled the "innate dignity" of the wifely role.

Needless to say, the art and science of pleasuring women advanced very little during this chaste period of our history.

In the twentieth century women have managed to reclaim their sexuality in a piecemeal fashion, approximately one erogenous zone per generation. Sigmund Freud got matters headed in the right direction by proclaiming that women did, indeed, have a sex drive. In fact, he believed that many neuroses were caused by the inhibition of that drive. But he created a significant setback for women by declaring that they had two kinds of orgasm: clitoral and vaginal. He regarded clitoral orgasms as "infantile and masculine." He wrote that "the sexual function of many women is crippled . . . by their obstinate clinging on to this excitability of the clitoris so they remain anesthetic in intercourse." In other words, a woman's interest in clitoral stimulation was a neurosis that kept her from having a mature, healthy vaginal orgasm.

This unfortunate doctrine was widely accepted by the medical profession. In a marriage manual written in 1931, a Dr. Greer wrote: "It [the clitoris] is highly sensitive, especially so in [women with] abnormal sexual appetite." He advised husbands to stay away from it.

Thirty years later sex researchers William H. Masters and Virginia E. Johnson launched a comprehensive survey of sex practices enabling us to base our understanding of female sexuality on scientific observation, not on conjecture. Masters and Johnson's primary conclusion was that there was only one kind of female orgasm. No matter how their female subjects were stimulated—by intercourse, vaginal penetration, or clitoral stimulation—their bodies appeared to respond in much the same way. Masters and Johnson believed there was only one kind of orgasm, a generic "sexual" orgasm, which they thought was always caused by either direct or indirect stimulation of the clitoris.

The duo made two other significant announcements. The first was that women could reach orgasm just as quickly as men—provided they received sufficient clitoral stimulation. The second was that virtually all women were capable of multiple orgasms. Despite the public nature of the laboratory setting, some of their female subjects were able to masturbate to orgasm six or more times in a matter of minutes.

Masters and Johnson's pronouncements touched off a revolution in female sexuality. In hundreds of "consciousness-raising" groups across the country, women encouraged each other to understand and explore their sexuality. Women who had been shamed in childhood for touching or looking at their genitals began boldly examining themselves with specula and mirrors.

The many women who had difficulty reaching orgasm through intercourse suddenly felt a new sense of entitlement. Instead of faking orgasms or enduring intercourse for their husbands' sake, they learned how to bring themselves to orgasm through clitoral stimulation and persuaded their partners to master the trick as well. It was no longer the role of male psychiatrists, husbands, medical doctors, or even sex researchers to define female sexuality; women were taking their sexuality into their own hands.

But the discovery of the central role of the clitoris was not the end of the revelations about female sexuality. In 1982 a book titled *The G Spot and Other Recent Discoveries About Human Sexuality* made a splash on the talk show circuit, bringing another female erogenous zone to the public's awareness. Written by Alice Ladas, John Perry, and Beverly Whipple, the book challenged what people then thought to be true—namely, that all female orgasms resulted from some form of clitoral stimulation. The authors maintained that there was a highly sensitive bean-shaped area of erectile tissue embedded in the front wall of the vagina called the Grafenberg spot or the G spot that was believed to produce a second kind of orgasm, a "vaginal" or "deep" orgasm.

In recent years a number of studies have confirmed the existence of the G spot. A survey of 1,245 nurses from the United States and Canada revealed that more than two thirds of the women were aware of an area of heightened sensitivity in their vaginas. Seventy-five percent of these women were able to reach orgasm through stimulation of this area alone.

With the addition of the G spot to the growing collection of female erogenous zones, we were brought full circle to Freud's original notion that women had two areas of genital sensitivity: the clitoris and the vagina. Only this time no one dared judge women according to their preference for one kind of stimulation or the other. The G spot was simply viewed as one more erogenous zone worthy of exploration.

In a hundred years we have drastically revised our view of female sexuality. Women, once thought of as shy, modest, virginal creatures, are now portrayed in the media as lusty temptresses. This modern view of women is clearly reflected in the women's magazines. On a recent trip to the grocery store, I spotted the following titles on the covers of mainstream women's magazines: "Sex with a Younger Man—New Sexual Thrills"; "Sex and Power—How to Have It All"; "Sexual Joy—Discover the Pleasures of Being Bad"; "Love Toys—Bring Back the Sizzle"; "Sexual Ecstasy—Dare to Go a Step Beyond"; "If You're Highly Sexed, Is One Lover Enough?"

Perhaps no phenomenon better capsulizes our more liberated view of female sexuality than the 1990's version of the Tupperware party. When today's suburban moms gather in each other's homes, it may not be plastic storage containers they're admiring. They may be ogling an exotic array of sex paraphernalia, including battery-operated vibrators, "split" panties, snap-crotch teddies, "shelf" (nipple-revealing) bras, and flavored lubricants. One woman I know is sending her three daughters to private colleges on the profit she makes from these in-home parties. She said that at a recent party one of the women joked about exciting her husband by doing cartwheels in her crotchless panties. "Everyone roared with laughter," said my friend. "That kind of reaction was unheard of ten years ago."

THE SEXUAL REPRESSION OF MEN

What about men? Has our view of male sexuality changed as dramatically over the years? In some ways men have been more fortunate in that society has never denied the fact that they have sexual desire. They have also been spared the frustration of trying to produce a mythical, female-defined orgasm or struggling to achieve orgasm without sufficient stimulation. However, there have been long periods in recent history when men, like women, have been made to feel guilty or immoral for expressing their sexuality.

During the 1800's and early 1900's, for example, men were exhorted to wage war against their "baser, animal nature." They were urged to be "continent," not just for religious and moral reasons but for health reasons as well. The human body was thought to be a closed system, with any unnecessary loss of bodily fluids jeopardizing a man's health and well-being. In a curious masculine equation, an ounce of semen was thought to equal forty ounces of blood, so orgasms had to be carefully meted out. An article that appeared in the prestigious *Boston Medical and Surgical Journal* in 1835 said that male "orgasms should be made but sparingly," for "sturdy manhood . . . loses its energy and bends under too frequent expenditure of this important secretion."

Health enthusiast Sylvester Graham carried this belief to the extreme, advising men to limit themselves to twelve carefully spaced orgasms a year. To help men stick to this Spartan regime, he advised them to eat bland foods, particularly whole grains, so as not to excite the nervous system—thus the "Graham" cracker.

Nocturnal emissions were also believed to be hazardous to a man's health. If a man persisted in "spilling his seed" at night, he was thought to be afflicted with a disease called spermatorrhoea. More than one emission a month was believed to result in "breathlessness, anxiety, bad digestion, brain fevers, and local irritation." The fact that some young men took this advice seriously is evident in the following excerpt from a letter that an anguished young man wrote to his physician:

> I have seen days and weeks that I did not wish to live. The emissions affect me more and more. I feel prostrated and greatly debilitated. . . . I have been paying attention to a lady that I love, and what am I to do? Would it not be insulting for me to propose marriage in my present condition? . . . Oh, sir! If I could but banish these feelings, and once more be restored to health, what is there that I would not give?

As extreme as the campaign against nocturnal emissions may seem to us today, it pales in comparison with the Victorian crusade against masturbation. Religious leaders, physicians, politicians, teachers, health writers—virtually all the authority figures of the time—thundered out their warnings to young men about the dire consequences of "self-pollution." Medical treatises produced "scientific evidence" that masturbation resulted in insanity, epilepsy, delayed physical development, loss of mental acuity, depression, flabby muscles, social awkwardness, acne, consumption, diabetes, jaundice. . . . The list went on and on. When all the possible health consequences were added up, masturbation was believed to be an indirect or even a direct cause of death. Our grandfathers and great-grandfathers were taught to be as fearful of masturbation as we today are afraid of AIDS.

EXORCISING THE GHOSTS OF OUR GREAT-GRANDPARENTS

The abusive repression of male and female sexuality began to abate in the early 1900's, but only by degree. Amazingly, only a little more than sixty years ago, husbands and wives were advised to sleep in separate beds. Dr. Greer stated in his 1931 marriage manual: "If married persons slept in different rooms the indulgence would only be thought of when there existed a natural, healthy appetite. Opportunity makes Importunity. No matter who else may sleep together, husband and wife should not."

Many of the people I interviewed for this book grew up in the shadow of this repression, and one of the unfortunate consequences is that they were given very little sex education. One woman said that the only thing her mother told her about sex was "There's something you'll have to do when you're married that you aren't going to like, and I don't mean the dishes." Another woman said, "It wasn't that sex was a taboo subject in my family; it didn't exist. There was nothing to talk about. As far as I knew, I lived in a completely asexual world." A man told me how bewildering it was to go through puberty and have no understanding of what was happening to him: "I felt as if I were the only person on earth with sexual feelings. It was strange, even frightening. I thought something was horribly wrong with me." Another man grew up feeling physically deformed because he was the only male in his family who had not been circumcised: "Nobody bothered to tell me why I was different. I thought I was diseased. When I was in junior high school, I used to lie in bed and sweat with worry."

It took me many years to banish the ghosts of repression from my own life. Like many people born in the 1940's, I grew up estranged from my body. I didn't even look at my genitals until I was in my last year of graduate school and was instructed to go home, get out a mirror, and see what I had. During sex, I would lie passively beneath my partner letting him make all the moves. It never occurred to me to do anything to add to his pleasure or to request anything different for myself.

In the first months of our relationship the normal thrusting was enough to bring me to orgasm. But as time went on, I required more stimulation. Since we never talked about sex, my partner didn't realize I was no longer fulfilled. When he tried to be more experimental—and that was what our lovemaking desperately needed—I resisted. One day he purchased an erotic video in the hope of inspiring us. I shamed him so mercilessly that he threw it in the trash. I didn't know that it was normal and natural for couples to be experimental in bed or that it can become a necessity.

I have found that a surprising amount of repression still exists in love relationships in the 1990's, even among young people. One of the primary ways it shows up is in the silence of women. In a recent study of ninety married women, only 41 percent said they felt comfortable asking their spouses for what they wanted sexually. This passivity is depriving many couples of a great deal of pleasure. Another study determined that sexually assertive women have "higher marital and sexual satisfaction, higher frequency of sexual activity, more orgasms, greater sexual desire, and more multiple orgasms." A third study compared a group of highly orgasmic women with women who had difficulty reaching orgasm. The two groups of women were indistinguishable in most ways. They had similar levels of sexual desire, they responded similarly to viewing erotic films, and they participated in many of the same sexual activities with their partners. The only significant difference between them was that the women with orgasmic difficulties felt uncomfortable asking for the kind of stimulation they required to reach orgasm.

One of the reasons that outspoken women are more sexually fulfilled is that the female sexual response is so varied. Regardless of the promises you read in some books, there is no one lovemaking position or technique that works for all women. In order to experience maximum pleasure, women have to be able to school their partners in what they like best.

I gained renewed appreciation for the great variety that exists among women when I invited eight women to discuss sexual technique. At one point in the conversation I asked them to go around the room and describe in detailed terms the lovemaking techniques they liked best. As you can see from this graphic excerpt, each woman had a unique set of instructions:

JANE: I've never had a "vaginal" orgasm, one without clitoral stimulation. Usually it's best for me to manipulate my own clitoris because I need a specific rhythm and pressure. Sometimes my husband can do it, and it's nice when he can because he enjoys it. But most of the time it needs to be me doing it. We've found several lovemaking positions that allow me to keep my hand on my clitoris. What I do is spread apart my lips with the left hand, while the other hand rubs with a circular motion. I use lubrication. I keep right on stimulating my clitoris until I reach orgasm.

MARION: The easiest, preferred way for me to reach orgasm is to have my husband lie flat on his back and for me to sit on top of him, like riding a horse. I'm on my knees. I keep his cock pushed to the front. I think that stimulates both my clitoris and my G spot. I control what gets stimulated by pushing front or leaning back. I'm going by my own sensations. Robert loves it that way. I can come in a lot of different ways, but that's the way I do it fastest and best.

JANE: Do you ever use clitoral stimulation at the same time you're having intercourse?

MARION: No, I don't need it. One thing I don't like is for Robert to be on top of me. I feel smothered. I always have to be on top. My husband is a big man. I don't like anybody on top of me, even when he's supporting his weight. I also like to be in control. And he prefers

it the way I want it. He always says, "Any way you want
it."

JANE: I really like it from behind.

NAOMI: Me, too.

JANE: But I don't come that way.

NAOMI: The best way for me to have an orgasm is not the
easiest. The best way is if I stimulate myself, or my husband does it at the same time, whatever, but after I have
the first orgasm, we have intercourse, and it feels absolutely wonderful. Then I can come again. It's the only
way I can have multiple orgasms. It is the most incredible feeling I've ever had. I've never heard of anyone
who does it the way I do.

GRACE: Well, we do something like that, too, only Jack
does it with his fingers. I stimulate my clitoris until I
come, and all the while he's stroking my G spot with his
fingers. He keeps massaging the G spot after I come,
and it sustains the orgasm. It's wonderful. I bet you're
getting the same stimulation through intercourse.

MARION: Robert taught me about the G spot first thing
when we got married. I didn't know what he was talking
about. That was nine years ago. My first husband didn't
know about it at all.

LINDA: I don't like anything with the hands. It's a basic
turnoff. I only like missionary-position intercourse. But
I come every time.

JANE: With no clitoral stimulation?

LINDA: With no clitoral stimulation. I've always been easily
orgasmic.

TONI: I have to have clitoral stimulation. But I recently
discovered that I respond more to vaginal stimulation if
we have sex in a side-to-side position. My leg is on top,
then his leg, then my leg, then his leg. Like scissors.
With the scissors position, I think my G spot gets stimulated more. Also, it's easy for me to reach my clitoris
in this position.

JANE: I've never had an orgasm just through intercourse.

Before I got married, I had sex with a lot of different men. And they had different sizes and shapes of penises, different rhythms, different staying power, but I didn't have an orgasm with any of them. It took being with one man for a long time and working out just the right kind of clitoral stimulation and not feeling embarrassed to ask for it.

BARBARA: The easiest way for me to come is if we're lying on our sides facing each other. Denton sucks my breasts, and I control the rhythm. But I have to work up to that. I don't like him to touch my breasts until I am turned on. Otherwise, it's a turnoff. But when I'm ready—and he gets me ready through oral sex—then I like being touched anywhere. One thing that's really important, and it's my easiest way to come, is for me to control the thrusting.

SUSAN: The vibrator is the easiest way for me. My husband came up with this wonderful vibrator technique, which is better than when I do it myself. He'll sit on the bed, and I'll sit close with my back to him. He'll put one arm around me and lovingly hold me, and with the other arm he reaches down and uses the vibrator. It's real nice. It's real nurturing. I'm being cuddled and held. There's a lot of skin against skin. It's real sexual, and I always come.

JEAN: So far nobody's talked much about breast stimulation. I'm most aroused when Greg touches my breasts. If I'm not interested in making love or I'm tired, all he has to do is rub my breasts and I get turned on. A couple of times I've had an orgasm just from that.

TONI: I'm jealous! I hardly feel anything when Dave touches my breasts. I seem to be missing that connection.

Many women have sexual preferences that are just as individual as the women in this group. In order to enjoy their bodies to the fullest, they need the courage and candor to make their needs known.

In my experience, women who require the use of vibrators or self-stimulation to reach orgasm may have the hardest time communicating their wishes to their partners. One of the outdated commandments governing the way we make love today is: "Thou shalt not touch thyself." All stimulation is supposed to come from intercourse or from the partner's ministrations. Yet many women need such a specific form of stimulation that it's difficult for their partners to provide it. One survey estimated that 30 percent of all women can reach orgasm only by stimulating themselves. In order to be fulfilled, they have to put aside feelings of inadequacy and shame about the way their body responds and say with integrity, "This is who I am. This is what I desire."

WHY MEN ARE RELUCTANT TO ASK FOR WHAT THEY WANT

Many men also have difficulty asking their partners for the kinds of lovemaking techniques they prefer. What keeps some men from being more forthright is the antiquated notion that a "real man" is not supposed to have any sexual needs other than for hot, frequent sex. If a man wants the lovemaking to be more intimate, more leisurely, or more romantic, there must be something wrong with him; those are "female" concerns. And heaven help him if he should need a special technique in order to maintain an erection or achieve orgasm. To admit he needs cooperation from his partner casts doubts upon his virility. One male client avoided sex for five years rather than ask his partner for oral sex, which for him was the only lovemaking technique that was guaranteed to produce orgasm.

Other men don't talk about sexual technique for the simple reason that they don't require anything other than intercourse to reach climax. But that doesn't mean they don't have a fondness for other sexual activities. Several days after I hosted the women's discussion group on sexual technique, I extended a similar invitation to a group of men. The men had an equally broad range of preferences:

MARK: First, I like my girlfriend to rub me on the chest. Lightly. I like my nipples kissed. Then, before long, I like my genitals played with, first with her hands, then her mouth. I don't like her to tease me by staying away from my penis too long. That's a turnoff. I like her to hold my penis in her hands and lick it while she's looking up at me. The eye contact is a real turn-on. If a woman can lick your cock while she looks you in the eye, you know that she likes your maleness.

ROBERT: I don't have any nipple sensitivity. I just get a big nothing.

SAM: I had this one woman who sort of—she put her mouth on my penis and left a lot of saliva on it. Left it real slick. Then she took her hand up over the head of my penis and then back down. It was great.

GLEN: I always like the same thing. I like my wife to give me head, as deep as she can. I especially like the feeling of touching the back of her throat. I like to hold her head and slowly work in and out of her mouth.

ROBERT: I like my balls to be stimulated while my wife is sucking on me. Lightly. Just brushing the skin.

GREG: For me, it's all the head of my cock. My testicles don't need to be involved.

SAM: I'm the exact opposite. I like my balls to be squeezed, manipulated, put in her mouth, nibbled. Licked. That's all nice.

MARK: Something I've noticed is that if you tell your wife you want something, she always does that one thing. You get that technique forever. I like some creativity. I like to be surprised.

GREG: It's the creativity that turns me on. The playfulness. I like my wife to do something I'm not expecting. Then, when she sees I'm liking it, I like her to back off. Tease

me. Make me beg. It makes this real connection between us. She's totally tuned in to how I'm responding.

In an ideal world we all would be intuitive, creative lovers, able
to discern exactly what our partners want. But few of us are clair-
voyant. We have to be told or shown. Sometimes our lovers can
communicate what they want with a moan or a sigh, but at times
more direct communication is necessary. The ability to talk about
our sexual desires comfortably and clearly is one of the essential
skills for Hot Monogamy. But communicating our desires is just the
beginning. We also have to override all the taboos and old messages
that keep us from reveling in our full range of sensual and sexual
pleasures. We have to develop the maturity and trust to allow our
partners to touch us, stimulate us, explore the entirety of our
bodies—to "know" us in the ordinary and the biblical sense of the
word.

The following exercises are designed to help you feel more
comfortable asking for and receiving the sexual techniques you like
best. The first one, the entitlement exercise, can be surprisingly
powerful. You are likely to gain some ground in your ability to give
and receive pleasure, even if you consider yourselves world-class
lovers.

In the second exercise you will be defining your "lovemap,"
the sexual techniques and activities that are most exciting or effective for you. Expect some resistance as you do this exercise. Making
a specific list of sexual requests goes against everything you see in
the movies and read in romance novels. If you have been together
for a number of years, there may be the added embarrassment of
sharing information that you wish you had communicated long ago.
Remarks like the following are often an indication of hidden resistance:

"I don't have time for this exercise."
"It will spoil the magic."
"It will make lovemaking too mechanical."
"I don't want to limit myself to a set of instructions."
"My needs are too complex to write down."

Work against your resistance and do the exercise anyway. If you acquire just one new piece of information about how to excite each other, consider your time well spent.

EXERCISE SECTION

EXERCISE 1: THE ENTITLEMENT EXERCISE

COMMENTS: Many people make vague requests for sexual techniques but don't give their partners specific, detailed instructions. This exercise will help you overcome any resistance you may have to getting exactly what you want.

The exercise has two parts. First, you will give your partner explicit instructions on how to rub your back, hands, or feet (your choice). This helps you learn to give clear, specific, and persistent instructions without the added complication of any sexual inhibitions. Next, you will tell your partner how to stimulate one of your erogenous zones. You can do the two parts of the exercise during the same session or in different sessions.

It is important that you take turns. As soon as one person gets ten minutes of massage or touching, switch roles. It is common for one partner to feel more comfortable being the giver, and the other to feel more comfortable being the receiver. Switching roles helps create a more equal partnership.

PART I: NONSEXUAL MASSAGE

DIRECTIONS: Take turns giving each other ten-minute massages on the back, feet, or hands. When it's your turn to be massaged, keep up a running commentary about what your partner is doing, either requesting a change or indicating approval. The goal is to train your partner to do it exactly right. *Don't stop short of total satisfaction.* You deserve to be pleasured exactly the way you want it.

Here is an example of a person giving explicit and persistent instructions for a back rub: "I'd like you to rub my back using massage oil. I'm most sore between the shoulder blades, so concentrate there. Yeah, that's the right place. Now, rub a little harder.

Harder still. I like it still harder. Yeah, that's great. You've got it. Oooh. Keep it up. Now, a little higher. Press right on that knot. No, you've lost it. Go down a little. Yeah, you found it again. Right there. That's a little too hard. Oooh, that's just right. Stay right there. Oh, yeah. Keep it up. That's just right.''

PART II: SEXUAL STIMULATION

DIRECTIONS: This is basically the same procedure as Part I, but this time you will be showing your partner how to stimulate you sexually. Pick an area of your body you would like stimulated. This could be your genitals, breasts, mouth, neck, ears, etc. Pretend that your partner has never touched you in this area before. Give your partner detailed instructions on what to do. You may need to supplement your words with a hands-on demonstration. The goal isn't to become aroused but to give clear, specific, and *persistent* instructions. (Once your partner is thoroughly "trained," you can dispense with the instructions and concentrate on the pleasure.)

Here's an example of a woman teaching her partner how to stroke her clitoris: "I'd like you to touch my clitoris. Use some lubricant. Spread my vaginal lips apart with one hand, and rub my clitoris with your other palm in a circular motion. Yeah, like that, only a little lighter. Still lighter. Just graze the top. Now a little faster. That's just right. Keep doing it just like that. That's great. A little harder. Now spread my lips farther apart. I like that feeling of pressure. Now use your index finger and middle finger. A little lighter and a little faster. Still lighter. Not back and forth but in a circle. Now try your thumb. Oh, I like that! That's perfect. That's just right.''

Here's an example of a man teaching his female partner how to stroke his genitals: "I'd like you to start by just stroking my balls very lightly. Just ruffle the hair. That's nice. That feels really good. Now dip your finger in lubricant and run it around the head of my cock. That feels so good. Now take your thumb and gently rub the underside of my cock head. In circles. More lubrication. A little harder. Yeah. Now grease up your whole hand and lightly run it up and down my shaft. Slower. Real slow. Really draw it out. Now squeeze harder. More oil. Come all the way over the head. Now just work the head. A little faster. Yeah.''

EXERCISE 2: CREATING YOUR LOVEMAP

COMMENTS: This exercise is designed to acquaint your partner with the full range of your sexual needs and desires—your "lovemap." If you have already talked at length about sexual technique, you may only need to discuss the fine points. If you have shared very little information, you can start with the basics. In either case, you will have the opportunity to explore new ground.

As I mentioned in the text, you are likely to experience some resistance as you do this exercise, but plunge ahead regardless.

DIRECTIONS: This is a private and personal assessment. At a later time you will be communicating portions of the inventory. (Some of you will feel comfortable sharing all your information with your partner right away, but I recommend that you keep it to yourself until you've read all the instructions.)

As you fill out the inventory, try to eliminate any moral judgment that stands in your way. Accept what your body is telling you, and set aside the "shoulds" and "should nots." Also, ignore any ongoing conflict with your partner about sexual technique. For now, let yourself go and freely acknowledge your desires.

As you describe what it is that you want from your partner, be specific. Saying "Kiss me" does not convey enough information. There are many different ways to kiss and many different places to kiss, and you probably have a specific kind of kissing in mind. The purpose of this exercise is to describe what you like in such detail that your partner can't get it wrong. Examples: "As we have intercourse, I would like you to kiss me quickly and teasingly on the mouth without using your tongue." "As I approach orgasm, I would like you to roll both of my nipples back and forth lightly between your fingers."

Put in all your preconditions. For example, a woman may want her nipples stimulated only during a particular phase of lovemaking or at a certain point in her menstrual cycle; otherwise it's an annoyance, not a turn-on. A man may want his penis stroked only if it is lubricated with oil or hand cream; otherwise he finds that it gets sore. Or you may be interested in oral sex only if your partner has showered recently.

You may find it hard to describe what you want. For example, you may want your penis or clitoris stroked in such a specific way you have a hard time translating it into words. Do the best you can, realizing you can always demonstrate the technique to your partner at a later date.

For greater clarity, this inventory is broken down into four sections: "Setting the Mood," "Growing Arousal," "Orgasm," and "Afterplay."

PART I: SETTING THE MOOD

First, you will be describing how you want your partner to get you in the mood for lovemaking. This is an area of technique that few couples talk about, and it can be the source of a great deal of conflict. Finding an effective, respectful way to interest each other in making love is important for a good sexual experience.

As you create this list, imagine that you are experiencing little or no desire but that your partner wants to make love. What can she or he do to make you interested in sex? Be specific. (In all sections of this inventory, I have provided some suggestions to stimulate your thinking. These are not meant to be exhaustive. You will have wishes that do not appear anywhere on these lists.)

To get me in the mood for sex, I would like you to (suggestions: tell me you're feeling sexy, talk to me suggestively, flirt, blow in my ear, rub your body against mine, tease, put on a certain kind of clothing [describe], give me a massage, make a special appointment for sex, tell me that you desire me, tell me that you love me, tell me what you find sexy about me, take off my clothes, compliment me, spend close, intimate time with me, set a romantic scene, help me around the house, make sure I'm in a relaxed mood, kiss me in this manner

. . . , touch me in this manner . . . , wait until I'm in a good mood, use certain "code words," light a candle, etc.)

_____
_____
_____
_____
_____
_____
_____
_____

Next, ask yourself what you can do for/to yourself to become more aroused. It's not always your partner's job to get you in a receptive mood; sometimes it helps if you assume some of the responsibility yourself. This is especially true for people who typically experience little or no spontaneous desire.

To get myself in the mood for lovemaking, I can (suggestions: read erotica, think about what I find sexy about my partner, think positive thoughts about my partner, read a sexy novel, take a shower/ bath, stimulate myself, think sexy thoughts, have a sexual fantasy, spend time by myself to relax and unwind, look at my partner's body, look at provocative pictures, watch a videotape, put on sexy clothing, take a nap, exercise, kiss my partner, arouse my partner in this manner, etc.)

_____
_____
_____
_____
_____
_____
_____

PART II: GROWING AROUSAL

Next, imagine you have succeeded in becoming aroused (or at least have a willingness to become aroused) through your own actions, your partner's actions, or a combination of both. What are some of the ways your partner can heighten your arousal and bring you close to orgasm? Be as specific as you can.

To arouse me to the point of orgasm, I would like you to (suggestions: kiss me in this manner and in these places . . . , be uninhibited, make sexy noises, talk to me in this manner . . . , be silent, touch me in this manner and in these places . . . , stimulate my genitals in this exact manner . . . , stimulate my breasts/nipples in this manner . . . , have intercourse with me in this/these manners [describe preferred positions], I like the rhythm, pressure, tempo of the thrusting to be . . . etc., have oral sex in this manner, stroke me lightly on my back, nuzzle my ears, kiss and bite me on the neck, show me that you are excited, share sex fantasies, I especially like these lovemaking positions under these conditions . . .)

_____

_____

_____

_____

_____

_____

_____

_____

_____

_____

_____

PART III: ORGASM

Now, imagine that you are at the brink of orgasm. What would you like your partner to do?

As I approach orgasm, I would like you to (suggestions: make sounds but no talking, talk in this manner, say my name, tell me you love me, touch me in this manner, have intercourse in these positions, vary the tempo and pressure of the thrusting in this manner, kiss or bite me in this manner, pinch my nipples, look at me, stimulate my clitoris in this manner, stimulate my G spot in this manner, stimulate my penis in this manner, stimulate my testicles in this manner, etc.)

_____

_____

_____

_____

_____

_____

_____

When I am actually experiencing orgasm, I want you to (suggestions: lie still, not stimulate me, squeeze the base of my penis, stroke my testicles, move to less direct clitoral stimulation, manipulate my G spot, squeeze my nipples, kiss me [where? how?], bite me, squeeze me, look at me, grab my buttocks, make noises, don't make noises, thrust harder, stop thrusting, etc.) [Note: Sometimes you may choose *not* to have an orgasm.]

_____

_____

_____

_____

_____

_____

_____

If I am interested in having more than one orgasm, I want you to (suggestions: wait a minute, then continue stimulating my clitoris, continue intercourse after my first orgasm, stroke my G spot, suck on my penis, hold me while I stimulate myself, etc.)

_____

_____

_____

_____

_____

PART IV: AFTERPLAY
   Now that you've reached orgasm, how would you like to end the experience?

After making love (suggestions: sometimes I have a powerful urge to go to sleep, I like to lie in your arms and talk, I like to kiss and caress each other, I want to become aroused again, I want to be kissed in this manner, I like to read, then go to sleep, I usually like to get up and do something else, other . . .)

_____

_____

_____

_____

_____

_____

_____

SHARING YOUR INVENTORY

Now that you have created this detailed inventory, it's time to do some analysis. First, go back over your inventory, and underline all your sexual needs and desires that your partner is already satisfying. As soon as you have a good opportunity (keeping in mind the guidelines discussed in Chapter 2, pages 38–39), let your partner know all the ways that he or she is currently pleasing you. Your goal is to train your partner to make love to you in the most pleasurable way possible, and one of the best ways to do this is through positive reinforcement. All too often we fail to reward our partners for what they are doing right. We take all their efforts for granted and focus, instead, on what they're doing wrong or omitting.

As you share your appreciation for your partner's lovemaking, you might use words like this: "I love the way you . . ." or "it really turns me on when you . . ." or "you've always known how I like . . ."; "you're so good at . . ."; "I get turned on every time you . . ."; "I appreciate the way you . . ."

Now go back through your list, and identify all the needs and desires that are not being satisfied within your relationship at the present time but that your partner was able to do for you at an earlier, perhaps more romantic stage of your relationship. For example, at one time your partner might have given you more back rubs or gone to the effort to dress more seductively or spent more time getting you aroused. Put a check mark by the items that used to be a part of your lovemaking.

Set aside some time to tell each other about what you used to enjoy about your lovemaking. Keep your statements positive. Say: "I really used to love it when you wore sexy lingerie to bed. You looked so provocative." Not: "How come you always come to bed in that frumpy nightgown?"

More positive examples: "We both used to be naked when we made love. I enjoyed all that skin." "Remember when we lit candles when we made love? It was so romantic." "We used to make love in the morning. That was such a nice time of day."

As you share these positive memories, look for activities and techniques that you both enjoyed and wish were still a part of your lovemaking routine. As soon as possible revive some of these practices.

Next, think about all the desires that your partner has never satisfied for you but that you believe he or she might be willing to satisfy if he or she knew exactly what you wanted. You may have been reluctant to share your desires, describe them in sufficient detail, or tell your partner how much you'd like them. Circle these items. Make separate lists of these special requests, and exchange them with your partner. You and your partner are encouraged to grant each other one of these requests every week or month. The person performing the technique is the one who gets to choose what to do. These are not obligations but gifts to each other.

Now think about all the desires that are not being satisfied within your relationship and that you believe your partner would have difficulty satisfying at this time. These desires may already be a source of conflict, or you may have never communicated them for fear of being rejected. (For example, you may have always wanted your partner to participate in oral sex, but he or she has not been willing. You may want your partner to share sexual fantasies, but you're afraid he or she would be offended. You want your partner to act more seductively, but he or she has been too inhibited. You want your partner to wear sexy underwear, but he or she has refused.) Put an X by those items. Hold these requests in reserve. As you become more adventuresome with your lovemaking and find yourself communicating more freely (this may take months), consider asking for one or more of these requests.

Finally, think about the way you currently make love and identify any techniques or activities that you actively dislike. During intercourse, your partner may talk when you wish she or he were silent or may be silent when you wish she or he would talk. Your partner may be too rough or too passive. Your partner may have bad breath or body odor. Your partner may rush through foreplay or afterplay.

What you want to do in this part of the exercise is let your partner know you would like something changed without being critical or hurting his or her feelings. One way to do this is to phrase your request using the word "instead," pointing out what you don't like and suggesting a positive alternative. Examples:

> *"Instead of touching my penis with a light, teasing touch, I would like you to grip it more firmly. Next time we're in bed, I'll show you how."*
>
> *"Instead of wet kisses, I would like you to kiss me more lightly."*
>
> *"Instead of brushing your teeth just in the morning, I'd appreciate it if you brushed them before coming to bed."*
>
> *"Instead of squeezing my whole breasts, I'd like you to pay more attention to the nipples. I like them to be squeezed quite firmly."*
>
> *"Instead of sucking on my clitoris, I'd like you to flick it from side to side with your tongue."*
>
> *"Instead of using saliva to lubricate your fingers, I'd like you to use K-Y jelly."*
>
> *"Instead of focusing just on my genitals, I'd like you to caress my whole body first."*
>
> *"Instead of falling asleep after we make love, I'd like you to hold me in your arms for a few minutes."*
>
> *"Instead of talking while we're making love, I'd like you to concentrate on the sensations."*

7

VARIETY

How to Have
More Fun in Bed

One of the most common complaints I hear from long-term monogamous couples is that their lovemaking lacks variety. Most of the time they make love in the very same way. A woman described her nightly routine this way: "We get into bed. We rarely kiss. He'll go right to oral sex. That will lubricate me. I'll reach orgasm. He'll penetrate, and three minutes later he'll reach orgasm. That's it. Who would want to do that again and again? It's so predictable. That's what drives me crazy. I don't find what we do very interesting."

A man found his love life equally humdrum: "My girlfriend and I have been living together for five years. Sex is very comfortable between us, but it isn't experimental anymore. We're afraid to be 'nasty' with each other. The sex we're going to have tomorrow night will be exactly like the sex we had four years ago. It's sad. I know I could go out with someone new and be erotic and do all kinds of wonderful things. I could tell a new lover, 'Let's try this!' 'I'd love it if you did that!' But with my girlfriend a sense of famil-

iarity closes me down. I really don't want an affair, but I'm tempted.
I long for the variety and the excitement." Unfortunately, the only
way he could imagine having a more exciting sex life was to have
an affair. He equated monogamy with monotony.

He's not alone. Having an affair is the way that millions of
people look for sexual excitement. There's no denying that sex with
a new person stimulates the appetite. Sexologists refer to this phenomenon as the Coolidge Effect, referring to the following incident
that may or may not have taken place between President and Mrs.
Coolidge. It seems that the President and his wife were being given
separate tours of a model government farm. When Mrs. Coolidge
toured the chicken yard, she stopped to admire a rooster that was
busily mating with one hen after another. The First Lady brazenly
asked the guide how many times a day the rooster performed his
duty. "Dozens of times," the guide replied. "Oh!" said Mrs. Coolidge, visibly impressed. "Would you mind telling that to the President when he comes by?" When the President's entourage came
to view the chicken yard, the guide dutifully reported that Mrs.
Coolidge wanted to draw his attention to the rooster's virility. The
President viewed the scene for a moment and then asked the guide,
"Does the rooster mate with the same hen over and over or with
different hens?"

"Why, different hens, of course," said the guide.

The President said with a smile: "Kindly convey *that* to Mrs.
Coolidge."

CREATING VARIETY WITHIN MONOGAMY

This story illustrates what many people know to be true: Sex with
someone new can be highly arousing. When the chemistry is right,
just a look or a touch or the sound of your lover's voice can make
you weak in the knees. This fever pitch can be maintained for
months or even years if the affair is kept secret. The element of
risk plus the fact that you can't be together as often as you'd like
sustains the erotic tension.

However, the question I am asking throughout this book is
whether or not it is possible to sustain passion in a monogamous,

long-term relationship. The answer is a resounding YES—provided you are willing to keep expanding the intimate and erotic boundaries of your relationship. With conscious effort and a willingness to change, you can experience passionate lovemaking on a regular basis.

Deepening your level of emotional intimacy (discussed at length in Chapter 5) may provide much of the missing aphrodisiac. Sex is never boring when you and your partner connect on an emotional plane and make love to each other's souls. In the previous chapter I talked about another factor—namely, the freedom to explore all the God-given pleasures of your body and to ask your partner for the kind of lovemaking techniques you like best. In this chapter I will be going one step farther and presenting a broad menu of sexual techniques to expand your lovemaking rituals. Like many couples, you may discover that Hot Monogamy lies in the realm of previously uncharted territory.

Just how well new lovemaking techniques can revive erotic interest was demonstrated in a recent study of a group of college students. The young men and women were shown the same sexually explicit film once a day for four days in a row. Most of the viewers were highly aroused the first day they viewed the film. By the third day their reactions were more muted. When the film was shown the fourth time, some of the coeds were actually bored. On the fifth day the researchers introduced a new film showing the same actors demonstrating a new lovemaking technique. The erotic response zoomed upward, almost reaching the level of day one.

If exploring new sexual activities can add so much excitement to a long-term relationship, why are so many couples slow to experiment? Some people are worried that trying new techniques will make them feel incompetent or foolish. Others are held back by messages left over from a repressed upbringing. Still others are put off by the seedy environment in which many sexual options are displayed. Going into a typical "adult" bookstore or videostore can be highly offensive to some people.

In an effort to give couples who come to my workshops more permission to explore the full range of sensual and sexual possibilities, I devote a portion of the seminar to talking about a wide variety of sexual techniques, sex games, sex toys, and erotica. So far no one has fallen asleep during this segment. To be offered reliable information about sexual variety in a safe, pleasant, wholesome setting is all the permission many couples need to become more experimental.

If a lack of permission or good information is all that's holding you back, then the following suggestions and resources may entice you to add more variety to your lovemaking.

DEFINING DIFFERENT LOVEMAKING STYLES

When people think about spicing up their love lives, they usually think about trying novel lovemaking positions or making love in unusual places. There's an even more basic way to add variety to your lovemaking, and that is to vary the amount of time and effort you put into your sexual encounters. Most couples settle rather quickly into one style of lovemaking. Each time they make love, they spend about the same amount of time and energy. Some couples can predict within a matter of minutes how long their encounters will last. ("Seventeen minutes," volunteered a woman at one of my seminars.) Although they may alternate between a few favorite positions, the overall effect is the same.

To relieve this monotony, I suggest that you have three or four distinct styles of lovemaking. One style may be quick and relatively uninvolved. It is ideally suited for times when only one of you is feeling aroused, when the hour is late, when the energy level is low, or when both of you are highly aroused and want to skip the preliminaries. Sometimes only one of you may want to reach orgasm. This style of lovemaking is commonly referred to as a quickie.

Quickies have a definite place in a love relationship. They can satisfy the needs of the more highly sexed partner, relieve physical tension, and add more spontaneity—especially when the quickie is a stealthy encounter in an unusual place like the kitchen, a walk-in closet, or the backyard. I know of one couple with teenage children who have made up for their lack of privacy by having quickies in the bathroom. They turn on the shower and overhead fan to disguise any noises and have a quick lovemaking session with no one the wiser. Many of the couples I've counseled don't use quickies often enough. Lovemaking doesn't always have to be a production.

The second style of lovemaking might take a moderate amount of time and effort—perhaps fifteen to thirty minutes. In this variation your goal may be for both of you to reach orgasm most of the time, so an adequate amount of time is required. This style of lovemaking often takes place in the bedroom at the end of the day or first thing in the morning. It's what most couples do most of the time.

There's nothing wrong with this garden-variety style of lovemaking. For one thing, it easily fits into a busy schedule. Furthermore, you can alternate between the two or three techniques that work best for you, with little need for conversation or negotiation. It's a comfortable, cozy, predictable way to make love. However, if that's *all* you do, then your sex life is likely to seem flat and uninspired.

The third style of lovemaking is more leisurely, lasting forty-five minutes to an hour or more. If your lives are busy, you may have to schedule it in advance. You may also want to do some scene setting, such as playing music, lighting candles, "dressing up," or spending time on preliminaries like a shared shower, massage, or teasing. Couples tend to have leisurely lovemaking sessions in the early stages of their relationships but allow them to slip from their repertoire after a few years.

The nice thing about making love in this prolonged fashion is that a little goes a long way. If you lead a busy life, you may have time for a lengthy encounter only once a month. However, one long session can sustain the intimacy for weeks. If you make no other change in your routine than add a dozen extended lovemaking events a year, you will notice a dramatic improvement in your enjoyment of sex.

The fourth style of lovemaking, which I call adventuresome sex, presents the greatest challenge for some people, and that is its purpose. Adventuresome sex takes you away from your everyday habits and adds a sense of risk and playfulness to the sexual experience. For some couples, this category might include gymnastic positions, sex games, sex toys, erotica, shared fantasies, or the use of various props, such as food, seductive clothing, feathers, or ice. Adventuresome sex can be hilarious as well as erotic. It can bond you together like no other activity.

Once you have defined the lovemaking styles that work best for you, I recommend that you give them names. One couple affectionately labeled their most fleeting style of lovemaking a "poke," a term found in the novel *Lonesome Dove.* Having labels makes it easier to convey your intentions. For example, if you ask your partner, "Are you interested in a quickie?" your partner will know you have a brief encounter in mind and can respond accordingly. On the other hand, if you ask, "Are you willing to go on a little adventure?" you alert your partner that you are in the mood for something a little more daring.

Another way to add variety to your lovemaking is to keep your partner informed of your changing needs and desires. Many people become less sexually inhibited in their adult years but fail to communicate this more liberal policy to their partners. Some years back I was working with a couple who came to me complaining of a lack of interest in sex. In one session I asked them, "Do the two of you have oral sex?"

They glanced at each other to see who would respond first. The woman said, "Not really."

I asked them, "Are you interested in oral sex?"

The man shook his head no; at the same time the woman nodded her head up and down.

Her husband looked at her in amazement. "You told me you wouldn't do oral sex!"

She answered, "That was seven years ago. I've changed my mind."

Another client told me that in her early twenties she would make love only in the missionary position. She's now in her fifties and says, "Today I don't think there's much that I'm not willing to do." Fortunately she's kept her husband informed of the warming trend.

EXPLORING THE G SPOT

Exploring a new erogenous zone is a delightful way to expand your lovemaking repertoire. All too many couples that I see limit their exploration to a few erogenous zones—typically the man's penis and the woman's breasts, clitoris, and vagina. One area that often gets overlooked is the woman's G spot. As I mentioned in the previous chapter, the G spot does indeed exist. Research has shown that all women have an area of sensitivity on the upper surface of the vagina. Stimulating this area is highly pleasurable for most—but not all—women.

The G spot is embedded in the front wall of the vagina behind the pubic bone, a short finger's length inside the opening. In an unstimulated state, the G spot is about the size of a dime and is difficult to detect—one of the reasons it tends to be bypassed. When stimulated, it swells to about the size of a half dollar and feels quite prominent through the vaginal wall, taking on a rubbery or spongelike texture that feels firmer and more textured than the surrounding area. It is often easiest to detect just before or during orgasm.

It can be difficult for a woman to stimulate her own G spot because she has to reach inside her vagina. Some women find it easier to reach from a squatting position. Another alternative is to purchase a specially designed G spot dildo or vibrator. These can be ordered through mail-order catalogs. (See Appendix B for more information.)

To stimulate the G spot with your fingers, insert one or more fingers inside your vagina. Firmly stroke the front wall of your vagina. The authors of the book *The G Spot* suggest that you imagine a clock face inside your vagina with twelve o'clock pointing to your navel. Most women locate the G spot between eleven and one. Because the urethra is also in that general area, you may at first interpret the sensation of G spot stimulation as a signal that you need to urinate. (You may want to empty your bladder before you begin the exercise.)

It is often easier for a woman's partner to stimulate the G spot because no contortions are necessary for him to insert his fingers into the vagina. To stimulate your partner's G spot, ask her to lie on her back with her knees lifted and spread apart while you insert one or two fingers *palm side up* into the vagina. Firmly sweep the upper wall of the vagina in a "come here" motion, about once a second, responding to your partner's feedback. You may not be able to distinguish the G spot from the surrounding area until the area becomes engorged. However, after a few minutes of firm stroking, the G spot should emerge as a denser, more prominent area.

A man volunteered the following description of how he stimulates his wife's G spot: "I think of my wife's vagina as a cave. If she's lying on her back, the G spot is on the ceiling of the cave. I put my middle finger in her vagina about up to the second joint. Then I bend my finger and stroke the top of the wall. If she's not very aroused, I don't feel much of anything. But after I stroke for a while, the tissue starts to firm up. It becomes shaped like a football or an ellipse, and it's about an inch and a half long. It seems to assume different shapes. Sometimes it's a ridge. Sometimes it's more spread out. I can clearly feel it, and my wife craves the feeling."

Some women experience little sensation the first few times the G spot is manually stimulated, so I suggest that you experiment a half dozen times, varying the pressure, speed, and kind of touch until you discover what works best. With sufficient practice many women can reach orgasm from G spot stimulation alone. (Some women ejaculate a colorless fluid when they reach orgasm through G spot stimulation. This is a natural, normal process. The ejaculate comes from the urethra, but it is not urine. It's a liquid produced by glands that surround the urethra.)

Once you've stimulated the G spot with your fingers, try out various lovemaking positions to see which ones exert the right kind of pressure on that area. Many women report that rear-entry positions or woman-on-top positions provide the most direct stimulation; some have long preferred these positions without realizing they were responding to G spot stimulation.

You can incorporate G spot stimulation into your lovemaking rituals in a wide variety of ways. A woman may find it easier to reach orgasm if her partner stimulates her G spot and clitoris at the same time. ("When my boyfriend does that to me," confessed one young woman, "you have to scrape me off the ceiling.") Some women find that lovemaking becomes more pleasurable when the G spot is stimulated prior to intercourse, engorging the tissue and making it more responsive to pressure from the penis. A woman can intensify her orgasms by adding G spot stimulation as she reaches orgasm. Some people call this a blended orgasm because it combines sensations from both the vagina and the clitoris.

Finally, sexual athletes can experiment with using the G spot to produce a blended, extended orgasm, one that results in not just multiple but almost continuous orgasms. To create an extended orgasm, stimulate the clitoris until the woman reaches orgasm. Then, as her vagina begins to contract in orgasm, transfer your attention to the G spot. When the contractions subside and the clitoris loses its hypersensitivity, resume clitoral stimulation until she peaks once again. And so on. And so on.

LOVEPLAY FOR MEN

There is an unfortunate tendency to shortchange men when it comes to sexual variety. There are several reasons for this. As I discussed in the previous chapter, most women require some form of clitoral or G spot stimulation in addition to vaginal penetration in order to reach orgasm. But the vast majority of men can climax from intercourse alone, so they don't need added attention. Second, we have long assigned women a passive role in lovemaking. A sex manual written in 1963, when I was a young bride, advised a man to reduce his wife "with his eyes, with his touch, and with the things he may say to her, to the imagined status of a small girl who is helpless and resigned in his hands." All too many couples have yet to break out of this traditional arrangement. Finally, as I mentioned before, some men have the mistaken notion that if they need more stimulation than they get from intercourse, something is wrong with them. One man said to me, "I don't like it if my wife stimulates me. That makes me think that I might need her help, and I don't like that."

Most men, however, love foreplay and feel they don't get

enough of it. Here are some comments from men that I've interviewed:

> *"I love women's bodies. I love everything about them: their breasts,*
> *their cunts, their skin, their hair, the way they walk. But I*
> *don't get the impression that women love men's bodies. I would*
> *like to know what it feels like to have a woman make love to*
> *me. I would like to lie there and enjoy all those wonderful*
> *feelings."*
> *"When my wife and I are making love, it's like I'm a bee and*
> *she's the flower. I'm buzzing around, and the flower's just wait-*
> *ing there to be pollinated. She's not very active. All the while*
> *we're having sex, she just lies there."*
> *"I would love to feel that my girlfriend wanted me as much as I*
> *want her. I would love to think she gets turned on by looking*
> *at my body and touching me."*

What can women do to lavish more attention on their male
partners? One way is to ask them. Many men will gladly volunteer
information. One woman who was married for twenty years finally
got up the courage to ask her husband how he would like her to
stimulate his testicles. He promptly gave her a demonstration. Since
then she's felt like a more accomplished lover, and her husband
has experienced an added dimension of pleasure.

Some men need coaxing to talk about their desires. One
woman said she got over her partner's reluctance by framing her
question this way: "Is there anything special you want me to do for
you tonight? Something I've never done before or haven't done in
a long time?" When a woman expresses her sexual curiosity, her
partner has more permission to share his longings.

When you run out of your partner's suggestions, I have some
other options for you to consider. One lovemaking technique for
men is called the scrotal tug. It involves a gentle pull on the testicles. Some men find this technique pleasurable in and of itself, but
more often it's used to prolong a man's arousal. Typically a man
doesn't ejaculate until his scrotum retracts and draws up close to
his body. Maintaining a gentle traction on the testicles keeps this

from happening, allowing a man to experience that delightful "cliff-hanging" sensation for a longer period of time.

To perform the scrotal tug, grasp the scrotal sac close to the man's body (just above the testicles) with your thumb and forefinger, making a ring shape. (You must do this before the testicles have elevated.) Do not squeeze the testicles themselves. Maintain a gentle downward traction while stimulating the penis with your mouth or hand. Your partner will tell you how firmly to pull.

Another male erogenous zone that is frequently overlooked is the prostate, a small gland, about the size of a walnut, just beneath the bladder. The prostate secretes prostatic fluid, the main component of semen. (Some physiologists maintain that a woman's G spot and a man's prostate gland are analogous glands, originating from the same embryonic tissue.)

There are two ways to stimulate the prostate: externally and internally. To stimulate it externally, press rhythmically into the perineum (the area between the anus and the testicles), with the ball of your thumb, being careful not to scratch your partner with your nails. Some books refer to this area as the external prostate spot. Some men like external prostate stimulation only when fully aroused. Some men don't like it at any time. Several men have reported to me that pressure on the external prostate spot helps them regain or maintain an erection. Ask. Experiment.

For those who are not opposed to anal stimulation, a more direct way to stimulate the prostate is to insert a well-lubricated finger into the rectum and press toward the front of the man's body. (Once again, be careful with your nails.) If you wish, you can wear latex gloves, wrap your finger in a condom, or use a one-finger sheath called a finger cot. (See Eve's Garden, page 286, in Appendix B for information on how to order finger cots.) Use lubrication with these devices as well. Some men enjoy internal prostate stimulation very much and can reach orgasm from this technique alone. Others find that external prostate stimulation intensifies their orgasms. Every body is different.

ORAL SEX

A discussion of sexual technique for men would not be complete without mentioning oral sex. Once regarded as a perversion, fellatio is now standard fare for most younger couples and is widely practiced by couples of all ages. However, most men would like even more oral sex than they are getting. When sex writer Susan Crain Bakos asked more than a thousand men whether or not they got enough oral sex, 75 percent of them said no.

I have talked with a number of women who were struggling to understand why their partners were so interested in fellatio. What many men have told me is that the oral stimulation of the penis is the most pleasurable form of loveplay for them. The mouth can exert more pressure than the vagina and can stimulate the penis in an endless variety of ways, including kissing, licking, and sucking. Also, during fellatio a man gets to lie back and devote all his attention to his own arousal, which intensifies the sensations. Finally, many men find that fellatio has an erotic, "forbidden" quality that heightens their pleasure. One man said simply, "I find everything about it exciting."

Some women object to fellatio because they're worried that the penis may harbor germs or bacteria, or they're turned off by the notion that the penis is a conduit for urine as well as semen. I reassure them that a freshly washed penis has fewer bacteria than the mouth. Other women are worried about gagging on the penis. Giving the woman control over the depth of penetration helps alleviate this worry. When a woman places her hand around the base of the man's penis, she can control how much of the shaft she takes into her mouth. She should also be the one to determine whether or not her partner ejaculates in her mouth. Some women have strong gag reflexes or do not like the taste of semen and cannot tolerate ejaculation.

Which oral techniques are most pleasing to men? As you can see by the following comments, it depends on the man:

"I like it best when my wife takes me as deeply into her mouth as possible. She puts Vaseline on her lips and uses firm pressure.

When I'm highly aroused, I like a gentle bite way down on the shaft. All the while she is gently stroking my testicles with her hand."

"The head of my penis is the most sensitive. I love it when she pops the head in and out of her mouth."

"I like gentle licks and nibbles all over the head."

"I like to start with a soft penis so she can put the whole thing in her mouth. I hold her head gently and control the motion. She keeps her teeth covered and uses hard pressure with her lips. When my penis gets hard, she puts her hand around the base of my cock. This feels like an extension of her mouth."

"She flicks her tongue across the underside of my cock, close to the head. Then I lie on my back as she bobs her head up and down on my shaft, using a lot of suction. The more action, the better."

"I like my girlfriend to suck more firmly on the upstroke than the downstroke."

"My wife sucks on the head of my penis while she masturbates the shaft with her hand."

"I'm lying on my side and my wife is lying on her side facing me, her head on a pillow. At first she sucks me actively while I lie still. When I get really aroused, I take her head gently in my hands and fuck her mouth as deep as she finds comfortable."

THE MANY REWARDS OF KEGEL EXERCISES

A research project you and your partner might try is to use Kegel exercises to enhance your mutual sexual pleasure. In 1948 a physician named Arnold Kegel developed a simple exercise to help women achieve better bladder control. It was designed to strengthen a small muscle on the pelvic floor called the pubococcygeal (PC) muscle, which is present in both men and women. Coincidentally the women reported that increasing the tone of the PC muscle gave them stronger and more frequent orgasms. (This fact was widely known in Indian, Chinese, and Arab cultures thousands of years ago.) Later studies have shown that a strong PC muscle may make it easier for a woman to reach orgasm from G spot stimulation alone.

In 1985 a team of researchers found another positive effect of Kegel exercises for women. They discovered that if women contracted the PC muscle every fifteen seconds or so while they were having a sexual fantasy, they became more highly aroused. This was true whether or not the women had practiced the exercise before. It wasn't having more toned PC muscles that contributed to their heightened arousal but simply the act of clenching them.

If a woman rhythmically tightens her PC muscle during intercourse, her partner will benefit as well. As she contracts the muscle, the vagina grips the penis more tightly, which her partner is likely to find highly pleasurable. The effect becomes more pronounced as the PC muscle becomes strengthened through regular exercise.

Men can also benefit from practicing Kegel exercises. Toning their PC muscles gives them more intense orgasms and improves their ejaculatory control. In order to gain more control over ejaculation, I advise men to practice during masturbation. When they sense they are about to ejaculate, they should push out with their PC muscles, which helps neutralize the orgasmic reflex and prolongs the state of arousal. Once a man masters this art, he can use it to prolong intercourse.

DIRECTIONS FOR KEGEL EXERCISES: A good way to locate your PC muscle is to stop your flow of urine midstream. The muscle cutting off the flow is the PC muscle. (The PC muscle is a short muscle that does not extend to the buttocks. Your buttocks muscles should remain relaxed during this exercise.) A way for a woman to locate her PC muscle is to tighten her vaginal muscles around her fingers, a dildo, or her partner's penis. The amount of pressure she can exert indicates the strength of the muscle.

When you first begin, tighten the PC muscle and hold for three seconds. (This will seem like a long time. Count: "One thousand one, one thousand two, one thousand three.") Then relax the muscle completely. (This is important. The more completely you relax the muscle, the more tightly you can clench it subsequent times.) Repeat five times. Repeat this sequence of five contractions several times. Increase the number of repetitions day by day until you are doing ten series of five three-second contractions each day. (Be careful not to overexercise the muscle at first. It can get sore.) It takes approximately two months for the muscle to be fully toned.

You can do the exercise anywhere: sitting at a computer, driving a car, standing in line at the grocery store, brushing your teeth. Having some sort of recording system will help you carry out your good intentions. (A friend of mine places a Post-It note on her computer and adds a slash mark for each set of five contractions.) If you perform your Kegels faithfully, your reward may be heightened arousal during intercourse and more intense orgasms— not to mention the elimination or prevention of bladder control problems.

PLAYING DRESS-UP

The Sharper Image, a company that specializes in electronics and high-tech gadgets, recently test-marketed two items of lingerie: a black lace hose and garter combination and a black lace body stocking. These two items alone added $1.5 million in "male" order sales. This sales figure doesn't surprise me. In one survey a thousand men were asked what turned them on most: dirty talk, X-rated videos, pornography, female masturbation, sexy lingerie, or "other." Of the men surveyed, 92 percent said they were most turned on by sexy lingerie. In an interesting footnote, 73 percent of these men said they relied on stimulation such as this to sustain their interest in a long-term relationship. In essence, a man who asks his partner to wear a lace teddy to bed may be saying to her, "Please help me be monogamous."

Some women are resistant to wearing seductive lingerie, however. Many a man has bought sexy clothes for his lover only to discover them hidden away in the back corner of the dresser drawer. Some women think sexy lingerie panders to sexist attitudes. Others are reluctant to wear revealing lingerie because they are uncomfortable about their weight or degree of physical fitness. Carol Hawkins, an executive officer in Undercover Wear, a women's home party lingerie company, says, "A lot of women tell me they will start wearing sexy clothes to bed when they lose twenty pounds." She urges them to do it anyway: "Your husband knows you're carrying that extra weight. You can't hide it, so you might as well package it well.''

The best way for women to enhance their figures, says Hawkins, is to buy their own lingerie: "Your lover doesn't know what will look best on you. He'll buy something that looks good in the ads." If you shop for yourself, you can play up your strong points. Some teddies, for example, are designed to support large breasts while others accentuate small ones. The cut can make all the difference. Most lingerie companies now carry a queen-size line designed to flatter fuller figures.

If women pick clothes that *they*, not their husbands, find erotic, they may wind up boosting their own libidos. I know a woman whose boyfriend kept urging her to wear sexy lingerie to bed, but she always refused. One day she and a friend happened to pass by a lingerie store and her friend persuaded her to go inside. At her friend's urging she picked out a couple of items and tried them on in the dressing room. When she tried on a bra that exposed her nipples, she was amazed to find herself becoming aroused. "I had no idea that *I* would be turned on by that stuff," she said. "I thought it was all for my boyfriend."

THE ALLURE OF THE "BODICE RIPPERS"

The erotica of choice for millions of women is likely to be found in the local supermarket, not Frederick's of Hollywood. I'm talking about the romance novel, which, in reality, should be renamed the erotic novel. Studies have revealed that women buy the paperback books not to read courtly tales of romance but to lose themselves in long, drawn-out tales of seduction.

In virtually all the romance novels the plot centers on the relentless seduction of a young, beautiful virgin by a handsome, exceedingly virile man. The heroine finds herself consumed with lust, seemingly against her will. By page 200 the heroine's virginity will be a thing of the past, and she will have enjoyed numerous heart-stopping orgasms. Even though many of these books are historical novels, the authors assume that the heroes have read Masters and Johnson and are well versed in clitoral stimulation. This expertise is hardly necessary, however, because all the heroines are vaginally orgasmic—first time, every time. Although the authors manage to drag out the lovemaking for many pages, they never use graphic terms. He strokes her "soft, moist petals." She fondles his "throbbing manhood."

An estimated twenty million women pay good money for this form of titillation. Romance novels account for 46 percent of the mass-market paperbacks sold in the United States, an estimated $750 million worth of sales in 1991.

There are some common misconceptions about the kind of woman who reads these novels. One might assume that the only romance she sees is between the embossed covers of her paperback. Not so. Two researchers recently tried to determine what distinguishes women who read romance novels from those who do not. They found no apparent difference in marital status, education, or income. The only notable difference between the two groups was in sexual activity. Surprisingly, women who read romance novels appear to experience greater sexual satisfaction and have sexual relations *twice as often* as those who do not. The researchers concluded that "erotic romances provide a form of sexual stimulation for their readers similar to that provided by sexual fantasies and that they are a form of 'softcore' pornography that women find socially acceptable and nonthreatening. . . . By grafting explicit sexual elements onto the existing Gothic novel form, a kind of erotica is created that has no social or emotional stigma for the reader."

I happen to be an advocate of romance novels. I believe that reading stories about lustful women can give a sexually inhibited woman the permission she needs to be a more passionate lover—especially when she reads the books last thing at night. I routinely make this suggestion during my workshops. A distinguished-looking woman came up to me during a break in a workshop to tell me she had never considered reading one of those "bodice rippers." "I have a Ph.D. in English," she said. "It would never occur to me even to glance at the cover of a romance novel." Then she surprised me by asking in a conspiratorial tone of voice, "Do you have any favorite authors?"

SEX TOYS

The so-called sex toys have zoomed in popularity in recent years. A 1978 *Redbook* survey of married women found that a mere 20 percent used some sort of "device" during lovemaking. In 1993 nearly 50 percent of the women who responded to a similar survey by *Ladies' Home Journal* acknowledged using erotic aids.

I view sex toys as just another way to give and receive pleasure. It's like making bread. You can knead dough with your hands, or you can use a mixer or a fancy bread machine. Whichever way you mix it, you come up with basic bread.

Vibrators are by far the most popular sex toy. Electric vibrators were first manufactured in this country in the early 1900's. It's not clear when the first woman thought to try one to ease the "muscle tension" between her legs, but the practice has grown steadily ever since. The appeal of vibrators is simple: When pressed against a woman's clitoris (not inserted in her vagina), they can produce a speedy orgasm. Many women who have difficulty climaxing experience their first orgasms with the help of a vibrator. Another reason for the popularity of vibrators is that they can be purchased without embarrassment from department stores, variety stores, and pharmacies.

Vibrators are often used for a woman's solitary pleasure, but an increasing number of couples are using them to supply clitoral stimulation during intercourse because a slim vibrator can be slipped between a couple more easily than a hand.

In my view, using a vibrator does not have to make sex mechanical or impersonal, especially if the couple finds some way to maintain skin or eye contact. To provide a feeling of closeness, I recommend that couples who use vibrators snuggle close together, look in each other's eyes, or caress each other with their free hands.

Vibrators can also be used when only the woman wishes to reach orgasm. One man described to me one of the ways he makes use of a vibrator: "When I'm tired and don't feel like doing anything—maybe I've had a grueling tennis match or something—and my girlfriend wants sex, I get out the vibrator. The vibrator is the female analogy to the quickie. It works every time. And my girlfriend doesn't complain."

There are three basic kinds of vibrators: coil-operated, motor-driven, and battery-operated. Coil-operated vibrators are run by electromagnetic coils. Typically the vibrators have two speeds and vibrate at either sixty or thirty cycles per second. Most coil-operated vibrators come equipped with snap-on attachments. If you purchase the vibrator from a mail-order catalog or a store that specializes in sex toys, you can order attachments specially designed for genital stimulation. (See Appendix B.) However, even most local variety stores now offer a soft, flexible nub attachment for those "special, hard-to-reach places."

The second kind of vibrator is the long, wand-shaped vibrator that is most often marketed as a back massager. It is driven by an electric motor and delivers a more intense pulse. Some women have a distinct preference for one kind of sensation or the other. An advantage of the wand vibrators is that you needn't feel embarrassed about leaving them on top of the dresser. However, they tend to be bulky and relatively noisy.

Battery-powered vibrators are smaller than either the coil or the wand vibrators and are usually penis-shaped. They are primarily sold through specialty catalogs or adult stores, although more discreet versions are now available in some department stores. Battery-powered vibrators deliver the least intense vibrations of the three kinds, and some women complain they don't deliver enough oomph. However, there are some advantages of the battery types: (1) Their smaller size makes them easier to conceal, and (2) they can be inserted into the vagina and used as a dildo as well as for clitoral stimulation.

Vibrators are not just for women anymore. Some men enjoy the added stimulation they get during intercourse when their partners are using vibrators. Other men use vibrators directly on the penis. (Several manufacturers provide a cuplike attachment designed for the head of the penis.) But although a growing number of men use vibrators, few that I have talked to give them rave reviews.

Dildos, another popular kind of sex toy, are phallic-shaped devices designed to be inserted in the vagina or the anus. They can be used for masturbation or to add variety to marital sex play. Unlike vibrators, they have to be ordered through sex catalogs or purchased at adult stores; that has kept many couples from experimenting with them.

Dildos come in all shapes, sizes, colors, materials, and textures. Some dildos are "representational"—i.e., they are made to look like penises. Others are whimsically designed in the shape of animals. (For some reason, beavers, kangaroos, whales, and dolphins are especially popular.) Top-of-the-line dildos are made out of silicone, which is flexible, retains body heat, and is nonporous for easy cleaning.

Sex toys require special care. Vibrators can be wiped off with a mild soap and water solution or wiped with alcohol. Dry thoroughly. Wash dildos in soap and water, and dry them before storing to prevent the growth of viruses and bacteria. Silicone toys can be boiled for up to five minutes. Some can even be sanitized in the top rack of the dishwasher! (Your sex toys should come with cleaning instructions.) If you share a sex toy with your partner, wash it between each use or cover it with a condom.

Joani Blank, a former sex therapist, has founded a company called Good Vibrations to sell a wide assortment of sex paraphernalia through the mail. Aesthetically pleasing, informative, and tasteful, the Good Vibrations catalog does away with the sleazy aura that has long permeated the industry. Good Vibrations, like several other companies, guarantees your confidentiality. Your order arrives in discreet packaging, and your name is never sold to another company. (See Appendix B for more information.)

Some cities now have sex paraphernalia stores with this more wholesome atmosphere. Well lit, pleasantly decorated, staffed by informed and helpful people, they make shopping for sex toys a more enjoyable experience. Many of these stores are owned and staffed by women, which is a plus for women shopping alone or wishing to accompany their partners. (See Appendix B for locations.)

EROTICA

A growing number of couples are spicing up their sex lives with erotic books, videos, and magazines. Single men are the traditional consumers of sexually explicit material, but women and couples are catching up. For example, of the 410 million adult videos rented in 1991, half of them were rented by women or by men accompanied by women.

Contrary to popular belief, many women respond to visual erotica just as strongly as men do. In one study erotic films were shown to a group of forty men and women, The sexual response of the participants was measured by various wires and probes, an indignity common to experiments of this nature. The data showed "strikingly similar male-female response patterns." The researchers concluded that "the commonly held view that males show a greater sexual responsivity to visual erotic stimuli than do females is not supported."

One woman explained to me why she liked to watch X-rated films: "My sex drive is asleep most of the time. When I watch an X-rated movie, it wakes up. I become less inhibited. It can be very freeing." Another woman reported that watching X-rated movies made her more accepting of her body. "After you've watched a dozen close-up shots, your own genitals begin to look a little less strange."

X-rated videos are a subject of a great deal of controversy, however. Some people object to them because they see a close link between pornography and violence against women. They argue that even when adult films contain no overt violence, they display an underlying disrespect or hostility toward women or portray them as objects for male gratification.

Another objection to the videos is that they glorify perfect bodies. Said a friend of mine: "I spent an hour watching an X-rated movie with my husband. The film featured these absolutely gorgeous women. I don't look that way. My friends don't look that way. When it was over, I didn't want my husband to touch me. The message I got from the movie was 'Be a *Playboy* centerfold or forget it.'" A female client made a similar comment: "I want my husband's attention directed to me—not some bimbo in a video. Especially when I will never look like her."

Some people don't like X-rated movies for yet another reason: The films bore them. They find the vast majority of these movies poorly produced, poorly written, and devoid of eroticism.

There are a significant number of couples who would enjoy watching erotic movies together if they could find ones that matched their tastes, morals, and sensibilities. In recent years a few video companies have begun producing erotic films that are less objectionable to some people. Candida Royalle, a former porn star, has formed Femme Productions to turn out what she calls "tasteful adult fare." Her movies are designed for women and couples and have been described as "R–X" rated. Although they contain explicit sex scenes, they are not demeaning to women. The actors treat each other respectfully, and the woman's sexual pleasure is just as important as the man's. One woman who reviewed one of Royalle's movies for this book commented: "I watched the whole thing and was never turned off. The love scene between the married couple was especially erotic. I was an inspired lover that night."

The same people who created the Good Vibrations sex toys catalog offer mail-order erotic videos as well. Called the Sexuality Library, this service labels movies according to a number of useful categories, including sensitivity to women's issues, quality of filmmaking, the type of sexual activity portrayed, and degree of explicitness. This rating system makes selecting an X-rated movie less of a grab bag.

The Sexuality Library also offers a wide array of books on human sexuality. Some of the books are of an educational nature, but others are purely erotic. The library features books on male sexuality, female sexuality, couples sexuality, sexual politics, erotic art, classic erotica, and sexual history. (See Appendix B.)

ANAL STIMULATION

Few people talk about anal stimulation, but approximately 40 percent of all heterosexual couples have done it at least once. The anus, like the vagina, has sensitive nerve endings, and some people enjoy those sensations. However, anal stimulation is one of those practices that divides people into two distinct camps: those who find it erotic and those who find it immoral, disgusting, unpleasant, or painful. The majority of women are in the latter camp. Of the more than forty thousand married women who responded to the 1993 *Ladies' Home Journal* survey, 89 percent indicated that anal sex was the one thing they would not do.

As you probably know, anal intercourse is an ideal way to transmit HIV. The anus is lined with a delicate membrane and does not self-lubricate like the vagina, so it can be easily abraded, allowing the absorption of the virus. Wearing a well-lubricated condom is an essential precaution, even for those couples who profess to be monogamous or who have taken the AIDS test.

For these reasons, I do not encourage anal intercourse. However, if both partners choose to engage in it, I recommend that the penis be sheathed in a condom lubricated with a water-based lubricant. There must be a high level of trust and communication between the partners, and the receiving partner should control the speed and depth of penetration.

LUBRICANTS

An increasing number of couples use personal lubricants during lovemaking. Many older women and women with scanty vaginal lubrication find them a necessity, but they are being used by younger couples as well. Prolonged, frequent, or vigorous intercourse can chafe the delicate vaginal walls and irritate the urethra, perhaps leading to a bladder infection. Lubricants provide an extra layer of protection. They are also handy for lubricating sex toys and for applying to the genitals during manual stimulation.

Years ago couples used petroleum jelly for personal lubrication. Then it was learned that petroleum-based products cling to the surface of the vagina, camouflaging or even encouraging yeast and bacteria growth. Another serious objection to oil-based jellies is that they degrade the latex in condoms, rendering them ineffective barriers against AIDS and other sexually transmitted diseases.

Water-based jellies (such as K-Y jelly) do not cause these problems. They are safe to use with condoms, do not promote the growth of bacteria or yeast, have a lower viscosity, and are non-staining. In the past few years a whole new generation of water-based jellies has come on the market. These superslippery space age lubricants have lubricious names such as Slip, Wet, Probe, and Astroglide. In my view, the premier lubricant is Astroglide, a clear, nonstaining, water-based lubricant with a faint sweet taste. It's the "slickest" of the lot, requiring only a small amount to reduce friction. Like the other lubricants now on the market, it has been thoroughly tested and doctor-approved. (Trying to decipher the product description of Astroglide requires a science degree: "The formulation uses a long-chain, nonabsorbent, water-soluble polymeric material as the thixotropic agent which negates the need for oil-based or emulsified creams that can de-fat sensitive dermal tissue. . . ." Perhaps that's why it's so expensive. But remember, a little goes a long way.)

You can purchase Astroglide and similar products in adult stores, in some pharmacies and clinics, and through mail-order catalogs. (See Appendix B.) Whichever water-based lubricant you use, make sure that it is sugar-free because sugar can promote bacterial growth.

SEX GAMES

There are many different kinds of sex games. Some come in boxes and can be bought in stores, but for the most part they tend to be silly or embarrassing. The best sex games may be the ones you invent yourselves.

One kind of homemade game is the shared sex fantasy, which involves acting out erotic fantasies with your partner. Here are some comments from couples who enjoy sex games:

> *"We pretend a lot. I'll pretend to be the virgin he's after. Or a prostitute. It turns us both on."*
> *"Once we pretended that I was a teenager breaking the rules by sneaking him into a girl's dorm. I pretended I was a virgin.*

*He had all the right lines. Tried to get me to drop my drawers.
I said, 'Will you respect me in the morning?'"*

*"I love to dress up like a prostitute. I'll say to my husband things
like 'Hi, honey, how are you doing tonight?' 'How much money
have you got?' 'Anything for you, sailor.' It's not me doing
that. I can't act that way unless we play these games. When I
do, boy, he loves every minute of it. He is putty in my hands."*

*"It makes me a lot sexier when I pretend to be someone else. I
don't have to take my inhibitions along with me."*

*"My wife likes to pretend that she's this young innocent. I'm an
older man who teaches her all about sex. I show her exactly
what to do to me. Then I initiate her through slow penetration.
We both get very excited."*

*"My boyfriend has wanted to tie me up during sex, but I'm not
interested. So what we do is pretend that I'm tied up while we're
making love. I get very excited by what he says he's doing to
me, but I don't have to do what I don't want to do. It stays
in the fantasy realm."*

When you create your own sex games, you can make them as
X-rated, R-rated, or "politically correct" as you wish. What's important is that you both agree on the nature of the adventure and
the outline of the plot. The goal is to create scenarios that excite
both of you.

Here are some classic scenarios:

Captain on a sailing ship and high-class passenger
Maid and demanding master
Strict schoolteacher and naughty student
School principal and seductive student
Patient in traction and horny nurse or doctor
Gardener and rich employer
Older woman, younger man
Older man, younger woman
Inquisitive doctor and innocent patient

However, more original scripts may come from your own imagination. The scenes that turn you on in your private imaginings are likely to be the ones that spark your interest in these shared adventures as well. The trick is to find a plot line that excites both of you.

One problem with sex games is that your partner may not respond the way your fantasy dictates. For example, your idea of a prostitute may be a woman with a heart of gold, but your partner plays the part of a bawdy tramp. There goes your fantasy. Advance planning will help the scene run more smoothly.

DEALING WITH A RELUCTANCE TO EXPERIMENT

One of the problems I encounter quite often in my practice is that one partner is more interested than the other in sexual experimentation. One partner wants oral sex, the other resists; one partner wants to play sex games, the other thinks the notion is "perverted"; one partner wants to experiment with dildos and vibrators, the other will have nothing to do with them.

My general advice is that if your partner wants a particular lovemaking technique very much and you don't have serious objections to it, give it a try. It is not likely that your partner has made a conscious decision to be excited by a given sexual activity. Most sexual preferences are a complex combination of physiology, personal history, and social conditioning, and this imprinting can be highly resistant to change.

It may be especially important to satisfy your partner's requests if she or he is experiencing nonerection, difficulty reaching orgasm, rapid ejaculation, or low sexual desire. It could be that the standard way you are making love does not satisfy your partner's needs. Giving your partner more (or less) physical stimulation, changing techniques or positions, or satisfying a compelling desire may allow him or her to function more normally. In particular, many men find that they require additional stimulus as they age and their penises become less responsive. A woman who is sensitive to this need and is willing to explore new sexual ground is bestowing a loving gift.

The first time you engage in a new sexual activity, it is normal to feel some awkwardness or anxiety. You may have a lot of unanswered questions: "What if I don't like it?" "What if my partner doesn't like it?" "What if I can't perform?" "What if my partner shames me for suggesting it?" "What if I find it embarrassing?" "What if it forces me to challenge some old messages or taboos?" In the face of so many unknowns, there is a strong pull to say no and return to the safe and familiar.

I have found that most people can overcome their qualms if they deal with them rationally. When they feel anxious, I encourage them to ask themselves, "Am I truly in danger?" By using their rational minds, they can decide whether or not their fears have any merit. If their fears are unfounded, they can rely on their maturity and commitment to the relationship to override them and go on with the activity. I call this technique the anxiety override, and it has helped many people become more adventuresome in their lovemaking.

If you go ahead and respond to your partner's request, you may discover there's a more self-serving reason for being experimental. There is often a fine line between what turns you on and what you avoid. Your most passionate experiences may lie just outside your comfort zone. Think of how you feel on a roller coaster as you climb that first hill. "I don't want to do this. Why did I do this?" Then—wheeeeee!—it's over and you want to do it again!

But a word of caution: If you experience a lot of anxiety, don't force yourself to continue. Either declare the activity off-limits or, if you wish to try again at a later time, get some professional help.

What can you do if you are on the other side of the situation and want your partner to be more experimental? The following list of suggestions will help you move step by step to a more varied love life.

1. *First, honestly examine your willingness to satisfy your* partner's *needs, both sexual and nonsexual.* Your partner may be withholding what you want sexually because you are withholding something he or she wants from you. Keep in mind the synergistic nature of this program. Ask your partner which chapters of the book and which exercises are especially important to him or her. If your partner

has been telling you, "I want more affection," or, "I want more intimate conversation," satisfy those needs first. If you make an effort to stretch into *your* areas of resistance, your partner is more likely to follow.

2. *Deepen the level of trust in your relationship.* For many people, trust is the key to becoming more experimental. They want to be assured that if they agree to break some new ground, they're not going to be forced, made fun of, taken advantage of, or made to do it again if they don't like it. One man said to me, "My greatest fear is that my wife is going to ask me to do something that I won't be able to perform." It takes time to develop trust. Be patient.

3. *Talk about the activity sometime when you are not making love.* Have a calm discussion about the activity in a neutral time and place. When you bring up a request immediately before or during lovemaking, you put your partner in a bind. He or she may not have the time or distance to think the decision through and is likely to respond with an automatic no.

4. *Explain to your partner how much the activity means to you.* Many people haven't bothered to tell their partners why they want to engage in a particular sexual activity. Lacking this information, their partners have less motivation. Explain what you want and why you want it. Example: "I would really like to use a vibrator when we make love. It's difficult for me to reach orgasm any other way. If we used a vibrator, I would spend a lot less time worrying about whether or not I reached orgasm and more time enjoying making love to you. I could lose myself in the experience." Or, "I would really like to go down on you. It would excite me to turn you on that way. It would turn me on, too. It's my number one fantasy. I think about it every time we make love."

5. *Find out what would make your partner more willing to grant your request.* Your partner may be more willing to do what you want if certain conditions are satisfied. For example, your partner may be more willing to watch an adult video with you if the film is R–X rated, not XXX. Or your partner may be more willing to perform oral sex if you are scrupulous about cleaning your genitals and/or use a flavored lubricant. It is in your best interest to satisfy any and all reasonable preconditions.

6. *Gradually work up to the activity.* Your partner is likely to feel more comfortable if you gradually introduce the activity. For example, if your partner is reluctant to perform fellatio, start out by asking her simply to look at, touch, or kiss your genitals. If your partner is reluctant to bring you to orgasm using a vibrator, begin by using it for only a few minutes. Through gradual change your partner may gradually overcome his or her resistance.

7. *Reward your partner for any movement in the right direction.* Don't expect dramatic changes. It may take time for your partner to become comfortable with a new activity. Give partial credit. Express your gratitude for every small change.

EXERCISE SECTION

EXERCISE 1: CREATING A SAFE PLAYGROUND

COMMENTS: This chapter has presented a number of ways to add variety to your sex life. Some of them may have appealed to you more than others. The goal of this exercise is to help you create a safe, enjoyable "playground," a menu of options that both of you find exciting.

One way to create this safe playground is to draw firm boundaries, each of you deciding what you are not willing to do at the present time. For example, one partner might exclude any form of anal stimulation or bondage; the other partner might rule out sex games and X-rated movies. Even though boundaries are drawn, a large number of possibilities remain.

DIRECTIONS: Below you will find a list of all the various techniques described in this chapter. First, underline those activities or techniques that are already a standard part of your lovemaking practices. Second, add any activities that I haven't mentioned that you would like to try. Finally, indicate your interest in trying out the new activities by circling a number from 0 to 6. A "0" indicates that you are firmly opposed to the technique at this time. A "6" indicates the idea excites you very much.

Compare scores with your partner, and then choose an activity that ranks high on *both* your lists. Experiment with it in the next few weeks. Repeat this process periodically to add variety to your lovemaking.

SUGGESTED ACTIVITIES

0 1 2 3 4 5 6   Varying your lovemaking styles
0 1 2 3 4 5 6   Adding more prolonged lovemaking sessions
0 1 2 3 4 5 6   Adding more quickies
0 1 2 3 4 5 6   Using a personal lubricant
0 1 2 3 4 5 6   Watching a sexually explicit film
0 1 2 3 4 5 6   Going to a store that sells erotica
0 1 2 3 4 5 6   Reading romance novels
0 1 2 3 4 5 6   Trying new lovemaking positions
0 1 2 3 4 5 6   Making love in unusual locations
0 1 2 3 4 5 6   Exploring the G spot
0 1 2 3 4 5 6   Experimenting with testicle stimulation
0 1 2 3 4 5 6   Fellatio
0 1 2 3 4 5 6   Cunnilingus
0 1 2 3 4 5 6   Anal stimulation
0 1 2 3 4 5 6   Using sexual props (food, feathers, ice, etc.)
0 1 2 3 4 5 6   The scrotal tug
0 1 2 3 4 5 6   Stimulating the prostate
0 1 2 3 4 5 6   Oral sex
0 1 2 3 4 5 6   Kegel exercises
0 1 2 3 4 5 6   Using sex toys
0 1 2 3 4 5 6   Wearing sexy clothes
0 1 2 3 4 5 6   Playing sex games
0 1 2 3 4 5 6   Reading erotic literature
0 1 2 3 4 5 6   Other _____
0 1 2 3 4 5 6   Other _____

8

CREATING LIFELONG ROMANCE

A man made this wistful comment on one of my surveys: "Every time I make love with my wife I am aware of a missing element of romance. I'd like more of it. She responds so impersonally. If I were to seek a new mate, romance would be high on my list of requirements." When romance is missing from a long-term relationship, people can experience a great sense of loss. They no longer feel as loved or desired by their partners, even when a commitment seems to be there. Romantic lovemaking seems to be especially important to women. In a recent study, 709 women were asked how they would change their sex lives. One of their top three requests was for more romance. Having a more romantic partner was more important to them than having more orgasms or having their partners be more communicative.

In order to understand romance, we need to make a clear distinction between *romance* and *the romantic love stage*. The romantic love stage is a predictable period of euphoria at the start of a love relationship. But what I mean by "romance" is an ongoing expression of love between two people. The romantic love stage is destined to end in a few months or years. Romance can go on forever.

The romantic love stage may be fleeting, but it plays an essential role in a love relationship, bonding two people together emotionally and physically to prepare them for the hard work of building a life together. To reinforce this bond, the body releases a chemical cocktail of peptides, creating a natural high. When people are "in love," they talk incessantly, forget to eat, and go to work on three hours' sleep. Colors seem brighter, the world friendlier, a boring job tolerable. Going to Wal-Mart can be an exhilarating experience when you're in love.

One of the primary ingredients in the love cocktail is phenylethylamine (PEA). Monkeys injected with PEA exhibit hypersexuality and "moonstruck" behavior—but only in the presence of another monkey. The same appears to be true for humans. When you're in love, you need to be with your partner in order to maintain your euphoria. Your spirits plummet when you're apart, a withdrawal that we call love sickness.

The romantic love stage also has a profound psychological component. When you're newly in love, a part of your unconscious mind begins to see your lover as the solution to all your emotional problems. Whatever Mommy and Daddy failed to provide in childhood is going to be offered by your new lover. Being in love is going to heal your childhood wounds and make you happy and whole. When this unspoken promise of lifelong nurturing is added to the drug-induced euphoria of romantic love, it becomes one of the most ecstatic experiences known to humankind.

But it doesn't last. Typically within three to six months reality begins to intrude. You run out of things to say. Your partner needs time alone. Your friends get lonesome. Your jobs demand attention. Money gets tight. The garbage needs emptying. . . . Your growing awareness of the world around you is an indication that the drug is beginning to wear off. As you ease back into a more normal mental state, you begin to see each other in a less favorable light. Your partner starts taking you for granted. You find some of your partner's habits annoying. Both of you become less willing to compromise, more inclined to withhold. This is the line of demarcation between romantic love and romance. This is where the work of the relationship begins.

The fact that romantic love is a discrete stage is easier to observe from a distance. When your friends fall in love, you can watch the fascinating process come and go. You can see the beginning and the inevitable end. I remember talking with a longtime friend when she was newly in love. She told me her boyfriend was so entranced with her that he would just sit and watch the way she moved. She talked at great length about his tenderness, his devotion, and his lovemaking skills. Not quite a year later I was hearing a different story. She said her boyfriend was still sitting around watching her move, but now it had become a source of irritation. "He's so lazy," she told me. "He has no motivation. All he does is sit and watch me work!" She also was beginning to feel hemmed in by what she now saw as his obsessive love and devotion: "I wish he would get excited about something besides me. He doesn't have any outside interests." She had come down from her romantic high and was seeing her lover in a new, harsh light.

As a marriage and family therapist with fifteen years' experience, I think it's time we expose romantic love for what it is: a delightful, short-lived, altered state of consciousness. It cannot be sustained. I have seen the seduction of romantic love lead people into disastrous relationships, splinter families, and destroy careers. I have witnessed the remorse and guilt of married adults who have fallen in love with new partners and left the marriage only to find out that romantic love is a brief stage. The illusion that the euphoric feelings for the new partner would last was exactly that: an illusion. I have heard from children, both young and old, who have experienced disappointment and shattered dreams as they watched their parents "fall out of love" and separate. It cannot be said too often: Romantic love is but a brief stage in the gradual unfolding of a mature relationship.

UNDERSTANDING ROMANCE

I view romance as an entirely different phenomenon. Romance is the way that you demonstrate your love and respect for your partner on an ongoing basis. Through your words and actions you let your partner know that he or she occupies a central place in your life. Every day we are confronted with examples of "special people" in the form of Hollywood stars, royalty, politicians, and lottery winners. We, too, want our day in the sun. When we're someone's sweetheart, we get to bask in that privileged position. Glen, fifty-eight, describes how he feels when his wife of sixteen years looks at him "in a romantic way": "Cyd has this particular way of looking at me that makes me feel so special. Her mouth has a certain smile that only I get on these occasions. It's not because of anything I did. It's just for who I am. I puff up and feel like a million dollars."

If romance feels so good, why do we have so little of it in our long-term relationships? One of the main reasons is that ongoing romance requires *commitment and conscious effort.* It demands that we think, plan, compromise, change, and mature. It requires that we give up our hope of finding the "perfect partner" and turn our attention to the task of loving and honoring our real life mate. It forces us to transcend our preoccupation with our own needs and desires and view life through the eyes of our partners.

Many of the people who come to me for counseling have a hard time doing this. Just this week I had a client say to me, "If I have to work on my marriage, I must have the wrong partner." Any two people who have managed to sustain loving feelings beyond the romantic love stage will tell you that they have worked on their relationship. They may feel like interrupting, but they listen instead. They may feel like yelling, but they use their calm voices. They may feel like being critical, but they learn to bite their tongues. They've accepted the fact that there are times when they have to carry the romantic ball on their own.

Unfortunately there is no biological drive to help you create ongoing romance, no euphoric drugs to make the work easier. You have to rely on conscious effort. There is also very little social support. Our culture does an admirable job of structuring the romantic love stage with the well-known rituals of dating, engagement, and weddings. But when you're home from the honeymoon, you're on your own. When the drug of romantic love begins to wear off, you're given very little advice about how to restore the good feelings. One of my primary jobs as a therapist is simply to give couples the information and support they need to create ongoing romance.

THE CARDINAL RULE OF ROMANCE

One of the fundamental pieces of advice I give couples about romance was underscored by a research project conducted by Arthur Aron, Ph.D., a researcher and lecturer at the University of California, Santa Cruz. In his experiment a man and a woman who had never met before were put in a private room together for ninety minutes. They were given a detailed set of instructions. First, they were supposed to exchange intimate information, such as their most embarrassing moment or how they would feel if they lost a parent. They were also instructed to look deeply into each other's eyes for two minutes without talking. Several times during the session a researcher would come into the room and ask them to "tell each other what you already like about each other." When the ninety minutes elapsed, the two subjects were escorted out separate doors so they would feel under no obligation to see each other again.

This single session was found to foster a deep sense of intimacy between strangers. In fact, the first two people who participated in the study got married six months later and invited Aron and his research assistants to the wedding.

Aron says that each of the elements of his experiment—mutual self-disclosure, eye-gazing, and knowing that the other person likes you—can lead to feelings of intimacy. But after twenty years of researching the phenomenon of love, he believes that the overwhelming predictor of whether or not you will love someone is the last one: *knowing that that person loves you.*

What I have concluded from research such as Aron's and from my own training and clinical practice is this: If you want to create ongoing romance, *find out what says "I love you" to your partner and do it.* This is not as simple as it sounds. We have a natural tendency to show love the way *we* want to be loved. We want to believe that my preferences are your preferences, my desires are your desires. This is rarely the case. One person's idea of romance may be hiking together through the Sierra Nevadas; another person's may be sharing a two-hour spending spree at Tiffany's. In order to create romance, these two individuals have to tailor their expressions of love to each other's sensibilities. If the person who likes expensive jewelry gives a pair of diamond cuff links to the partner who lives in jeans and hiking boots, the unspoken message is not "I love you" but "I wish you were more like me." *To be a true romantic, you have to see the world through your partner's eyes.*

I've talked with a number of people who have learned to express their love in this "partner-specific" way. I asked Sylvia, twenty-six, a professional hairstylist: "What is the most romantic thing your husband has ever done for you?" She replied, "You're going to think this is crazy, but it's something that my husband did one day when I was sick. I went to work with a sore throat. By midmorning I was feeling terrible. I called my husband and told him all I could think about was going home, getting into my pajamas, and crawling into bed. On the way home I was running a fever. I felt even worse when I remembered I hadn't finished the laundry. My favorite pajamas were in the washer, and the sheets were stripped off the bed. When I got home, I went into the bedroom and was surprised to see that the bed was made up with clean flannel sheets and that my pajamas had been dried and folded and placed on the bed. My husband had come home from lunch to do those things for me. Physical comfort is not a big deal for him. He doesn't like to be 'coddled.' But he knows that I do. That day I felt deeply and truly loved."

When you are in the romantic love stage, you can rely on traditional gifts like roses and candy. But after you've been living together for a number of years, your gestures of love have to reflect a more intimate knowledge of each other. Here's another example. One afternoon Jose called his girlfriend, Angie, and invited her to join him and some of their friends at a restaurant after work. Jose met their friends at the restaurant and waited for Angie. Fifteen minutes went by, and she hadn't arrived. Angie was usually quite punctual, so Jose began to worry. Then it occurred to him that Angie might have lost her way. He knew she had a terrible sense of direction. He left the restaurant and began searching for her.

He found her several blocks away, asking strangers for directions. Angie was deeply touched by his thoughtfulness. "I would have found the restaurant eventually," she said, "but he knows that I hate to be lost. He wanted to spare me the ordeal."

ADDING EXCITEMENT TO YOUR ROMANCE

Another important ingredient in the creation of lifelong romance is excitement. Excitement restores the love drug, PEA, to your system. It gets your heart racing and your adrenaline flowing, intensifying your emotional bond. A couple in their mid-fifties gave their relationship an unanticipated jolt of excitement by taking an ocean-going kayak trip off the coast of British Columbia. They were skilled kayakers but had never attempted such a rigorous trip. One afternoon a sudden storm came up, catching them midway between two islands. Before they could reach the safety of shore, they were paddling their way through five-foot swells. They managed to thread their way through the waves without capsizing, but their hearts were beating in their throats. When they talked to me about this adventure, I could see how much it meant to them to have shared such a dramatic moment together.

But you don't have to risk your life to have a renewed spirit of adventure. There are a host of less dangerous possibilities. Two friends of mine, Joanne and Paul, married for fourteen years, found that their love for each other was rekindled during a two-week vacation in Berlin. They left their two young children in the care of a relative so they could spend some much-needed time together. Each morning they got on the subway, map in hand, and began exploring the city. Neither of them spoke German, and they had no tour guide or itinerary. "We didn't know where we were headed or what we would find," said Joanne.

The two weeks they spent roaming around Berlin had more impact on their relationship than they had anticipated. "We knew we needed time away from the kids," said Joanne, "but something happened between us that was more significant than simply spending time together. When we got back to the States, we found that our resentments had all but disappeared. And it wasn't because we had talked about them or tried to work them out. They just weren't an issue anymore."

Joanne and Paul took that trip three years ago, yet they still feel closer to each other today. They had found a way to step outside the bounds of their normal routine and allow some excitement into their lives, reforging the bond between them that had been worn away by the tedium of daily life.

Adventure can also be found closer to home. One man found a way to make his relationship more exciting by inviting his wife to accompany him on a midnight escapade. He and his wife had just bought a lot on a lake in an exclusive neighborhood with twenty-four-hour security. Although they owned the property, they had yet to get the code for the entrance gate. At eleven o'clock one night J.J. told Shanna to dress warmly because they were going on a little trip. He refused to tell her where they were going. He drove to within a quarter of a mile of the entrance gate, parked the car, and got out. He reached in the back seat for a thermos and told Shanna to follow him. When they approached the locked gate, J.J. got on the ground and wiggled under it. Shanna followed, and the two of them ran down the road, giggling like kids. They arrived at their boat dock to enjoy hot chocolate and the full moon as it crested over the hill.

SEX AND ADVENTURE

When there is a sense of shared adventure between you and your partner, there is also likely to be a stronger current of sexuality, an intriguing fact that was demonstrated in a research experiment involving a group of young men. The only thing the men were told before the day of the experiment was that they were going to participate in an "experiment in learning." When they arrived at the laboratory, they were given some good news and some bad news. The good news was that a strikingly beautiful research assistant was going to lead each of them through the experiment. The bad news was that she was going to be administering electric shocks to study the relationship between pain and learning. Following this unsettling announcement, the men were divided into two groups. The men in Group I were told that they had been designated the control group and would receive barely noticeable electric shocks. Those in Group II were told that they were the guinea pigs and were going to experience considerable pain.

Before the supposed experiment began, the beautiful research assistant mingled with the men, answering any questions they might have. When she left, a male researcher approached each man individually to ask him in confidence how he felt about the young woman. The men in Group II who had been told they were going to receive painful shocks found her far more sexy and attractive than the less anxious men in Group I. The researchers concluded that adrenaline not only makes the heart beat faster but stimulates sexual desire as well. In a burst of eloquence rarely seen in professional journals, the researchers concluded that "passion is like any other form of excitement, and must glide uneasily between the shoals of boredom and terror, navigating to keep firmly in the current of excitement."

If your long-term love relationship is heading toward the shoals of boredom, I urge you to find some way to make your life together less predictable and routine. Adding a spirit of adventure to your relationship is an excellent way to keep romance and passion alive.

THE IMPORTANCE OF PHYSICAL AFFECTION

Physical affection is another integral part of romance. Kissing, holding hands, snuggling, and patting each other are some of the many ways that couples express their love. Physical affection is the daily reinforcement of the pair bond, the "glue" that holds a relationship together.

Regrettably, physical affection is in short supply in many love relationships. Recently I asked five hundred people the question "What is it that your partner doesn't understand about your sexuality?" One of the most common responses was that their partners didn't give them enough physical affection. Here are some typical remarks:

"My husband seems fairly sensitive to me when we make love. However, he isn't affectionate during the day. He doesn't surprise me with a hug and a kiss when I'm putting away the groceries. During the evening he isolates himself. He sprawls out on the couch and leaves no room for me to sit. It makes me feel unloved and alone. Then, when he approaches me at night for sex, I feel resentful. I think, 'He doesn't really love me. He just wants sex.' "

"About the only time Greg would touch me was in public. In private he would be irritated if I grabbed him for a hug or patted him. He didn't even like to kiss. Imagine, not liking to kiss! I never felt safely loved in that relationship. There was never that comfortable space that I imagine exists when you have enough nurturing."

"Touching is very important to me. To be married and not have that in place was difficult. I believe that was the greatest rejection of all."

"My wife isn't as affectionate as she used to be. Sometimes I wonder why I come home at night. I don't feel that there's anyone there who loves me. She is willing to have sex, but I don't feel her heart is in it. I feel she's just doing it to 'service me.' "

In my survey, as in others, more women expressed a need for physical affection than men. Advice columnist Ann Landers came up with a similar conclusion. In a much-talked-about column she asked: "Would you be content to be held close and treated tenderly and forget about 'the act'?" Seventy-two percent of the more than ninety thousand women who responded said yes. What was most surprising was that almost half of those who said yes were under forty years of age.

Why do women as a group seem to place a higher value on physical affection than men do? At birth there is no apparent difference between the sexes. Both male and female infants have the same overpowering need for physical contact. Babies who are totally deprived of physical affection either die or grow up with psychosocial dwarfism, a condition that stunts the body and mind. Children of both sexes need the life-affirming touch of their caretakers in order to survive and thrive.

But girl babies may receive more physical affection than boy babies. A researcher observed forty-two mothers and their newborn infants during their stay at a maternity hospital, filming their interaction with a videocamera. When she analyzed the film frame by frame, she found little difference in the way the mothers treated their infants on the basis of birth order, weight, or degree of prematurity. However, she found a marked difference based on sex. In a given period the mothers touched their girl babies an average of 23.7 times and their boy babies only 16.2 times, only two thirds as much.

As our boys grow older, we may not only skimp on the amount of physical affection we give them but unwittingly limit the amount of affection they give others. Following a masculine code that is thousands of years old, we raise our male children to be tough, resilient, and independent. We tell little boys as young as three or four years of age, "Tough it out," "Play with the pain," "Stop that bellyaching," "Stop being a sissy," "Figure it out for yourself," "Don't come crying to me!" "Defend yourself!" and "You're acting like a girl." If we go against the mainstream and encourage a boy to be gentle and caring, he is likely to be the target of verbal abuse on the playground. Sensitive and affectionate boys—boys who have the very qualities that most women say they would like in their husbands—are often labeled "wimps" or "sissies" or worse by their playmates. Boys learn early to conceal their vulnerability behind a thick skin. It's no wonder that when they grow up to be men, they require less affection than women and are less likely to dole it out. Like plants that have to withstand the rigors of a cold climate, they've been hardened off.

If a woman wants her male partner to be more affectionate, it's important that she tailor her touching to his individual needs. My husband and I have very different preferences when it comes to touching, which I discovered one day while we were driving in the car. I was sitting with my arm over his shoulder, and occasionally I'd give him a love pat or two. It occurred to me to ask him if he liked to be patted this way.

"No, not really," he said. "To me, patting is what you do to a child or a pet. I'd rather be rubbed or massaged."

"That's interesting," I replied. "I love to be patted. To me it is nurturing and reassuring. Rubbing feels sexual to me, which is fine sometimes. But often I just want affection." Since then I've withheld the urge to pat, substituting a rub or massage in its place. I also get more pats now that he knows what I like. When working with couples, I often ask: "Does your partner know how to touch you?" If the answer is no, I ask them to demonstrate what they like. Don't assume that your partner knows. Check it out.

Sometimes a man who appears to resist affection may have a greater need to be touched than he realizes. Sue Anne, who has been living with Aaron for several years, told of this incident: "It was the end of a long week. Aaron and I both had killer schedules. I was in the laundry room complaining to myself when he came in and said, 'You sound like you need to be held.' He took me to the bedroom and held me in his arms. As he held me, he began to talk about his own rough week. The more he talked, the more I realized that *he* was the one who needed to be held. We switched roles, and he lay in my arms longer than he ever has before."

Aaron was projecting his own need to be nurtured onto Sue Anne. Nonsexual physical holding is important to both sexes. If you add just five minutes of mutual holding to your relationship on a regular basis, you are likely to experience a deeper level of emotional bonding.

ADDITIONAL PRINCIPLES OF ROMANCE

As I reflect on all the loving acts I've observed between couples, a number of additional insights stand out. One of them is that *romance takes daily effort.* There is a very special couple that I see each year at meetings and social events sponsored by one of my professional organizations. She is a school counselor, and he is an accountant. He's not there for business purposes; he's there as her partner. One time I mentioned to the woman, Mary Bird, that she and her husband looked so happy together. She said, "Well, thank you for noticing. Yes, we are happy. Every day when I first wake up,

I ask myself, 'What can I do for Carl today?' It's just a habit I have formed over the years. Every day I do something just to please him." The love these two have for each other is obvious, even to a stranger. There is a synchronicity between them, a knowing of each other that only comes through time, intention, and knowledge.

Something else I've observed over and over again is that *romance requires that you be mindful.* You can't use the same old techniques and expect fresh or profound results. One couple knew their relationship was in trouble when the wife bought her husband a wallet for their anniversary in March and then another one for his birthday in May. They ended up in my office for therapy.

For maximum effect, *romance involves an element of surprise.* We rarely get surprises as adults. As children we had surprise birthday parties, surprise holiday presents, surprise events orchestrated by adults. Life was full of surprises. Not so in adulthood. This makes it all the more meaningful to be pleasantly surprised—especially by one who loves you. My friend Diane knew that Phil would be arriving at his hotel in Grand Rapids in the middle of a long travel week. She called ahead to the hotel and arranged to have his favorite beer cooling on ice in his room. To complete the welcome, she mailed ahead a jar of her homemade salsa and a bag of blue cornmeal tortilla chips that Phil loved. When he walked into his room, there was his favorite snack waiting for him.

Romance does not have to cost money. In this day and age when time is at a premium, going that extra mile can have a tremendous impact on your partner. When the recession hit, Blain had to move his business home to cut costs. There was no unused space, so he had to turn the garage into an office. He was moving, remodeling, and trying to make a living all at the same time. One evening after a three-day road trip he drove into the driveway dreading the mess he had left in his partially finished office. When he walked into the garage, what awaited him was a freshly painted office with tidy shelves and a clean floor. His wife had taken vacation days to stay home and finish the work he had begun.

Another characteristic of ongoing romance is mutual respect. Imagine for a moment that you and your partner have just been introduced to each other by a friend and are left alone to get acquainted. You both are feeling rushed and preoccupied. You don't listen very well to each other. You interrupt each other and anticipate each other's words. You make fleeting eye contact. Before long one of you is reading a newspaper and the other is watching TV. Do you think you would be attracted to each other? Would you be favorably impressed? Would you want to make love to each other? Would you want to live with this person for the rest of your life?

Compare this imaginary encounter to the way you interact with your partner on a daily basis. Does your busyness or lack of focus make you unintentionally rude to each other?

Romance is playful and flirtatious. I asked a group of middle-aged men what said "romance" to them, and they all agreed that playfulness was one of the key ingredients:

CHRIS: When I think of romance, I think of coquettishness. A certain playfulness. I like to be teased. Seduced.

PATRICK: There's kind of a creativity involved, too. There you are, plodding along, doing your thing, and your lover takes you away from all of that. The surprise phone call. "Let's do something different." It's a relief. It's youthful. It's like being a colt, being filled with energy.

JIM: If a woman is playful, I don't care if she's one hundred and twenty. I'm going to get horny.

When you are spontaneous and playful with your partner, it brings back memories of the romantic love stage, when every day was a discovery. It gets you out of your rut and makes you look at each other in a new way.

The same awakening can occur when your relationship is going through a crisis. All of a sudden there is a new level of intimacy, a deeper honesty. But you don't have to wait for a crisis to develop to see each other anew. You can be romantic and playful on an ongoing basis. Jeff and Katy were in their hot tub one night in their usual unclothed state when she turned to him and said, "Let's do something different. How could we make this more fun?" They both thought for a minute. Then she suggested, "I know! Let's run around the house naked!" The words were barely out of her mouth when Jeff jumped out of the tub and took off running. Katy took off after him, squealing and giggling like a kid. When they recounted this escapade to me, it still brought blushes to their cheeks.

Showing your sentimental, sensitive side deepens the level of romance. A man stood up at the end of one of my talks and told me about something his wife had done for him: "I was called to active duty during Desert Storm. I had two days' notice, and I was gone eight months. Valentine's Day rolled around, and my wife sent me a white teddy bear holding a little heart that said 'I Love You.' Despite what some of the macho Navy guys around me may have thought, I left that teddy bear on my bunk every day. That was the most romantic long-distance thing my wife could have done for me."

Writing love letters is a time-honored way to describe your sensitive thoughts and feelings and expose your vulnerability. It's a way to go on record with your love. Your willingness to be vulnerable calls forth compassion and tenderness in your partner, which inspire more love from you. It takes only one person to get the ball rolling.

Poems are a variation on this theme. Several people have talked to me about being deeply touched by their partners' poetry. When I asked one person, "What is the most romantic thing anyone has done for you?" she answered: "My boyfriend writes revealing poetry. I am so moved because he trusts me enough to let me see the tender side of him." Another individual said that her husband took one of her poems and turned it into the opening for one of his screenplays.

Sometimes romance involves designing your own *special occasions and celebrations,* creating rituals that are known only to you. One couple, married twenty-four years, confided to me that they celebrate the date they first made love. This is more significant to them than the day they got married. Another couple celebrates the day of the year they first met. One man still has the pajama bottoms his bashful bride made him buy on their honeymoon. He wears them periodically as a reminder to her of the delightful ways in which she has changed.

Couples who stay in love may have *symbols* that carry special meaning to them. Early in their relationship Sol and Darla were walking in the woods and came upon a pair of mating turtles. Sol remarked, "Isn't it remarkable that a male turtle and a female turtle happened to find each other in such an unlikely place, and here we are to witness it?" For a few minutes they watched the turtles in their slow-motion mating ritual. A week later Sol slipped a ceramic turtle into Carla's hand as they sat in a movie theater. Turtles have become a symbol of their delight at having found each other.

Although some women complain that the male view of romance always seems to have an underlying sexual motive, it would be wrong to separate sex from romance altogether. *Sexuality* can be an appropriate and meaningful part of romance, as my friend Martin discovered. He came home to a dark house one night and noticed a faint glow coming from the dining room. He walked cautiously toward the back of the house. As he entered the alcove, he saw that the table was beautifully set with candles and flowers. He was about to call out to his wife when he heard her voice behind him. "Are you ready to eat?" she asked. He turned and saw her dressed in black hose, high-heeled shoes, and a small apron. She carried a plate of food in each hand. They had to warm the food up later in the microwave.

Some men have gone to the Marabel Morgan school of romance as well. When Heidi came home from work, she saw her husband's shoes and socks by the front door. Annoyed, she picked them up to take them upstairs. On the stairs she tripped over his jacket and tie. She found her husband's shirt and pants strewn across the top landing. She finally caught on to what was going on when she saw his briefs draped over the doorknob. She opened the door with a smile to see her husband lying naked on the bed, dozens of candles lighting up the room.

Some of the most romantic stories I've heard have had to do with *intimate knowledge of the partner's history*. One of my clients was struggling to come up with a present for her husband's sixtieth birthday. He was a "man who had everything." After days of pondering she thought about an old photograph that had been taken of him when he was eight years old. She got out the photo and studied the little boy standing proudly erect in his brand-new cowboy shoes. Even though she had never seen her husband wear cowboy boots in the forty-one years she had known him, she sensed the nostalgia might still be there. She shopped around and found a pair of boots that were a close replica of the ones in the picture. When he opened his gift, tears came to his eyes, and he looked as if he had encountered a long-lost friend. Now, eight years later, he still wears those cowboy boots and has added three pairs to his collection.

We all are tied to our histories. When our partners pay homage to our pasts, they can touch us profoundly. The children in us bond with them on a deep, unconscious level.

DEALING WITH A RESISTANCE TO ROMANCE

If your partner is not as romantic as you would like, there is much you can do to encourage more open displays of love. The first principle to remember is *positive reinforcement*: Any action that is reinforced positively tends to increase in frequency. Reinforce any and all romantic gestures in the way your partner likes best, whether with a smile, a kiss, or a warm thank-you. Don't wait for perfection. Focus on what you are getting, not on what you are missing. Romantic love that goes unrecognized withers and dies on the vine.

The second principle is to *refrain from punishment.* If you criticize, nag, or gripe about your partner's lack of romantic attention, you increase the possibility that he or she will withhold even more or will respond with a forced, insincere gesture just to please you.

Finally, as I stressed at the beginning of this chapter, *find out what says "I love you" to your partner and do it.* (Exercises 1 and 2 at the end of this chapter will lead you through this process step by step.) The best way to help your partner become more romantic is to tailor your own expressions of love to his or her unique needs and desires. Your uncritical display of love and acceptance may help heal some of your partner's hidden emotional wounds, helping create the romantic partner you long for.

Some of you may have the opposite problem—namely, that you find yourself rejecting the romantic attention of your partner. On some level, you don't believe you deserve that much love. Bonnie, thirty-three, talked about the difficulty she had accepting one of her partner's romantic gestures: "One time I came home to find that Lennie had cooked a surprise dinner. The table was set by the pool; candles were floating in the water. But I couldn't get into it. I had fantasized about that sort of thing a hundred times, but I couldn't accept it was happening to me."

It is often the case that people who resist romance were deprived of love and attention as young children. When their partners do nice things for them, they experience a cognitive dissonance; their partners' view of them does not match their own bleak appraisal. They may also find that their partners' demonstrations of love make them more aware of the pain of earlier years. In a recent workshop I was helping a couple do the mirroring exercise when the woman began to cry. Both she and her mate were confused by her tears because the exercise had been going very well and a feeling of deep intimacy was developing between them. I asked the woman, "What are your tears about?"

"I don't know," she replied.

"Do they feel like tears of sorrow or happiness?" I asked.

"Both," she sobbed. "I am happy to feel close to Steve, but a part of me believes I don't deserve it. I've never felt this close to anyone before."

I asked her to put her head on her husband's shoulder and to let herself cry. I explained that if she could release some of those tumultuous feelings, she would gradually feel more comfortable with deep levels of intimacy. In the comfort of her husband's arms she was able to release some of the grief she had harbored for so many years. The next time intimacy develops between them, it is likely she will find it easier to accept.

I can identify with people who are resistant to romance because this has been one of my issues. My father wasn't around when I was growing up, and there were times when my mother wasn't emotionally available. A part of me interpreted their physical and emotional absence to mean that I was unworthy of love. Later in life, when a man showed love for me, I would be suspicious of him and put him to the test. If he passed the first test, I would give him a more difficult one. At times I would push him to the limits with my resistance. Several men told me, "You're a hard person to love," and they were right.

One of the things that helped me break through my resistance has been a loving husband, who has persisted in showing his love in concrete ways. I didn't make it easy for him. For example, when we first met, he went to great lengths to find exotic boutiques so he could satisfy my taste for unusual clothing and jewelry. Each time he told me about a new store, I would hasten there myself and buy up the things that were most appealing to me. After a while there would be nothing left in the store that I truly liked. As his presents became less frequent, I would criticize him. Thankfully he caught on to my game and helped me see how I was sabotaging his efforts. I began to see that my childhood had taught me that I didn't deserve loving attention and that if I was going to have it, I would have to do it myself. Through my husband's unflagging efforts, I finally learned that I was a lovable person and that I could count on his romantic attention.

Since then he has continued to treat me to frequent displays of love. A few days ago I was dragging myself into the house after spending six days conducting back-to-back workshops. It was nine o'clock at night, and I was tired, jet-lagged, and in no mood for romance. The smell of fresh bread drew me into the kitchen. There was my husband, ladling out a bowl of homemade cream of chicken soup, my favorite soup. It had taken my husband all afternoon to make the soup and the bread, and he had timed the bread so it would be ready to take out of the oven five minutes before I was due to walk in the door. I felt instantly revived. We had a late intimate supper, catching up on all the news. As we were heading for bed, I said to him, "Now *that* was my idea of foreplay." We went to bed and proceeded to make love—not because I felt obliged to him but because I truly wanted to make love to him. It was yet another example of the power of romance and of the surprising way that all the nine elements of a love relationship are intertwined.

EXERCISE SECTION

EXERCISE 1: DEFINING WHAT SAYS "I LOVE YOU."

COMMENTS: This first exercise will help you decide which traditional romantic gestures are most meaningful to you. If you wish, add notes in the margin to shed more light on your responses. (The next exercise will help you define your more unique desires.)

DIRECTIONS: Rate each of the following romantic gestures on a scale from 0 to 4. (There's a separate checklist for each of you.)

0 = no interest
1 = little interest
2 = some interest
3 = much interest
4 = highest interest

PARTNER 1:

_____ 1. Preparing a special meal for me
_____ 2. Bathing me
_____ 3. Telling me "I love you"
_____ 4. Doing a chore without being asked
_____ 5. Asking me to go for a walk
_____ 6. Giving me a back rub
_____ 7. Giving me a card
_____ 8. Giving me flowers
_____ 9. Opening the car door for me
_____ 10. Looking deeply in my eyes
_____ 11. Kissing me
_____ 12. Praising me in front of others
_____ 13. Giving me a thoughtful, inexpensive gift
_____ 14. Giving me an expensive gift
_____ 15. Writing me love notes
_____ 16. Showing up at work for a surprise visit
_____ 17. Taking me out to eat
_____ 18. Snuggling in bed
_____ 19. Carrying packages for me

_____ 20. Listening to music together

_____ 21. Calling me endearing names

_____ 22. Giving me a surprise birthday party

_____ 23. Planning a surprise vacation

_____ 24. Giving me romantic clothing

_____ 25. Writing me a love letter

_____ 26. Writing me a poem

_____ 27. Going on a picnic together

_____ 28. Taking a shower together

_____ 29. Sitting in a hot tub together

_____ 30. Putting effort into celebrating our anniversary

_____ 31. Putting effort into celebrating my birthday

_____ 32. Putting effort into celebrating Valentine's Day

_____ 33. Giving me a special gift at Christmas

_____ 34. Going away for a weekend together

_____ 35. Staying home together with no interruptions

_____ 36. Sleeping in together

_____ 37. Going to a movie

_____ 38. Taking me to a sporting event

_____ 39. Cuddling on the couch

_____ 40. Holding hands

_____ 41. Hugging me

_____ 42. Accompanying me to a cultural event

_____ 43. Sitting by the fireplace together

_____ 44. Lighting candles

_____ 45. Playing games with me

PARTNER 2:

_____ 1. Preparing a special meal for me

_____ 2. Bathing me

_____ 3. Telling me "I love you"

_____ 4. Doing a chore without being asked

_____ 5. Asking me to go for a walk

_____ 6. Giving me a back rub

_____ 7. Giving me a card

_____ 8. Giving me flowers

_____ 9. Opening the car door for me

_____ 10. Looking deeply in my eyes
_____ 11. Kissing me
_____ 12. Praising me in front of others
_____ 13. Giving me a thoughtful, inexpensive gift
_____ 14. Giving me an expensive gift
_____ 15. Writing me love notes
_____ 16. Showing up at work for a surprise visit
_____ 17. Taking me out to eat
_____ 18. Snuggling in bed
_____ 19. Carrying packages for me
_____ 20. Listening to music together
_____ 21. Calling me endearing names
_____ 22. Giving me a surprise birthday party
_____ 23. Planning a surprise vacation
_____ 24. Giving me romantic clothing
_____ 25. Writing me a love letter
_____ 26. Writing me a poem
_____ 27. Going on a picnic together
_____ 28. Taking a shower together
_____ 29. Sitting in a hot tub together
_____ 30. Putting effort into celebrating our anniversary
_____ 31. Putting effort into celebrating my birthday
_____ 32. Putting effort into celebrating Valentine's Day
_____ 33. Giving me a special gift at Christmas
_____ 34. Going away for a weekend together
_____ 35. Staying home together with no interruptions
_____ 36. Sleeping in together
_____ 37. Going to a movie
_____ 38. Accompanying me to a sporting event
_____ 39. Cuddling on the couch
_____ 40. Holding hands
_____ 41. Hugging me
_____ 42. Accompanying me to a cultural event
_____ 43. Sitting by the fireplace together
_____ 44. Lighting candles
_____ 45. Playing games with me

EXERCISE 2: PERSONAL PREFERENCES

In addition to the general list above, each one of us longs to be touched in highly personal ways. Below, list ten activities that would make you feel loved. (This may require some quiet reflection.) Be specific, and state each one in positive terms so your partner will know exactly what you long for. Examples:

> *"I would love you to meet me at the airport gate when I am not expecting you."*
> *"I would enjoy having my feet massaged for half an hour."*
> *"Join me on a weeklong backpacking trip."*
> *"I would like to spend a weekend together in a hotel."*
> *"Take a sailing class with me."*

Make your lists separately without reading each other's.

PARTNER 1:

1. _____

2. _____

3. _____

4. _____

5. _____

6. _____

7. _____

8. _____

9. _____

10. _____
_____

PARTNER 2:

1. _____
_____

2. _____
_____

3. _____
_____

4. _____
_____

5. _____
_____

6. _____
_____

7. _____
_____

8. _____
_____

9. _____
_____

10. _____
_____

Once you have completed your lists, share them with your partner. Discuss them to make sure each person's wishes are clearly understood. It's up to you whether or not you grant one of your partner's wishes. Do not compete or keep score. The exercise is designed merely to inform and motivate you.

EXERCISE 3: PLANNING AN ANNIVERSARY CELEBRATION

COMMENTS: Below you will find a list of questions to help you plan an anniversary celebration that has special significance to both of you.

DIRECTIONS: As you begin to plan your next anniversary celebration, consider the following questions:

- Which locations have special significance to you?
- Which dates or times of year are most important to you? (These may or may not coincide with your wedding date.)
- Are there any other people you wish to include in the celebration?
- Which symbols or objects have special significance to you?
- Which activities do you both enjoy?
- Do you have special shared memories about any particular kind of food, music, flowers, etc.?
- Are there any vows, poems, spiritual or literary passages that are important to both of you?
- What are the conditions that make you feel most closely connected to each other? (Examples: being in a natural setting, exploring a new city/country together, taking a cruise, relaxing on the beach, etc.)

EXERCISE 4: A ROMANTIC CALENDAR

COMMENTS: With a little effort you can celebrate your relationship all twelve months of the year. Here's a monthly calendar of activities to inspire you.

DIRECTIONS: Read the following suggestions. Underline or highlight any suggestions that you respond to positively. Have your partner do the same. Make a plan to enact some of the suggestions that appeal to both of you.

January: This is the month we celebrate the beginning of a new year. What better time to celebrate your relationship? New Year's Eve is especially important to some couples. Whom you kiss at midnight has ritualistic significance. New Year's Day is a natural time to celebrate and reaffirm your commitment. One couple I know write an annual relationship contract and renegotiate the terms on January 1. Goal setting is also appropriate during this month of beginnings. Set aside dates for leisurely lovemaking, private time together, and shared vacations.

February: Valentine's Day is a day for lovers, but we have diluted it in recent decades by including children, teachers, and friends. To get back to basics, make sure you focus your energy on your sweetheart. Perhaps you might send your lover a card or a small gift each week of February. Or make Valentine's Day an occasion by taking time off from work and spending the day together. Dress up and go dancing or to a special restaurant. Revisit locations that have special significance for you. Write a heartfelt letter of love.

March: No matter what part of the country you're in, the weather is likely to be bad. March may be a good time to plan an evening in front of the fireplace or to have a candlelight dinner. If you both like indoor sporting events, buy tickets and treat yourselves to an evening of excitement. When it's cold outside, a long hot bath together can warm you up in more ways than one. Spend an evening going through your old pictures and recalling the fun times you've had together.

April: With April come spring and new beginnings. This is the month to venture outdoors as a twosome for a walk, hike, bike ride, or stroll through the park. Being a homemaker for so many years, I can't think of spring without thinking of spring cleaning. Going through your belongings and weeding out extraneous items can be a time of bonding. Yes, some people find this romantic, especially the pragmatists.

May: May is the month of flowers, a true symbol of romantic love. Surprise your partner by bringing home a flat of bedding plants and planting them together. Planting a tree can serve as a symbol of your love throughout the years. Of course, there is the option of giving your partner cut flowers or a plant for home or work. Don't forget that men like to receive flowers, too.

June: This is the traditional month for weddings and commitments. What better time to renew your vows through word or deed? A simple sentence like, "I'm looking forward to growing older with you" or "I'm glad you're in my life" will long be remembered.

July: Celebrate the height of summer with some hot sex. Take a risk. Make love outdoors; have sex in every room in the house during this month. Go on a picnic. Spread out a blanket and watch the stars at night. Get in the water. Have a squirt gun fight. Play with each other.

August: Make sure that you have some vacation time for just the two of you before the busy fall season descends upon you. If you have children, spending time alone with your partner sends an important message to them. Your children need to know that you are a priority in each other's lives. Knowing that you love each other makes them feel safe and gives them permission to form an intimate bond when they become young adults.

September: Those tasks that you've been putting off all summer finally have to be dealt with. This may be the perfect time for a pragmatic gesture of love. Clean your partner's car. (Or pay to have someone else "detail" it.) Clean out the garage. Pick up after yourself without being reminded. Stack the dishes in the dishwasher the way your *partner* likes it done. Sharpen the kitchen knives while watching a football game. Give your partner some extra affection when the pressure mounts. Leave love notes in unlikely places as a reminder of your support. Go to a football game and eat junk food for the fun of it.

October: Since this is the month for Halloween, why not experience some romantic "acting out"? You might reenact how you and your partner met or go to a public place and pretend that you're just meeting each other. Costumes of all kinds can be fun. Surprise your lover with a bouquet of autumn leaves. Have a fall picnic that features hot cider, a hearty casserole or soup, and fresh bread. The parks and national forests are delightfully empty in the fall, so consider an off-season camping trip. It gets dark early, and you'll have to snuggle together to keep warm—ideal conditions for a leisurely lovemaking session.

November: The eleventh month of the year is the time to give thanks, and what could be more romantic than taking this time to thank your mate for all she or he does for you? You could do this in a little speech at the Thanksgiving dinner or make it more private, behind closed doors. A card or letter expressing your thanks is likely to become a keepsake.

December: The last month of the year is full of lights and festivities. It's traditionally a time for children, church or synagogue, relatives, and office parties. If you're not mindful, the rush of the holiday season can keep you and your lover apart. Reserve some time for the two of you. Also, be respectful of each other's separate holiday traditions. Ask your partner: "What food has special meaning to you? What decorations bring back the fondest memories? What holiday traditions from the past would you like to re-create?"

Help each other out with holiday chores. Make this a "his and her" holiday season, not a female tour de force. Put special thought into your gifts for each other. One couple I know has stopped buying each other separate gifts and goes shopping together for one shared gift. They enjoy spending this time together and find that it reduces the pressure to come up with a "perfect gift."

EXERCISE 5: A PERSONAL GUIDE TO THE HOLIDAYS

COMMENTS: Many couples make each other guess exactly what a particular holiday or special occasion means to them. If their partners guess wrong, they're in hot water.

The truth is, most people have a unique emotional response to each holiday. One woman thinks Mother's Day is nothing but a commercial ploy and would rather ignore the whole thing; another feels deeply hurt if her husband fails to surprise her with a gift. One man wants a big party on his birthday; another would rather celebrate alone with his family. One woman thinks Halloween is for children and trick-or-treating; another wants to go to adult parties and spend hours constructing an elaborate costume. Some people enjoy receiving utilitarian Christmas gifts; others believe that a utilitarian gift is grounds for divorce.

This exercise puts an end to the mind reading and demands that you be explicit about your feelings about each holiday and state exactly how you want your partner to respond.

DIRECTIONS: Look at the following list of major holidays, and check the ones that you celebrate. Add any that I've overlooked. Answer the questions after each holiday that you have checked. Share your responses and elaborate on them.

PARTNER 1:

VALENTINE'S DAY
What significance (if any) does this holiday/celebration have for you?

_____

What would you like your partner to do for/with you?

_____

PASSOVER
What significance (if any) does this holiday/celebration have for you?

_____

What would you like your partner to do for/with you?

_____

EASTER
What significance (if any) does this holiday/celebration have for you?

_____

What would you like your partner to do for/with you?

_____

YOUR BIRTHDAY
What significance (if any) does this holiday/celebration have for
you?

What would you like your partner to do for/with you?

MOTHER'S DAY
What significance (if any) does this holiday/celebration have for
you?

What would you like your partner to do for/with you?

MEMORIAL DAY
What significance (if any) does this holiday/celebration have for
you?

What would you like your partner to do for/with you?

FATHER'S DAY
What significance (if any) does this holiday/celebration have for
you?

What would you like your partner to do for/with you?

YOUR ANNIVERSARY
What significance (if any) does this holiday/celebration have for
you?

What would you like your partner to do for/with you?

FOURTH OF JULY
What significance (if any) does this holiday/celebration have for you?

_____

What would you like your partner to do for/with you?

_____

LABOR DAY
What significance (if any) does this holiday/celebration have for you?

_____

What would you like your partner to do for/with you?

_____

HALLOWEEN
What significance (if any) does this holiday/celebration have for you?

_____

What would you like your partner to do for/with you?

_____

THANKSGIVING DAY
What significance (if any) does this holiday/celebration have for you?

_____

What would you like your partner to do for/with you?

_____

HANUKKAH
What significance (if any) does this holiday/celebration have for you?

_____

What would you like your partner to do for/with you?

_____

CHRISTMAS
What significance (if any) does this holiday/celebration have for
you?

What would you like your partner to do for/with you?

NEW YEAR'S
What significance (if any) does this holiday/celebration have for
you?

What would you like your partner to do for/with you?

OTHER HOLIDAYS OR SPECIAL OCCASIONS

PARTNER 2:

VALENTINE'S DAY
What significance (if any) does this holiday/celebration have for
you?

What would you like your partner to do for/with you?

PASSOVER
What significance (if any) does this holiday/celebration have for
you?

What would you like your partner to do for/with you?

EASTER
What significance (if any) does this holiday/celebration have for
you?

What would you like your partner to do for/with you?

_____

YOUR BIRTHDAY
What significance (if any) does this holiday/celebration have for you?

_____

What would you like your partner to do for/with you?

_____

MOTHER'S DAY
What significance (if any) does this holiday/celebration have for you?

_____

What would you like your partner to do for/with you?

_____

MEMORIAL DAY
What significance (if any) does this holiday/celebration have for you?

_____

What would you like your partner to do for/with you?

_____

FATHER'S DAY
What significance (if any) does this holiday/celebration have for you?

_____

What would you like your partner to do for/with you?

_____

YOUR ANNIVERSARY
What significance (if any) does this holiday/celebration have for you?

_____

What would you like your partner to do for/with you?

_____

FOURTH OF JULY
What significance (if any) does this holiday/celebration have for you?

_____

What would you like your partner to do for/with you?

_____

LABOR DAY
What significance (if any) does this holiday/celebration have for you?

_____

What would you like your partner to do for/with you?

_____

HALLOWEEN
What significance (if any) does this holiday/celebration have for you?

_____

What would you like your partner to do for/with you?

_____

THANKSGIVING DAY
What significance (if any) does this holiday/celebration have for you?

_____

What would you like your partner to do for/with you?

_____

HANUKKAH
What significance (if any) does this holiday/celebration have for you?

_____

What would you like your partner to do for/with you?

_____

CHRISTMAS
What significance (if any) does this holiday/celebration have for you?

_____

What would you like your partner to do for/with you?

_____

NEW YEAR'S
What significance (if any) does this holiday/celebration have for you?

_____

What would you like your partner to do for/with you?

_____

OTHER HOLIDAYS OR SPECIAL OCCASIONS

_____

_____

EXERCISE 6: CREATING A ROMANTIC LOVEMAKING RITUAL

COMMENTS: One way to make your lovemaking more meaningful is to create a ritual to prepare you for a romantic, intimate experience. Developing a ritual demonstrates your ability to create something unique and personal, which may verge on the sacred.

DIRECTIONS: When the two of you are in a quiet, intimate mood, spend some time devising a ritual to perform before lovemaking that will heighten your awareness of each other and deepen the bond between you. Your ritual can be as simple as lighting a candle or looking each other in the eyes for a few moments, or it may be more elaborate, involving some of the following elements:

Candles
Special music
Special lighting
Flowers
Eye gazing

Massage
Playing musical instruments or singing
Incense
Reciting poetry
Reading favorite passages or quotations
Reading passages from the Bible

9

SEX AND BODY IMAGE

We are a nation obsessed with our bodies. More than ever before, we are dieting, exercising, counting fat grams, getting hair implants, and paying large sums of money to be nipped, tucked, padded, and sucked. Image is everything. Yet, in spite of our efforts, we don't like what we see in the mirror. More than 85 percent of the people who responded to a body image survey conducted by *Psychology Today* magazine were concerned about their appearance. Nearly 35 percent had *significant* problems with the way they looked. Sadly, the people who took this survey were more unhappy with their appearances than those who had taken a similar survey thirteen years earlier.

It probably comes as no surprise to you that there is a significant difference in the way that men and women view their bodies. Take a moment to refer back to the results of your Sexual Style Survey on pages 21–35. If you are a typical couple, the man's score will be higher than the woman's. I can often tell the sex of the person who filled out a survey just by glancing at the body image category. One woman who had a very low body image was puzzled by her husband's much higher score. "He never says anything bad about his body," she said disbelievingly. "He just won't criticize himself. He's getting a paunchy tummy. He has skinny little bird legs. His legs are really pale. And he's getting flabby because he no longer works out. But he doesn't worry about those things! It's really weird." She was dumbfounded that her husband could have a less than perfect body and be content with it.

I am disheartened to see that people who tend to have the lowest body images of all are young women in their teens and twenties. A majority of those lovely young women you see with sleek bodies, velvet skin, and shiny hair are highly critical of their looks. This comes as no surprise to a friend of mine, the mother of a beautiful nineteen-year-old daughter named Martha who turns heads whenever she enters a room. Men and women alike stop their conversations to watch her walk by. She has even modeled for one of the fitness magazines. Yet Martha is dismayed with her appearance. She's obsessed with dieting, and the fact that her stomach has a slight curve to it has turned her into a compulsive jogger.

Regrettably there are signs that men as a group are also growing less accepting of their looks. The sale of men's cosmetics has grown to a $2.5 billion annual business as millions of men have started moussing their hair, "combing out the gray," and finishing off their toilette with "foundation cream" and hair spray. Twenty percent of all plastic surgery is now performed on men, four times what it was ten years ago. Face-lifts for men are becoming increasingly common, and a surprising number of men are opting for pectoral and calf implants to bulk up muscles that are slow to respond to exercise. Said one man who was recovering from his third round of cosmetic surgery: "You start looking more closely, you see a lot that needs fixing."

SEX, BODY IMAGE, AND VIDEOTAPES

There's no doubt that the various media play a major role in our obsession with body image. Every time we glance at a billboard, open a magazine, or turn on the TV we are confronted with images of beautiful people—those truly exceptional bodies that catch a photographer's eye. From the woman who co-anchors the six o'clock news to the man who models fly casting equipment in the sports catalog, we are surrounded by unusually good-looking people.

It doesn't help that our culture makes a clear association between being beautiful and being worthy of love. The romantic lead in a play, TV show, or movie is always handsome or beautiful. Actors with ordinary bodies and features are assigned "character" roles. The message that we get from the media is that we have to be extraordinarily beautiful to be worthy of love. Here's the way novelist Kathleen E. Woodiwiss describes her main character in her romance novel *Shanna*: "Her beauty was such that his knees grew weak. . . . Her pale honey-hued hair, caught in a mass of loose ringlets, cascaded over her shoulders and down her back. . . . Her features seemed perfect, the nose straight and finely boned. The soft brown brows arched away from eyes that were clear and sea-green, brilliant against the thick fringe of jet-black lashes."

What man could possibly hope to win such a beauty? Why, a man whose face was "handsome, recklessly so, with magnificent dark brows that curved neatly, a straight, thin nose; a firm but sensuous mouth. The lean line of his jaw showed strength and flexed with the movement of the muscles there. . . . Ruark was slim yet sturdy and moved with almost sensuous grace. He had wide shoulders, narrow hips, trim waist, and trim belly."

The beautiful people portrayed in books such as these are almost always young. The hero can be in his thirties or even forties—provided he is sufficiently muscular, lean, and handsome. But in order for a heroine to be credible, she has to be in her late teens or twenties. In those rare instances when the main female character is (heaven forbid) over thirty, she is stunningly well preserved. She is slim, firm, and flat-bellied, and amazingly, her succulent breasts haven't lost an inch of altitude since high school. Here's how Janet Dailey describes the face of her middle-aged heroine in her book *The Glory Game*: "She looked thirty; an unkind eye might have guessed thirty-seven, but people were always surprised when she admitted she was forty-two. Her skin had a fresh, youthful glow, lightly tanned by Florida sunshine . . . many discreetly looked, but there were no scars near the hairline to betray nips and tucks taken to correct sagging flesh.''

I keep thumbing through the books for a heroine *I* can identify with: one who's fifty and has fine hair, thin lips, small breasts, and dry skin. So far no luck.

One of the hazards of trying to measure up to our cultural standards of beauty, especially feminine beauty, is that they change from decade to decade. When Twiggy came on the scene in the sixties, we began idolizing the thin, prepubescent female body, the kind of body that was called scrawny or skinny when I was growing up. To achieve this desired flatness, gaunt fashion models wrapped their already minuscule breasts in bandages and ordinary women subjected themselves to an endless series of brand-name diets. Then came a new standard of beauty: Woman were supposed to have a thin, prepubescent body *with large breasts.* To achieve this anatomical oddity, thousands of women dieted themselves down to a tiny dress size and then paid thousands of dollars for breast implants. Now there are signs that the emaciated waif look is coming back.

I realized how obsessed we've become with thinness when I went shopping with a young woman who was recovering from a life-threatening battle with anorexia. We had to search all over town to find a pair of pants small enough to fit her emaciated body. We finally found a pair of 00 slacks in a petite woman's shop. (I discovered that day that the lower range of women's sizes goes 5, 3, 1, 0, and 00.) The clerk who helped my friend try on the tiny pair of pants kept commenting on my friend's "cute" body. "Tell me," she gushed, "what's your secret for staying so thin?" I thought: "Starvation, compulsive exercise, and vomiting."

WOMEN, SEX, AND BODY IMAGE

Considering the culture's obsession with beauty, youth, and thinness, it's not surprising that so many women are unhappy with their appearances. When their bodies show ordinary signs of wear and tear or when they are embellished with the natural padding that comes with maturity, they are filled with despair.

But what effect does this have on their sexuality? To find out, I asked a group of women to discuss sex and body image. Here's a portion of that conversation:

PAT LOVE: When has anyone here really enjoyed her body or thought it was sexy?

SANDY: Do we have to talk about this? [Laughter]

ELLEN: I liked my body once. I had the flu and a bad case of diarrhea for three weeks. I lost twenty-five pounds. I went down to a hundred and fifteen pounds. I'm five-seven. I was able to wear my roommate's bright red pants. I felt sexy then. If you look good in a pair of tight pants, that's sexy.

MARGARET: I've always been thin, but it hasn't made me feel sexy. I've felt very unfeminine because of it: masculine and unattractive.

BETTY: That amazes me. I've always thought you look like Grace Kelly!

MARGARET: Don't be absurd. I've always felt very masculine. I've been embarrassed all my life about having small breasts. The guys teased me when I was growing up about having "bird legs."

TONI: I had guys tease me for having large breasts. My cousin and I were known as the "boobsy" twins.

MARGARET: When people tell me I have nice-looking anything, I think they're lying. There's an old tape that I grew up with. I had a cousin who was known as the pretty one. I was known as the smart one. People used to say things to me like, "When you're eighteen, you're really going to be pretty," which I interpreted to mean, "You're not pretty now." I became eighteen, and nothing happened. No big change or anything. I did not feel attractive; therefore, I did not look attractive.

MELONY: I was thinking that the way you were teased as a child never leaves you. You never get over it. I was very thin. I was about a hundred pounds forever. Kids would say to me, "Stick your tongue out and turn sideways and you'll look like a zipper." All that stuff. I showed them. Now I'm too fat. [Laughter]

NANCY: The only time I liked my body was when I was nursing my kids. That's the only time I had breasts.

DEBORAH: I am so upset about my face that I had cold laser stimulation to help me get rid of my double frown. I wear a piece of tape at night to get rid of my forehead wrinkles. I almost paid money for plastic surgery. They were going to smooth down the wrinkles and clip the nerve so I couldn't frown. But the doctor couldn't assure me that I would like the way my face felt when it was done. My boyfriend didn't care about the wrinkles. He said, "I don't want you to have a plastic face."

SANDY: I like my legs, but my knees have dropped. I've been thinking about having them fixed.

PAT LOVE: Here's what I want to know: Is your ability to be sexual and relaxed, to lose yourself in the lovemaking affected by your body image?

VOICE: Absolutely.

VOICE: Sure.

VOICE: Yes.

ELLEN: I felt sexy when I lost all that weight.

SHELLY: The fact that I'm so fat blocks my sexuality. I don't want to get in certain lovemaking positions. My husband reaches over to touch me and I say, "Don't touch me." I hate the way I feel.

NANCY: Do you feel comfortable having your husband see you naked?

SHELLY: No! Absolutely not. This morning I got up, and even though I had on a nightshirt, I wrapped an afghan around me. My husband looked at me and said, "You know, you don't have to do that." But I did. For me. That's how bad I feel about myself. Even though he is very, very kind to me. The other night he joked, "I want to have sex, but I promise not to touch you. I'll keep both my hands behind my head.'' [Laughter] He and I can joke about it, but I still feel very uncomfortable every time he touches me.

When a woman is unhappy with her body for any reason—she thinks she's too fat, too thin, too "hippy," too short-legged, too thick-waisted, too busty, or too flat—it can have a deadening effect on her sexuality. In a study of 123 women, researchers found a strong correlation between body image and sexual desire. Women who had negative views of their bodies not only were less interested in making love, but were more restricted in their range of sexual activities and had more difficulty becoming aroused and reaching orgasm.

A year ago I worked briefly with a woman named Marion who was a striking example of how low body image can affect virtually every aspect of one's sexuality. When Marion analyzed her Sexual Style Survey, she realized that her negative body image lowered her score in every single category. She scored low in the sensuality category because, in her words, "I'm not going to let him run his hands all over *this* body!" She scored low on the technique section because "I don't feel as free as I used to before I gained all the weight. If I'm up on top, he'll see all these bulges and folds." Her romance score was at the bottom of the scale. "The thing about romance," she explained, "is that I don't feel I deserve my husband's love. The other day I said to him, 'I wouldn't be surprised if you found me so gross you would go out and find someone else.' "

Sadly, her negative body image not only made her a more inhibited sexual partner but made her feel unworthy of love. She had built a wall of mirrors between herself and her husband, each mirror reflecting back to her a negative, distorted image of her body.

MEN, SEX, AND BODY IMAGE

I have yet to meet a man who was as inhibited by his appearance as most women seem to be. Although many men have concerns about the way they look, they are less likely to let it interfere with their lovemaking. A few men even asked me why body image was a part of the Hot Monogamy program. Asked one man: "What does body image have to do with sex?"

There is only one aspect of body image in which men are more concerned than women, and that is in the appearance of their genitals. While many women find their genitalia unattractive—in fact, a majority of the women surveyed in one particular study regarded their genitalia as the "ugliest" part of their anatomy"—few women spend much time worrying about what lies between their legs. "Fortunately," one woman wrote on her survey, "all those folds and orifices are hidden from view."

Male genitals, however, hang out in plain view, and most men are highly aware of them. This self-consciousness is accentuated by the messages men get from the media. Says Bernie Zilbergeld in his book *The New Male Sexuality:* "Penises in fantasyland come in only three sizes: large, extra large, and so big you can't get them through the door. 'Massive,' 'huge' and 'enormous' are commonly mentioned in fiction." In an interview Zilbergeld added, "Freud is partly right about penis envy. It exists, but only among men. Every man I've met wants someone else's penis or a mythical penis." Some men are so distraught about the size of their penises that they resort to using mechanical pumps—devices that have no lasting effect on penis size but can damage sensitive erectile tissue.

Whether you are male or female, it's difficult to feel sexy when you feel your body doesn't measure up. If you're heavy, if you were born with short legs or a thick torso, if you're not tall, or busty, or muscular, or well endowed, it's easy to feel you are not sexually attractive or don't deserve to be loved.

UNREALISTIC STANDARDS ABOUT OUR PARTNERS

The unrealistic standards of beauty perpetuated by our culture can also affect the way we view our partners. I have talked with numerous men and women who are unhappy with their partners' appearance. Excess weight is a big issue for some men. In many of the couples' workshops I've given, there has been at least one man who's complained about his wife's weight. Typically he'll say something like this: "If she'd just lose some weight . . . I'm not as attracted to her as I used to be. When I married her, she didn't look like this. She knows I want her to lose weight." Some men expect their wives to maintain the figures they had as young brides. Sadly a small percentage of these men find that they're no longer sexually attracted to their "overweight" wives. A man that I'm seeing in private sessions is wrestling with this issue. He said to me, "My wife's had two kids. She's put on weight. Her breasts sag. I love her, but she doesn't excite me anymore. I'm not proud of this, and I'm careful not to say anything about it to her. But she senses it anyway."

Some people demand nothing short of perfection. One woman complained to me that her twenty-nine-year-old husband was losing his sex appeal because he had gained a few pounds. When I had a chance to meet him, I was stunned by his striking good looks. Other people have confessed to me they will date only exceptionally attractive people.

During an all-male discussion group I listened to a middle-aged man named Mick candidly talk about his obsession with bodily perfection. "It's hard for a woman to have a good body after age twenty-five," he said. "So now I'm dating women who are twenty years younger than I am." Not surprisingly he found many of the young women "immature," one of the reasons he's never married.

He did his best to explain his preoccupation with beautiful women. "I think I was imprinted with *Playboy* magazine," he said. "I'm serious. I stared at Playboy Bunnies for thousands of hours when I was young. I masturbated to them. In college I had a whole collage of them on my wall. I went to bed staring at beautiful bodies, and I woke up to them every morning. There's an imprint on my consciousness of what a sexy woman is supposed to look like. It's really screwed me up around women. A woman is walking down the street, and I'm attracted to her because she looks like the package. And I don't even know her. And if a woman doesn't look like the package, I find I'm not interested in her. There's this one woman that I've been dating and I like her a lot, but I'm not attracted to her sexually. I know it sounds stupid for me to say this, but her breasts don't appeal to me."

His candor encouraged several other men to speak up. Here's a part of that interchange:

TONY: Those images we see of beautiful women can be really powerful. It still affects me, even though I'm in my fifties. The COSMO girl—she's beautiful, air-brushed, young, sexy. When you get with a real woman and live with her day and night, she's got blemishes. She gains weight. She gets sick. She's a real person. You have to put away your fantasies.

ALLEN: Men are sold this bill of goods about how women are supposed to look. A woman who's eighteen years old is supposed to stay that way the rest of her life, and we've been sold that. That's bullshit!

WAYNE: I have a friend who tells me that he's no longer attracted to his wife. He says, "I like thin women with firm breasts." His wife used to be thin. But she's gained weight and her breasts have become huge since nursing the baby. He says that when she puts on her spandex clothes and stuff, there are bulges. I know what he's doing in his mind. There's some mythical woman out there, and he's comparing his wife with her.

Clearly these men were not happy about the way they'd been manipulated by the media. The airbrushed perfection of the Playboy Bunny came to their minds unbidden, frustrating their ability to find satisfaction with their real-life partners.

LETTING GO OF UNREALISTIC STANDARDS

Whether you are distressed about your own appearance or unhappy with the appearance of your partner, you have to find some way to become more accepting if you want to enjoy your sexuality to the fullest. You have to find some way to love yourself and make love to your partner *just as you are now.*

One way to become more accepting of your bodies is to compare the idealized images you have in your head with ordinary human beings. I gained a new appreciation for both male and female bodies when I spent a weekend at a family nudist camp. A friend of mine who is a nudist invited me to accompany her and her husband to their favorite camp. The only awkward moment for me was when I was taking off my clothes after driving through the gate. After that I felt as if I were at any other resort. People were shooting pool, playing Ping-Pong, swimming, lounging by the lake—all nude. I saw people with fat bodies, thin bodies, old bodies, and young bodies. The motto of the camp was "Every body is beautiful," and the people around me, having absorbed this philosophy, carried themselves with uncommon grace. I can still picture my friend, who has what she calls a "marshmallow stomach," walking around proud as a peacock wearing only a necklace and earrings. I've felt more kindly toward my own body ever since.

Another friend of mine who is a very heavy woman had a similar experience when she visited a spiritual retreat on the West Coast. The retreat had outdoor baths, and most people bathed in the nude. She said, "Before I got there, I had a lot of fears about the nudity. I didn't know if I could handle it. I like to pretend that my clothes hide all my fat." She felt very self-conscious the first day she went to the baths, but by the second day she had much less anxiety. "Nobody was paying much attention to me," she said. "I thought, 'If two hundred people can look at me and accept the way I look, why can't I?'" By the end of the week she felt totally at ease. She said, "The people who stood out were the ones wearing bathing suits."

If you don't have an opportunity to visit a nudist camp, a nude swimming beach, or a public bathing area, you can visit a health club frequented by a broad cross section of people (not one that caters just to physical fitness buffs and twenty-somethings). A glance around the dressing room will acquaint you with all the infinite varieties of human flesh.

Excess weight is an issue that plagues many people. One way to become more accepting of your body weight is to become more educated about the consequences of dieting. Only a small percentage of the population is born with the long-limbed, slender, attenuated bodies we have come to admire. The rest of us struggle mightily to achieve those elusive proportions through dieting. But as we now know, only 5 percent of all dieters manage to lose weight and keep it off. The other 95 percent either fail to reach their goal or reach their goal over and over again through a relentless process called yo-yo dieting that is harmful to the heart and can reduce muscle and bone mass. While it is physically possible to eat low-fat foods and exercise your way to a lean body, it requires a commitment of time and energy that many people cannot or will not make. To demand that of ourselves or our partners may not be realistic. Although we should all eat healthy, low-fat foods and get enough exercise to ensure good health, we need to put an end to our self-destructive obsession with thinness.

WHAT PEOPLE REALLY WANT IN A LOVER

Once you start letting go of unrealistic standards of beauty, you can begin to appreciate what *really* makes people sexually attractive. The media drill the message into our heads that sexy people are young, slim, firm, and classically beautiful; we labor under the illusion that we have to look that way to be sexy. But that's not what I heard from the majority of people I interviewed for this book. I heard over and over that it is *responsiveness*, not *attractiveness*, that makes a person a memorable lover:

> *"Passion is the most important element to me in sex. Being with beautiful women who were not passionate was not a turn-on for me. But being with women who did not fit the* Playboy *image at all but were passionate was very exciting."*
>
> *"The fears my wife has about gaining weight and losing her attractiveness are groundless as far as I'm concerned. She's forty-seven, and I know that as long as I touch her and kiss her and she responds with passion, the other stuff is not going to matter."*
>
> *"If she squirms when I touch her, that's enough."*
>
> *"What I really value in a lover is if he is full of attention. I want him to be paying attention to me, to how I'm feeling, to what I want. How he looks hardly matters."*

"What I want is a man who is willing to be intimate. He can be thin, fat, have a ten-inch cock or a four-inch cock. I don't care about any of that. I just want him to be emotionally available."
"My wife really lets go during sex. I love it when she openly enjoys what I'm doing to her. Thank God she doesn't let the fact that she's overweight diminish her pleasure or mine."

As this last person's remarks show, if you allow your feelings of inadequacy about your appearance to interfere with your sexual responsiveness or your ability to be intimate, you may be depriving your partner of what he or she truly values in a lover. Ultimately a relaxed, emotionally present, and turned-on lover is more physically arousing to most people than a lover with a perfect body.

ADORNMENT

People with negative body images tend to err in one of two directions. Either they are careless about their physical appearance or they devote excessive amounts of time and energy to trying to look better.

People who are careless with their physical appearance broadcast their negative body image loudly and clearly: "Because I don't have a perfect body, I don't deserve a good haircut." "Because I'm overweight, I don't deserve to buy good clothes or take care of them." "Because I have lines and wrinkles, I'm not worthy of adornment."

People project much more positive images when they put conscious effort into their appearances. When the color of your clothes flatters your coloring, when your clothes fit well, when your clothes are well cared for, you make a strong first impression. It doesn't matter if you are old or young, tall or short, fat or thin, plain-looking or beautiful. The effort you put into looking good says, "I care about me. I'm worth the effort." When this attitude is reflected in your posture and the way you walk, the effect can be stunning. People are drawn to you. They think you must lead an interesting, full life. They want to spend time with you.

You were given only one body. Whatever its present size or

shape, it's the only body you have. Dress it up and take it out! When you look as good as you possibly can, you will feel better about yourself, which will ultimately make you feel more sexually alive.

It may also be wise to put more effort into how you look at home, a lesson a friend of mine learned a few years ago. She was newly remarried, and her first husband was over at the house picking up their children for a weekend visit. She went upstairs for a few minutes, and when she came back down, she overheard her first husband say to her second husband, "She may look good to you now, but just wait a few months. Soon she'll be wearing baggy sweatpants during the day and coming to bed in an old flannel nightgown. And you'd better get used to seeing her in curlers because she wears them *all* the time."

My friend got the message. To this day her second husband has never seen her look frumpy. She said to me, "It's not that I dress up at home. I wear casual clothes. But he's never seen me look *bad*."

Coming to bed freshly showered and wearing beautiful lingerie or elegant cotton or silk pajamas is another way to say, "I care about me." Lingerie comes in all sizes. If you've been neglecting to dress up for your late-night dates, consider treating yourself to some new clothes. It's just one more way to show respect for your wonderful body.

There are some people, however, who need to spend *less* time with their appearances. They are so insecure about their looks that they spend inordinate amounts of time fixing their hair, choosing which clothes to wear, and "putting on their faces." If you err in this direction, you need to stay away from mirrors and focus on what people really appreciate about you. Most people are going to be far more tolerant of your appearance than you are.

You might also consider diverting some of the energy you put into your appearance into being more physically active. One of the conclusions of the *Psychology Today* survey mentioned earlier was that people who cared about fitness and health had more positive feelings about their overall appearance than those who focused primarily on the way they looked. A regular exercise program not only improved their physical appearance but improved the ways they *felt* about the way they looked. "As one respondent so aptly summed up, 'I like my body, though it would certainly win no beauty contests. I take care of it because without it I could not exist. The beauty in me is really the beauty of me.' " Terri Sutton, writing in the Minneapolis/St. Paul alternative newspaper called *City Pages*, echoed these sentiments: ". . . my preferred method to revalue my body is to use it. That means dancing in it, walking with it, running, jumping, having sex, feeling it hurt, feeling its strength, appreciating its resiliency—living in it to the point where I don't say 'it' but rather 'me.' "

OVERCOMING PENIS ENVY

What can you do if you are a man who feels inadequate about the size or shape of his penis? First and foremost, make sure that you have accurate information about penis size. The vast majority of penises are between five and seven inches when fully erect. In a flaccid state they are around three to four inches. You may be feeling inadequate because you are comparing yourself with the celebrated phalluses of porn stars.

Another way to become more accepting about your genitals is to get a better perspective—literally. When you look down at your own penis, your view is foreshortened. When you look across the locker room at another man's penis, you view it straight on, so it may appear to be longer than yours. (This could be why two out of three men estimate their own penises to be undersize.)

But even if your penis is smaller than average, that doesn't have to affect your ability to bring pleasure to your mate. The nerves in the vagina are clustered in the two inches closest to the vaginal opening in the area called the G spot. (For more about the G spot, turn to page 152.) A penis that is four inches long when erect is going to stimulate the G spot just as well as a penis that is seven inches long.

I also want to assure you that penis size is not an issue for most women. I have never had a female client tell me in couple's therapy or in a private session that she thought her partner's penis was too small. One of my male clients worried for the entire twenty years of his marriage about the smallness of his penis. When he finally got up the courage to talk about it in couple's counseling, his wife remarked: "I have never, ever thought your penis was too small. We've always seemed a perfect fit."

My clinical observations are backed up by various studies. A survey reported in *The Kinsey Institute New Report on Sex* found that women were more concerned about finding a partner with "firm muscle tone, well-groomed hair, a clear complexion, and white teeth" than they were about finding a mate with a large penis. Shampooing your hair and brushing your teeth more often are likely to be more thrilling to your mate than finding a magical way to lengthen your penis.

HELPING YOUR PARTNER BECOME MORE SELF-ACCEPTING

What can you do to help your *partner* have a more positive body image? First of all, make sure that you're not adding to the problem by being overly critical. Many people wrongly believe that criticism will help their partners lose weight or become more diligent about exercising: "You're getting fat." "You shouldn't be eating that." "Look at you. You're a pig." One man took unflattering pictures of his wife and posted them on the refrigerator to convince her she needed to lose weight. This kind of behavior will only lower your partner's self-esteem and drive a wedge between you. Even subtle messages like complimenting your partner for losing weight or looking thin can deliver the hidden message that he or she was unacceptable before. The best way to help your partner have a better body image is to send out a continual message of acceptance.

To help you do this, make a detailed mental or written list of all the ways you value your partner as a lover, including any aspects of your partner's body you find attractive. Be honest in your appraisal. Your partner will know whether or not you are telling the truth.

Once you have composed your list, begin giving compliments. Many of us stop complimenting our partners once the courtship period is over. We all need to hear that we're loved and appreciated—over and over again.

Here are some examples of appreciative comments:

"I love it when you get really turned on."
"You make love to my penis in the nicest way."
"You know just what to do to bring me to orgasm."
"You are the best lover I've ever had."
"I really like your hair. It's so soft and glossy."
"You have the nicest hands."
"I love to feel the skin on your inner thighs. It's like velvet."
"Your lips are so succulent."
"I like the way you smell."
"I like to cuddle up against you. You are so warm and soft."
"I have always loved your eyes."
"You are so strong. I love to feel the muscles on your back."
"I love the way your penis feels. It's hard and soft and smooth all at the same time."
"I love the way you walk."

EXERCISE SECTION

EXERCISE 1: VISUALIZING BODY ACCEPTANCE

COMMENTS: This first exercise is a powerful one that can help you change deep-seated beliefs about the way you look. It uses a process called creative visualization. Many of you are already familiar with this technique. Simply stated, creative visualization involves getting into a state of deep relaxation and then imprinting your mind with a positive message. People use this technique to excel in sports, stop smoking, lose weight, and instill desired habits.

This particular exercise is designed for people who want to improve their body image and become more sexually responsive. I urge you to use it. You are likely to become more accepting of your physical appearance after five or six repetitions. This, in turn, will result in greater sexual desire or in feeling more freedom to ex-

periment with sexual technique. Remember that all the nine areas
of this program are interconnected.

DIRECTIONS: Read the following script into a tape recorder. Add
soothing background music if you wish. (If you'd rather listen to
someone else's voice, have a friend read the script.) Play back the
tape when you are in a quiet, restful environment and can guarantee you will not be interrupted for at least thirty minutes.

You will note that there are places throughout the script where
a pause is indicated. The number of dots gives an approximate
indication of how long you should pause: . . . = 5 seconds, ... =
10 seconds, ... = 15 seconds, and so on.

Script: Lie down on a soft, comfortable surface . . . Loosen
any restrictive clothing . . . Close your eyes and begin to
focus on the sounds around you . . . . Relax your body
and let it sink into the bed or carpet. As you continue to
relax, focus on your breathing. Feel the air coming into
your body and going out of your body . . . . With each
exhale, let go and let yourself relax even more . . . . Take
in a deep breath, and hold it until you feel some tension
. . . Exhale, relaxing even more. Now take three deep
breaths, holding your breath each time until you feel tension; then slowly breathe out through your nose until
there is no more air in your lungs . . . . Now
imagine that you are floating above your body and can
look down on your body . . . Get a clear look at your body
. . . . As you look at your body, listen to the thoughts that
you normally have about your body, whether they are negative or positive. Listen to the messages you have about
your face . . . your eyes . . . your nose . . . your mouth . . .
Listen to your messages. Now look at your hair. What are
your messages about your hair? . . . Begin traveling down
your body, looking at your arms . . . Now focus on your
hands . . . For a moment experience how you feel about
your hands as you look at them from a distance. You may
find that these are old messages, new messages, or a blend

of old and new messages. Travel down from your shoulders, taking the time that you need to think about your back . . . your chest or breasts . . . . your torso. Look and listen. Experience your normal messages about your upper body, all the messages . . .

Now focus on your waist . . . Listen to the way you feel about your waist. Your hips . . . your buttocks . . . your stomach . . . Take a moment to relax even more deeply. Breathe deeply in and out. Now continue with your inventory. What are the messages about your genitals? . . . Hear all the messages, past and present, about your sexual organs . . . Think about your thighs . . . your knees, calves, and ankles. Let your body melt into relaxation. Let your tension drain out of your body into the bed or the floor. Get a clear look at your legs . . . your feet . . . and your toes. Now scan your entire body, and listen to all the messages past and present . . . .

Now think about some of the most negative messages you tell yourself about your body . . . Highlight one of those messages . . . Stay in touch with that message. Imagine yourself making love and try to determine how this message interferes with your lovemaking . . . Highlight another negative message, and think about how it affects your lovemaking . . . Now listen to a negative message about your body that even you have been afraid to hear. Your worst fear about the way you look . . .

Once you have thought about how all these messages affect your lovemaking, imagine yourself making love feeling proud, excited, adequate, comfortable about every aspect of your body—just as it is now. Your body hasn't changed; only your attitude has changed . . . How might your lovemaking change if you felt positive about every part of your body? Watch yourself. Watch how you respond when you feel more accepting of your body . . . Watch your partner's reaction to the way you have changed . . .

Breathe deeply . . . Now begin to travel to a safe place

. . . It's a very special place. It may be a place that you've been to before, or it may be a place that you create in your mind's eye. Travel to this safe place. Relax and look around you . . . See it in vivid color . . . Hear the sounds of this place . . . Feel what it is like to be relaxed and safe in this special place. As you relax in this special place, look off into the distance and see a very wise and loving person coming toward you . . . This may be a person you know, or it may be a stranger . . . It's a very safe, wise, loving person . . . You invite this person to come and sit in front of you. The person begins to talk about what you would have to give up if you were to see the beauty of your body . . . what challenges would lie before you if you accepted your body exactly as it is now . . . You may have to give up the fantasy of being something that you are not . . . . . You might have to accept the knowledge that you are a sexual person . . . You may have to face the grief of the loss of youth . . . You may have to face the grief of never having had a perfect body . . . You may have to accept the fact that others are attracted to you . . . You may have to deal with your sexual energy . . . You may have to challenge society's narrow attitudes . . . You may have to start living your life the way you want to live it . . . . Listen to this wise person . . .

Now ask the wise person, "How am I beautiful, not just in body but in soul?" . . . Listen as the wise person tells you, "I see your beauty. You cannot hide it from me. I see deep within you an energy for life. I see the uniqueness that makes me want to come closer to you. I see a body that deserves to be taken care off, nurtured, touched, stimulated, adored. I see a body that is a sexual body, a body that deserves to give and receive exquisite sexual pleasure. I see a body that will only pass through this earth one time in this form. I see a miracle."

As the wise person continues to talk about your body, you listen and begin to experience the miracle of your own body. You become aware of the usefulness of your hands, the strength of your arms, the energy in your legs, the complexity of your senses. You realize that all of the different parts and senses of your body are most alive during lovemaking and that your body yearns for and deserves this pleasure. Your whole body responds to sexual pleasure. Your whole body hungers for touch and affection. Your whole body responds in a sexual, sensual manner.

Now see yourself thanking the wise person for being there. You receive a final message about your beautiful, unique miracle of a body . . . . . See yourself going back home, traveling now from this safe place, knowing that you can come back anytime that you want or need to. You are taking with you a new love and appreciation for your body. You take all of these positive messages and can now apply them to your daily life and your love life. See your partner responding in a positive way to these changes . . . See yourself enjoying your body, feeling the aliveness and energy . . . See your body relax and open up to your partner's loving touch . . . See yourself making love with this delightful body, this body, which is your body—just as it is now, transformed by your love and acceptance . . .

Now slowly stretch your arms and legs . . . take a deep, cleansing breath, and then begin breathing a little more quickly. Breathe energy into your body . . . Now open your eyes and go back to your daily life, knowing that this new love of your body comes with you.

Note: For information about purchasing a recorded version of this and other tapes, contact me at my office in Austin, Texas. You'll find my address and phone number just before the appendices.

EXERCISE 2: SELF-ACCEPTANCE THROUGH SELF-VIEWING

COMMENTS: You are not likely to feel comfortable having your partner see you naked if you're not comfortable looking at yourself. One way to become more accepting of your body is to spend some time studying yourself in the mirror.

DIRECTIONS: When you know you're not going to be interrupted, go into your bathroom or bedroom and take off all your clothes. Stand in front of a mirror, and look at your body from all possible angles. Touch your body, and feel its warmth, its hardness, its softness. Pat your body, and think positive thoughts about it. Say to yourself, "This is my body. I love my body."

Repeat this exercise every week or so until you truly feel comfortable with what you see in the mirror.

Eventually you may want to go one step farther and invite your partner to study your naked body as well. Once you have allowed your partner to survey every inch of your body, you will no longer feel the need to cover up and hide.

EXERCISE 3: PRAISING YOUR PARTNER AS A LOVER

COMMENTS: You probably have many positive thoughts about your partner as a lover that you have never communicated or haven't communicated in recent months. This is your opportunity to bolster your partner's self-image.

DIRECTIONS: Over the next few days, think about all the things you enjoy about making love with your partner, including any positive thoughts you have about his or her body. (You might want to refer to pages 227–28 for suggestions.)

Write down these comments in the space provided below or on a separate sheet of paper, and make a point to communicate them on a regular basis. As I mentioned earlier, it's important that you be completely honest in your assessment.

1. What I value about you as a lover:

_____

_____

2. What I enjoy about your body:

_____

_____

10

BECOMING A MORE SENSUOUS LOVER

I listened with fascination as a man in one of my discussion groups described a former girlfriend to us: "What I loved about her was how she communicated with her body. The way she touched me told me, 'You and I are going on a little trip. I'm going to take you down this lane and this lane.' It's as if she were inside my skin, feeling what I'm feeling. She could bring me up, bring me up, bring me up, then drop me back down. Then she'd bring me up again. Then over the top. It was all done without words. It was heavenly." Another friend of mine wistfully recalled a lover from her college days. "What I remember most about him was how comfortable he was with his body. He was never ashamed or embarrassed. He was totally at ease in his skin. We would make love all afternoon. I was drugged with pleasure."

It's not surprising that both these idyllic experiences occurred in brief affairs, not long-term relationships. Sensuality—the ability to be comfortable in one's body, suspend time, and communicate through the skin—is what is missing in many marriages. After a couple spends a few years living together, the sense of immediacy disappears. All too often husbands and wives go to bed feeling distracted and numb, reflexively groping for each other's genitals. The unspoken goal is to go from neutral to orgasm in fifteen minutes, like a car zooming from zero to sixty.

"Spectatoring" is a term sex therapists use to describe what happens when people feel disconnected during lovemaking. A person who is afflicted with this common syndrome spends more time thinking about problems at work or household chores than about the partner lying right beside him or her. If spectatoring becomes chronic, sexual problems tend to arise. A distracted man may have erection difficulties, and a preoccupied woman may find it hard to reach orgasm.

When people feel cut off from their senses while making love, they usually experience sensory deprivation in their daily lives as well. They go through the day feeling numb and unresponsive. In an effort to feel, they turn up the stereo, douse themselves with strong fragrances, and eat large quantities of sweet, salty, or spicy food. Paradoxically, the more they assault their senses, the more cut off they feel.

Why are so many of us estranged from our senses? In our early years we were highly sensual beings. If you have forgotten, spend some time with a one-year-old. She learns about her environment by *sensing* her surroundings. She squishes her food with her hands. She pops everything in her mouth. She splashes in the warm, sudsy dishwater as long as you'll let her. One hot summer day, as I was watering the flowers in my backyard with a garden hose, my toddler grandson eyed me cautiously and edged toward the water. When he saw my look of approval, he stuck his hand in the spray. Seeing the grin on my face, he plunged in his whole arm. Then with a joyful yelp he ran through the stream of water. He ran through the water again and again until he was soaking wet and laughing with glee. He was at one with his universe.

Around the age of three or four most children are gradually weaned away from this natural sensuality. Their caretakers tell them:

"Don't play with your food."
"Go wash your hands."
"Stop making those noises."
"Get that out of your mouth."
"Don't stare at that lady."
"Keep your hands to yourself."
"Put that smelly dog outside."
"Get up off the floor!"
"Don't touch yourself there!"
"Look at you! You've gotten yourself all wet."

As they become young adults, they are rewarded for shutting out the world even further and focusing their energy on getting good grades, good jobs, and good money. In their free time, modern society encourages them to interface with radios, TVs, computers, plastic, cars, and concrete. All the while they are growing more and more estranged from their bodies. They are jolted back to their senses in the first few months or years of a love relationship, but then their perceptions become dulled once again.

TIME, ATTENTION, AND SELF-INDULGENCE: THE MISSING DIMENSIONS

There are no shortcuts to bringing back the sensuality to your lovemaking. By its very nature, sensual lovemaking requires generous amounts of time. For many of us, this means we have to make sex a higher priority in our lives. Our schedules are so tightly packed that, as my colleague Marvin Allen says, "We have to catch every green light." Our sex lives suffer the most. Lovemaking doesn't pay the bills, further our career goals, or cross off any household chores, so we relegate it to the bottom of the list. Once the house is clean, the yard's been mowed, the kids are in bed, and the office homework is done, we'll see if we have any time left over for sex. Sex may be in the forefront of our brains, but it's an afterthought in our schedules. A recent *Ladies' Home Journal* survey revealed that married women are making love less often now than they did ten years ago. Almost three fourths of the working women who responded to the survey said they didn't have enough time for sex.

Reserving a one-hour block of *quality* time once a week for sex may increase your satisfaction with your lovemaking more than any other change you can make. You don't have to use this time for lovemaking if neither of you is in the mood. Think of it as an "opportunity" for sex. If you choose, you can spend the time massaging each other, going for a walk, or having an intimate conversation. But if conditions are right, you will have enough time for a sensual, satisfying experience.

Susan Delaney-Mech, M.D., psychiatrist and sex therapist in private practice in Plano, Texas, advises her clients to write down their appointments for sex on the calendar—in ink. "People tend to erase appointments that are made in pencil," she explains, "but they keep the ones written in ink." (The therapist who taught her this technique referred to it as the "Bic" Cure, after the name of the ballpoint pen.) She also counsels her clients to prepare themselves physically, emotionally, and spiritually for the sexual encounter. "I recommend that couples make an effort to think only positive thoughts about each other in the twenty-four hours prior to making love. I encourage them to think about why they married each other. I encourage them to get in a spirit of gratefulness. And they are to avoid thinking about the faults of their partners—or the faults of their in-laws." If they fantasize about sex, she urges them to fantasize about making love to their partners, not other people. The results? "Couples who follow these recommendations are delighted with the results," she says.

I have found this to be true in my practice as well. Few couples realize the power they have to create a loving sexual encounter. By reserving a time to make love and then deliberately creating a positive attitude, you can greatly increase your ability to give and receive pleasure. Once these mental habits are firmly established, you begin to transform your bedroom into a sanctuary—a place of comfort, safety, and sensuality.

Another requirement for sensuous lovemaking is that you must give yourself permission to luxuriate in your own physical pleasure. A woman in one of my discussion groups put it beautifully: "In order for me truly to enjoy sex, I have to think of myself as a princess. I have to accept all the pleasure and luxury that are offered to me. I have to feel worthy of being made love to." She wasn't advocating being a passive or selfish lover. She realized that for her, as for many people, the real challenge was to open up and embrace her own pleasure.

Ironically, many people whom I see in my practice have more trouble receiving pleasure than giving it. One of the more revealing exercises in my weekend workshops is called the entitlement exercise. (Instructions for this exercise appear on pages 136–38.) It's deceptively simple. In part one of the exercise I instruct the couples to go to their hotel rooms and take turns massaging each other's feet or shoulders for ten minutes, giving their partners continual feedback about what they like and don't like. The more self-indulgent the receiver becomes, the higher marks he or she gets on the exercise.

This is surprisingly hard for many people to do. One woman commented, "I had no problem giving Bob a massage. But when it was my turn, I found myself watching the clock. I was worried about taking more than my fifteen minutes. I was the oldest child of four. I was taught that it's selfish to take. And if someone gives you something, you have to be grateful for whatever it is. You can't influence what they do for you." Her partner, meanwhile, had his own reason for resisting the exercise: "I was worried that Gloria didn't really want to massage me. I was glad you asked us to do it for just ten minutes. That's the only way I could allow myself to relax into it." Not surprisingly both Bob and Gloria complained of low sexual desire and routinely went for weeks without making love.

My partner and I had a breakthrough when I finally felt entitled to receive regular massages. I had hinted many times to him that I love massages, but I had never requested them with much conviction. Deep down I thought it was too much to ask. Then one day I began to think about all the ways I had stretched into my own resistance in order to fulfill his needs. Working on the many areas of my sexuality, I had become a much more available and passionate lover. But I had made little progress in bringing my own needs and desires to the table. When this realization had time to sink in, I felt more entitled to receiving massages and was finally able to ask for them in such a way that my partner could truly hear me. I'm happy to say that weekly massages are now a regular part of my life. I learned once again that when I ask for something with courage and conviction, my wishes often come true.

REVELING IN THE FIVE SENSES

To enjoy your sensuality fully, all five of your senses need to be in the receiving mode. Many of us limit ourselves to one or two. One of my most sensuous experiences took place years ago when I was a passenger on a friend's motorcycle late at night. I was wary of riding the bike, especially in the dark, and my anxiety seemed to heighten my senses. I sat with my arms wrapped around my partner's waist, swaying with him, curve after curve. Our bodies felt welded together. I was aware of the warm summer air whipping my hair. I felt the air currents change from warm to cool as the road left the open meadows and dipped into forest glades. The smells in the air went from musk to floral, woodland to water. When we stopped to admire the moon, I heard the night creatures singing their songs. My body was alive with sensation.

In recent years my partner and I have found that by systematically exploring all our senses, we can bring this same wide-awake quality to our lovemaking. In the remainder of this chapter I'll take you on a guided tour of your five senses, giving you specific advice for adding new sensuality to your lovemaking.

The *sense of smell* is an integral part of our sexuality. Semen, vaginal lubrication, perspiration, and saliva all carry a natural fragrance, and some people find these odors highly erotic. Napoleon ended a letter to Josephine with these provocative lines: "I will be arriving in Paris tomorrow evening. Don't wash."

It isn't just the amorous French who are intoxicated by natural scents. Anthropologist Helen Fisher reports in her book *The Anatomy of Love* that "in Shakespeare's day, a woman held a peeled apple under her arm until the fruit became saturated with her scent; then she presented this 'love apple' to her lover to inhale. Today, in certain areas of Greece and the Balkans, men are known to tuck their handkerchiefs under their armpits and present them with a flourish to their female partners at the start of a dance." The men swear by the results.

In our more fastidious (some might say "uptight") culture, we coat our armpits with deodorant, suck on breath fresheners, douche away vaginal secretions, wear disposable panty liners, shower with deodorant soap—and wish everyone else did as well. The thought of *enjoying* our body odors seems decidedly perverse.

Whether you enjoy body odors or adhere to the "squeaky clean" school of lovemaking is a highly individual matter. However, there are some overall gender differences in the way we respond to odors. As a rule, women have keener senses of smell than men, a sensitivity that is heightened during ovulation. Women can also have stronger reactions to certain body odors, such as bad breath, perspiration, and the smell of a "seasoned" body. Women are a hundred times more sensitive to a compound called Exaltolide, which has an odor very similar to men's sexual musk. Men, on the other hand, tend to react more negatively to artificial scents, especially those that their mates broadcast freely around the living area. In most households it is the woman who anoints herself with cologne, perfumes the linen, sprays the air with "fresheners," and luxuriates in an herbal bath. This characteristic has also been observed in very young children. Girl babies have been observed playing with perfumed rattles for a longer period of time than boy babies do.

Aromatherapy, the therapeutic use of various scents, was studied extensively by the ancient Chinese, East Indians, and Egyptians and is now a legitimate medical subspecialty in France. Aromatherapy is in its infancy in the United States, but so far researchers have managed to put lab rats to sleep with oil of lavender. Human subjects exposed to the oil have become more relaxed and tranquil. (Could this be why our grandmothers tucked lavender sachets in the linens?) In our materialistic culture it's not surprising that most of the aroma research in this country is devoted to studying the effect that perfume has on our spending habits. Researchers have learned that perfuming the air in a department store causes shoppers to linger longer and spend more money. However, one group of researchers is currently trying to isolate the main chemicals in human musk, hoping to concoct a reliable aphrodisiac. If they succeed, the seductive perfume ads of the future may be based on fact, not fantasy. In the meantime, you may have to indulge in some olfactory research with your flesh-and-blood partner.

The *sense of sight* can add greatly to your libidinous pleasures. In one of my interviews a man surprised me by turning his attention to the outfit I was wearing, giving me an education in the art of sensual observation. "Look at what you've got on," he said. "Your clothes are very sensual. They're very feminine and sexy. You wouldn't see a man wearing shiny material of that nature or those bright colors. Even though your top is very loose, the pants cling tightly to your legs. What you have on is designed to attract, to draw attention to your body." For him, his eyes were an erogenous zone. He had learned to increase his pleasure by turning the visual world into erotica.

As a rule, men are highly sensitive to visual stimulation. In their younger years the sight of their naked partners may be all they need to become fully erect. I've heard many women complain that they dare not undress in front of their mates unless they have time for sex. Men, more often than women, are likely to want the lights left on during lovemaking so they can watch the show. They find that the physical joining of their bodies, the appearance of aroused genitals, and the sight of a woman experiencing orgasm can be highly arousing.

Some women have the same reaction, but others find the visual world a distraction. By turning out the lights or closing their eyes, they can intensify their physical sensations. If you and your partner are in opposite camps, the soft glow of candles or dimmable lights will help you find a compromise.

Looking deeply into your lover's eyes is another way to maximize sensual pleasure. Eye gazing has been observed in primates just prior to intercourse and is referred to by zoologists as the copulatory gaze. Humans practice this ritual as well. If you're in doubt, spend some time in a singles' bar. Several cultures have adopted the use of the veil to try to control this mating behavior. Many partners in long-term relationships could be said to be wearing an invisible veil because they avoid each other's gazes for all but a few fleeting moments. If you are willing to risk intense intimacy with your partner, try maintaining the copulatory gaze for a full sixty seconds the next time you make love.

Pictures, magazines, and photographs provide a warehouse of stimulation for those who are turned on by their eyes. Although tastes vary, most of us can be aroused by visual erotica. For some, the picture might depict a couple in a romantic relationship; for others, the physical act of making love. Still others are excited by photographs or drawings of the human body.

Movies and videos add another dimension to visual stimulation. Couples have mentioned to me a number of Hollywood films that have excited them, including *The Postman Always Rings Twice, Body Heat, Picnic, The Big Easy, The Sea of Love, Nine½ Weeks*, and *Blue Velvet*. In laboratory experiments, erotic videos have proved a potent source of stimulation for both men and women, creating a higher level of arousal than any other form of erotica, including audiotapes, photographs, and the written word.

Another way to indulge your sense of sight is to put more effort into the decoration of your bedroom. When you go to bed tonight, look around the room. Do the colors soothe or excite you? Is the bed welcoming? Do you have mood lighting? The right artwork can help create a romantic or erotic mood, and strategically placed mirrors can give you a whole new perspective on your lovemaking. Buying a new bedspread, sheets, or duvet can both enhance your sensual pleasure and declare your lovemaking a major priority in your life. A word of caution: Both of you should take part in the decorating of the bedroom. All too often female sensibilities hold sway. This is yet another area of your relationship in which consultation and compromise are important.

Of all the senses, the *sense of touch* is the one central to lovemaking. The feel of flesh against flesh is a delight that simultaneously reassures, bonds, and excites. When you are sensitive to touch, a simple caress or brush of the lips can send a tingling warmth throughout your entire body.

A man described one of his most memorable sexual encounters in this manner: "We didn't even have intercourse. There were three couples necking in my friend's car. I was so excited and so

hard. My girlfriend and I must have kissed for two hours. It started
with just a little touch of my tongue on her lips. I ran my tongue
around the outside and then inside her mouth. She started giving
me tongue. I was on fire. I started sucking on her tongue when she
put it in my mouth. She started sucking on mine. It was like fucking
her mouth and having her fuck mine. I stuck my tongue deeper
and deeper inside her. I wanted to climb inside.''

To restore the electricity to your sense of touch, you may need
to be more experimental than you were years ago. Simply kissing
your long-term partner may no longer push you over the edge when
repetition and familiarity have dulled your senses. To reexperience
that backseat-of-the-car eroticism, you may need to step outside
your normal routine and introduce some unusual materials into
your lovemaking, such as feathers, fur, silk, warm jets of water,
whipped cream, warm towels, even ice. Ralph, a talkative, friendly
sort, told me about one of his most recent erotic pleasures. His
partner of twelve years asked him if he wanted to try some "cool
sex." He said he wasn't sure what she meant, but if it had anything
to do with sex, he was willing to try. They proceeded to make love
in much the same way they had done in the past. At the moment
of orgasm his partner reached under the bed, pulled out some ice
wrapped in a towel, and placed it on Ralph's scrotum. He described
the experience as "otherworldly." Just to recall it sends shivers up
his spine.

As you work to revive your sense of touch, be sure to take into
consideration the unique sensibilities of your partner. Some people
like a light touch; others, firm. Some people like to be teased; others like to get down to business. As always, these preferences need
to be clearly communicated.

Then there is *aural stimulation*. Many couples fail to take advantage of the mood-altering effect of music. Music not only can
"soothe a savage breast" but can awaken the erotic savage as well.
It's been years since I saw the movie *10*, but I still remember the
sexual tension of Ravel's *Bolero*. Bring a tape player into your bedroom, and explore the potential that music has to soothe, relax,
and excite you.

Some of you may also want to investigate music's ability to take you back in time. A friend of mine spent many hours in her high school days dancing and making out to Johnny Mathis's records. One night she put a tape of his music on the tape deck just before she and her partner slipped into bed. The nostalgia of the music completely changed their style of lovemaking. "For years we'd been spending very little time kissing. We'd go right to oral sex. That night we kissed each other for half an hour before making love. I was sixteen all over again, but this time I could 'go all the way.' "

Making music together can be a delight. Who has not been stirred by a bride and groom singing to each other at a wedding? I once had a lover who played the guitar and sang to me in bed. I'll never forget that part of our relationship.

If you listen carefully, you can also hear music in lovemaking sounds, becoming aroused by each other's heartbeat and breathing. You can be stimulated by the succulent sounds of fellatio, cunnilingus, or intercourse and ignited by the involuntary moans your partner makes at the moment of orgasm.

The sounds of love can also involve words, including endearing expressions, exciting pillow talk, and hot phrases. Some lovers tantalize each other with explicit descriptions of what they intend to do to each other. Phone sex can be a wonderful turn-on. One couple confided to me that they start the verbal foreplay at breakfast and make "obscene" calls to each other at work. By the time they climb into bed at night, they're already halfway there.

There are some gender differences to consider with the sense of hearing as well. Once again women tend to respond more acutely. The slightest sound can rivet a woman's attention—or distract her. In most households it's the woman who is likely to say, "Turn down that TV/radio/stereo." One woman told me that playing soft music while making love helps her screen out distractions. Another woman found even soft music an unwelcome intrusion.

Also, many women prefer romantic or sentimental conversations in bed to explicit sex talk. What excites a friend of mine most of all is having her husband whisper in her ear how much he loves her. It's vital that you take into consideration your partner's preferred vocabulary. Consider easing out of your comfort zone and using the words and phrases most exciting to him or her. They may not be a turn-on for you, but they will elicit a warm response from your partner.

No matter what you say to your partner, direct eye contact can double the impact of your words. The tone of your voice can also make a big difference. Lowering the pitch of your voice and slowing down the pace of your delivery can turn a simple phrase like "I want you" into foreplay.

Our *sense of taste* serves a dual function, tuning us into both touch and taste. For this reason, anything we do with our mouths has a double impact. Sucking is an instinct we are born with and stays with us all of our lives. Many grown-ups like to suck on lollipops, Popsicles, hard candies, beer or soft drinks in bottles, or cigarettes. Right now, stick your finger in your mouth and suck it. See how good it feels? Suck hard, then soft, fast, then slow. Switch your focus to your finger. Experience the inside of your mouth from the vantage point of the one being sucked. Feel the soft lining. Experience the motion of being drawn in tightly, then released. Now imagine your mate sucking your fingers, ears, knees, toes, or genitals. Your whole body can come alive when it is sucked.

Licking is another universal oral pleasure. The deft use of the tongue can turn a simple hello kiss into "Wow! I'm glad to see you!" Licking and sucking the penis or clitoris are highly erotic for many people, providing them with their most intense sexual experiences. Licking and sucking the nipples can arouse both men and women. A few lucky people can reach orgasm through nipple stimulation alone.

Some lovers thrill to the sensation of love bites or nibbling, a behavior common throughout the animal kingdom. When cats mate, for example, there is an orgy of biting, hissing, and wrestling. Try a few experimental nibbles on your mate and observe the reaction.

Edible lubricants can add flavor to your lovemaking. People who are new at oral sex may find that a flavored lubricant helps reduce their inhibitions. Other couples swear by honey, chocolate, or whipped cream.

Eating by itself is a sensuous experience. When seasoned with conscious eroticism, it can quickly become X-rated. If you don't

believe me, rent the movie *Tom Jones* or *Nine½ Weeks*. Feeding each
other, watching each other eat, or simply sharing a meal can
delight, nurture, and excite.

THE MIND: THE SIXTH SENSE

The brain, of course, is the most powerful sex organ of all. Your
partner may be a highly skilled lover, but if your mind is distracted,
you will feel little or nothing at all. On the other hand, if you are
having highly erotic thoughts, a flick of the tongue can send you
over the top. Lovemaking is one of those many occasions in life
when "you must be present to win."

Although you may not realize it, most people regularly experience three distinct mental states during lovemaking: (1) distracted or negative, (2) receptive or neutral, and (3) enhanced or
eroticized. Some people find that they are distracted most of the
time they make love. They worry about the messy room, the upcoming tax audit, their heavy thighs, their partner's baldness, their
lack of sexual desire. *It is not possible to be fully aroused when you are
dwelling on negative or competing thoughts.*

Many people believe they have little control over their frame
of mind, but this is not the case. There are some proven ways to
create a more receptive or eroticized frame of mind. To begin with,
it helps to build in some transition time from your daily life, creating a buffer zone that gives you time to let go of mental distractions. Joan, a screenwriter, came to me because she was having
difficulty reaching orgasm. At first she thought the problem was a
lack of desire. Then she realized that it was a lack of mental attention. She often worked at her screenwriting right up until bedtime.
When her partner approached her for sex, she was so wired that it
was hard for her not to bat his hand away. "I was still in a work
mode," she said. She found she was much more receptive if she
spent half an hour unwinding from work before climbing into bed.

Meditating, stretching, doing yoga, exchanging massages, or
simply lying down for a few minutes and focusing on your breathing
are excellent ways to make the transition from daily life. The effect
of deep relaxation before, during, or after lovemaking can trans-

port you to another world. (For specific instructions, see Exercises 2 and 3 at the end of this chapter.)

Sex therapists prescribe a specific technique called sensate focus to help couples shut out mental distractions, take the pressure off performance, and focus more on physical pleasure. Designed by Masters and Johnson, the exercise involves taking turns caressing each other's bodies. The partner being touched concentrates on the point of contact, shutting out distracting thoughts. The goal is not to become sexually aroused but to relax and experience the sensations. The fact that the genitals are not stimulated during sensate focus is one of the keys to its success. When your partner stimulates your genitals, you tend to focus on building to orgasm. You may grasp at sensation, trying to reach a goal. When orgasm is no longer the issue, you can relax and sink into the realm of pure feelings.

Many people use sexual fantasies or mental imagery to create a more receptive state of mind. Years ago it was thought that only men indulged in erotic fantasies, but the 1973 publication of Nancy Friday's book *My Secret Garden*, a compendium of women's sexual musings, put that notion to rest. From more recent research we know that approximately 85 percent of all men and women fantasize during intercourse at least some of the time, while 25 percent fantasize often. A small but significant percentage of people, primarily women, find that they cannot reach orgasm unless they fantasize.

Sexual fantasies can serve a number of purposes, including:

Heightening your level of arousal while you are masturbating
Serving as a rehearsal for new sexual activities
Allowing you to experience the forbidden
Blocking out mental distractions
Intensifying sexual desire
Adding variety to your lovemaking

Although sexual fantasies are commonplace, approximately 25 percent of those who fantasize feel guilty, ashamed, or inadequate for doing so. Some people are caught up in the myth that if two people love each other, they shouldn't have to fantasize. They think that fantasies are an admission of personal inadequacy or a sign that the relationship has lost its appeal. In reality, studies show that people who fantasize the most during sex are the most satisfied with their sex lives. They report the greatest sexual satisfaction, the most orgasms, the least sexual guilt, the most positive sexual attitudes, and the fewest sexual difficulties.

As long as a person can distinguish between fantasy and reality, I believe that fantasies pose little problem. There are two exceptions: (1) If a fantasy causes you significant embarrassment, anxiety, or guilt, it is likely to have a negative effect on your lovemaking, and (2) if you engage in fantasy much of the time during lovemaking, you will find it difficult to connect emotionally and spiritually with your partner. I encourage people who use sexual fantasies to make eye contact with their partners at some time while making love. Looking in each other's eyes at the moment of orgasm can be an especially moving experience.

Another way to enhance your level of arousal is to use mental imagery. By mental imagery I mean creating a picture in your mind of what you are experiencing in the moment. For example, if you are having intercourse, you can close your eyes and visualize the penis moving in and out of the vagina. If you are having oral sex, you can create a vivid picture in your mind of what that looks like. Your mind becomes a camera, creating X-rated close-up shots. When you use mental imagery, you're not mentally distancing yourself from your partner; you're merely accentuating what's really going on. This enhanced, eroticized frame of mind may take you to new heights of pleasure.

EXERCISE SECTION

The following checklist will help you gauge how fully you are taking advantage of your sensual potential. (There are two checklists, one for each of you.)

EXERCISE 1: SENSUALITY CHECKLIST

PARTNER 1: Read the following statements and decide how well each one describes your current practices:

> 0 = never
> 1 = rarely
> 2 = some of the time
> 3 = most of the time
> 4 = all of the time

1. I practice hygiene habits that please my partner.
   0   1   2   3   4
2. I focus on the physical sensations while we are making love.
   0   1   2   3   4
3. I take advantage of music to enhance our lovemaking.
   0   1   2   3   4
4. I use specific sounds or words to arouse my partner.
   0   1   2   3   4
5. I use a variety of forms of touching while making love to my partner.
   0   1   2   3   4
6. Massage is a part of my lovemaking technique.
   0   1   2   3   4
7. I know what kind of touch pleases my partner.
   0   1   2   3   4
8. I am aware of my partner's preference for natural fragrances or other scents.
   0   1   2   3   4
9. I use different aromas to enhance our lovemaking.
   0   1   2   3   4
10. I make use of visual stimulation (movies, pictures, books, clothing) to arouse my partner.
    0   1   2   3   4
11. I look at my partner while making love.
    0   1   2   3   4

12. I use mealtime to begin the romantic process.
0   1   2   3   4

13. I use the versatility of my mouth to arouse my partner.
0   1   2   3   4

14. I take time to enjoy the afterglow of our lovemaking.
0   1   2   3   4

15. I have ways to intensify my mental concentration during lovemaking.
0   1   2   3   4

PARTNER 2: Read the following statements and decide how well each one describes your current practices:

> 0 = never
> 1 = rarely
> 2 = some of the time
> 3 = most of the time
> 4 = all of the time

1. I practice hygiene habits that please my partner.
0   1   2   3   4

2. I focus on the physical sensations while we are making love.
0   1   2   3   4

3. I take advantage of music to enhance our lovemaking.
0   1   2   3   4

4. I use specific sounds or words to arouse my partner.
0   1   2   3   4

5. I use a variety of forms of touching while making love to my partner.
0   1   2   3   4

6. Massage is a part of my lovemaking technique.
0   1   2   3   4

7. I know what kind of touch pleases my partner.
0   1   2   3   4

8. I am aware of my partner's preference for natural fragrances or other scents.
0   1   2   3   4

9. I use different aromas to enhance our lovemaking.
   0   1   2   3   4
10. I make use of visual stimulation (movies, pictures, books, clothing) to arouse my partner.
   0   1   2   3   4
11. I look at my partner while making love.
   0   1   2   3   4
12. I use mealtime to begin the romantic process.
   0   1   2   3   4
13. I use the versatility of my mouth to arouse my partner.
   0   1   2   3   4
14. I take time to enjoy the afterglow of our lovemaking.
   0   1   2   3   4
15. I have ways to intensify my mental concentration during lovemaking.
   0   1   2   3   4

EXERCISE 2: SELF-FOCUS

COMMENTS: This simple exercise is designed to help you relax and concentrate on bodily sensations. It takes about five minutes. Consider practicing this exercise at the beginning of your next lovemaking session.

DIRECTIONS:

1. Place yourself in a comfortable position. Lie down or find a posture you can maintain without strain or pressure.

2. Loosen any restrictive clothing.

3. Close your eyes and pay attention to your breathing. Concentrate on the air flowing in and out of your lungs. Each time you exhale, deepen your relaxation.

4. If thoughts distract you, let them float by and go back to focusing on your breathing.

5. Continue for approximately five minutes.

EXERCISE 3: PARTNER FOCUS

COMMENTS: The purpose of this exercise is to relax you and to increase your nonverbal connection with your partner.

DIRECTIONS:

1. Lie on your back beside your partner with your feet pointed in opposite directions.
2. Place your hand nearest your partner on his or her chest.
3. Lie very still, close your eyes, and focus on your partner's breathing.
4. Begin to synchronize breathing with your partner. Do this for approximately five minutes.
5. Talk about what this was like with your partner.

EXERCISE 4: GAZING

COMMENTS: This exercise will deepen your level of intimacy by helping you become more comfortable looking into each other's eyes.

DIRECTIONS:

1. Begin by holding your gaze into each other's eyes a few seconds longer than you normally do.
2. At some future date, gradually increase your gaze to ten seconds. (At first this may seem like a very long time.)
3. When you are comfortable with prolonged eye contact, experiment looking into each other's eyes at the moment of orgasm. There are no words to describe this experience.

EXERCISE 5: WARDROBE CONSULTANT

COMMENTS: Many people have distinct preferences about their partners' style of dress. This exercise is designed to give your partner information about the apparel that pleases you most. It could give the phrase "dress for success" new meaning.

DIRECTIONS:

1. At an agreed-upon time, go to your partner's closet or dresser and point out articles of clothing you find the most pleasing.
2. Pick out the sexiest outfit.
3. Pick out the most romantic outfit.
4. Point out the outfit you like the least.

EXERCISE 6: MAKING SCENTS

COMMENTS: The purpose of this exercise is to help you and your partner decide which artificial scents (if any) to have around the house and/or use in your lovemaking.

DIRECTIONS:

1. Gather all the fragrances you currently have around the home. Explore the bathroom and bedroom for soaps, lotions, deodorants, hair sprays, shampoos, mousses, cream rinses, colognes, perfumes, and aftershaves. Also collect any scented candles, incense, potpourri, sachets, and room "fresheners" or deodorizers.
2. Individually, take a whiff of each one and rate them on a scale of 1 to 10. "1" means you hate it. "10" means you love it or it turns you on. Consider eliminating all fragrances that score below a 5 on either one of your scales.
3. Together, visit a store that specializes in fragrances or an alternative grocery or health food store that carries massage oils, essential oils, and fragrant lotions. Rate fragrances on the 1 to 10 scale. Find ones that you both enjoy.

EXERCISE 7: MAKING YOUR OWN "HOUSE BLEND" MASSAGE OIL

COMMENTS: This exercise is an extension of the previous one. It gives you instructions for creating your own uniquely scented massage oil.

DIRECTIONS:

1. Together, visit a store that carries essential oils. (This could be a natural-foods store or a New Age store.)

2. Buy a bottle of unscented almond oil, a massage oil preferred by many professional masseuses, or another massage oil of your choice.

3. Test all the available essential oils to find the one that is most pleasing to both of you. Purchase one or more of your favorites.

4. At home, add the essential oil to your massage oil drop by drop until you reach the desired concentration. (After a few minutes, you will become habituated to the smell and will no longer be an accurate judge of amounts. Refresh your sense of smell by leaving the room or going outside for a few minutes. Then continue.)

Note: You may want to try out your house blend massage oil on the following exercise.

EXERCISE 8: AN EROTIC MASSAGE

COMMENTS: This chapter would not be complete without an exercise using massage. Touch is so basic to safety, trust, and bonding that it is difficult to overstate its power. Massage is one of the most nurturing, loving, and potentially erotic forms of touch.

I do not recommend back-to-back massages, meaning that as soon as you finish giving a massage, you become the receiver. It is better to focus on the pleasure of giving or receiving and return the favor later.

Most people prefer to be massaged with an oil or lotion. You can use almond oil, baby oil, or vegetable oil. Hand lotions and moisturizing lotions also function admirably. (Don't let the fact that you don't have any specialized "massage" oil keep you from attempting this exercise.)

The following massage is excerpted from the delightful book *Romantic Massage* by Anne Kent Rush. Rush calls it the "Connecting" massage because it's designed to help you "learn to reopen erotic feelings throughout your whole body." You do this by touching an erogenous zone with one hand while your other hand gently massages an area that is not as sensitive. You massage the two areas simultaneously until your partner reaches a high level of arousal. Then you remove your hand from the erotic zone while continuing to massage the other area. Rush says that if you do this frequently, the "newly sensitized areas will become as excitable as the genital or other area." Her directions continue:

> Your partner lies on his or her back on a bed, massage table, or covered pad on the floor in a warm room. Cover your partner with a light film of massage oil. The proportion of how exquisite the strokes feel seems to increase with how light your touch is. The speed will vary some with each individual's taste, but usually should be quite slow.
>
> Sit on your partner's right side [that is, to the right of your partner] facing his or her abdomen. Place both hands, palms down, on the abdomen and begin *very* lightly and *very* slowly making large circles on this area with your whole hand. Continue these circles for a while.
>
> Now slowly separate your hands, moving one palm down the inside of your partner's leg and the other up the chest. Your right hand moving across the chest traces a line from the abdomen, across the ribs, over the left [the near] nipple, over the left pectoral muscle arc, and into the armpit. *At the same time* your left hand moves from the abdomen, over the hip, down the inside of the thigh, inside the calf, across the ankle, ending up in the arch of your partner's left foot.
>
> Much of the success of this stroke depends on timing: your hands should be crossing the thigh and ribs at the same time and should also reach the armpit and foot arch simultaneously. Now, make slow *light* circles in each arch with your two hands in time; stay with this light motion a while.
>
> Now begin the return trip. Retrace your paths toward the abdomen, moving still slowly and feather lightly.

(Cross the thigh and side simultaneously.) End with a few more circles on the abdomen.

Repeat this stroke on your partner's right side.

Rush recommends that you create your own strokes for connecting "the mouth and the nipples, the perineum and the back of the neck, the mouth and the genitals, the palms of the hands and the bottom centers of your feet, the tip of the nose and the nipples."

EXERCISE 9: HEAVENLY HOVERING

COMMENTS: Hovering, which involves the lightest of touch, is done by holding your hands just above the surface of your mate's skin, brushing the fine hair. Many people find this a tantalizing experience. It can send chills up your spine and make you squirm with sensation. For the toucher, it is a rare opportunity to focus completely on your mate. It can be a very sensual and loving experience.

DIRECTIONS:

1. Decide which one of you will receive the hovering first.
2. The receiver decides how much flesh to expose.
3. The receiver lies down on a comfortable surface and closes his or her eyes.
4. The active partner sits comfortably in the best position for reaching the most body areas. During the hovering he or she changes position as needed to keep a comfortable posture.
5. Hovering movements are ever so slow and delicate. Image that you are transferring heat energy from your hands to your partner.

EXERCISE 10: TOM JONES REVISITED

COMMENTS: This is a playful exercise you can perform at home or in public depending upon your sense of indiscretion. You are going to use food to send your partner an erotic message. The message has three parts: (1) Here's what I want to do to you; (2) here's what I want you to do to me; (3) here's what we can do together.

You will deliver these messages one at a time by using food in a mime-like manner.

DIRECTIONS:

1. Take turns showing each other "Here's what I want to do to you sexually." Use food, fingers, utensils, and sounds of eating to illustrate your preferences. No words allowed.

2. Next, show each other "Here's what I want you to do to me sexually."

3. "Here's what we can do together sexually."

4. Don't forget to chew and swallow.

11

S₂I

The Formula For
Lasting Passion

In the previous chapters you've explored eight of the nine separate facets of your sexuality. As you have seen, each of these elements has an important role to play in creating a satisfying, lasting love relationship. *Talking freely about sex* helps you communicate your sexual needs and wishes. *Sexual desire* motivates you to be sexual and intensifies the lovemaking experience. *Verbal and emotions intimacy* allows you to share your inner reality with your partner. *Sexual technique* arouses both you and your mate. *Variety* keeps freshness and excitement in your lovemaking. *Romance* creates lasting feelings of love and connection. A positive *body image* helps you relax and focus on physical pleasure. *Sensuality* transforms sex into a luxurious, whole body experience.

In this final chapter I want to step back and look at the larger picture, not just the parts. What happens when you are functioning well in all eight of these areas? What's the payoff for working to create good communication skills, a positive body image, customized lovemaking techniques, a willingness to romance your partner, and an appreciation for the sensual side of lovemaking?

The answer is *passion*, which I define as a blend of sexual arousal and emotional intimacy. Take a moment to look back at your score in the passion category of the Sexual Style Survey, pages 21–35. Now review for a moment the survey statements that correspond to the passion category:

7. I make an effort to feel emotionally close to my partner while making love.

13. I express feelings of love for my partner during lovemaking.

27. One of my goals is to feel united with my partner during lovemaking.

37. I am a passionate lover.

43. I experience spiritual connection with my partner during lovemaking.

47. During lovemaking I freely surrender to sexual passion.

58. I look my partner in the eyes while we are making love.

As you can see, the common denominator in all these statements is the combination of sexual arousal with love for your partner. When you feel emotionally connected with your partner during lovemaking, you are no longer two separate individuals moving independently toward orgasm; you are partners on a fantastic voyage. Your partner's arousal fuels your arousal as you take turns lifting each other higher and higher into ecstasy. There is a freshness to your lovemaking, a suspension of time, a total absorption in the present. At peak moments you feel at one with your partner, and the words "I love you" may flow spontaneously from your lips.

I have asked a number of people to describe what these passionate moments are like for them. Although everyone acknowledged that passion transcends words, a few people made valiant attempts to describe those peak experiences to me:

"For me the best sex is when I feel completely open to my partner. Even though I may cry and laugh at the same time, it doesn't have to do with sorrow or deprivation. It has to do with discovering a new realm. It's like finding a second floor of the house when I didn't know there was a second floor."

"Sex can be the sweetest, most exquisite experience. I start moving uncontrollably. I go into an altered state. Something else takes over. My lover and I are driven along. It's a ride. And it's just the most incredible thing in the world. We're gone. It's all instinctual. Do you understand?"

"For me sex is an opening. My woman has opened up to me. I go inside. I become every phallic object there ever was. I feel it throughout my whole body. My whole body becomes rigid and stiff and I am phallus and my lover is a flower that opens up and takes me in. It's about power. It's about strength. And at the same time it's about the vulnerability of being so very close to her."

"Sex for a woman is very intrusive. I don't mean that in a bad sense. But he goes into you. You have to open up to him. You have to be receptive physically. Invite him in. And he has to open up emotionally and let you inside of him. Men can be so protective of themselves. My husband is extraordinarily powerful yet has the capacity to be extraordinarily vulnerable. We envelop each other."

"I can't describe it. There have been moments when I felt my partner and I were in the space of ecstasy. She was right there with me. To be way out there in space and to look in her eyes and see that she's way out there, too. For that split second—and it's not necessarily the moment of orgasm—we're both right there and we're at one with the universe."

I have had the audacity to try to reduce this spiritual epiphany to a mere formula: S_2I—two *S*exually expressive people joined by *I*ntimacy. To form this interpersonal molecule, both partners have to experience intense levels of arousal. Either they are naturally blessed with ample amounts of physical desire or they have found what it takes to become more highly aroused. What binds them together is intimacy. They don't merely want to experience sexual pleasure; they want to pleasure each other. They don't merely want to have sex; they want to make love.

Most of the couples I see are missing at least one part of this formula. It is quite common for one person in a love relationship to be more focused on sex and the other person to be more focused on intimacy. All too often the person with the high sex drive resists intimacy, and the person with the ability to be emotionally intimate resists sexuality. Clearly this arrangement doesn't work. It's one of those instances when two halves don't make a whole. In order to experience passion, both individuals have to transcend their limitations. The person with the high sex drive has to become more emotionally available, and the person with the intimacy skills has to become more sexually charged.

When people don't work to overcome their limitations, the relationship is stalemated. I listened to a man talk about how frustrating it was to live with a woman who made no effort to compensate for her low sexual desire: "Sex to me has been real close to the divine. And I don't mean religion. It's an excitement and a liberation from whatever it is I stay bound up in. It's a way out of me, a way to connect to the world. But I can't have that now. My wife is very muted sexually. She hardly moves. She doesn't make any sounds. She may reach orgasm, but I never know it. I love her. Our relationship is sweet. But I haven't been able to get to those passionate places I like to go to because I need someone to work off of, to work with, to go up the ladder." Passion requires two people in a crescendo. It's a movement up and out of yourself. In order to have your lovemaking connect you with the universe and the divine, you need a sexually expressive partner.

People who live with partners who are *emotionally* blocked can feel just as deprived. An acquaintance of mine was married for twenty-one years to a man who was unable to share his emotions during lovemaking. She said to me, "My husband had a lot of sexual desire, but he lacked passion and spirit, which kept the lovemaking mechanical. Early in the marriage he told me that sex was sex and love was love and they were separate. I went through most of the marriage believing he was right. Our lovemaking was seldom spontaneous, and there was *no soul.* Then I had a relationship with a man who was both sexual and intimate. It was incredible. It was . . . spiritual."

HOT SEX VERSUS PASSIONATE SEX

Some couples have the incomplete formula S_2. In this variation, both partners are sexually charged, but they are rarely intimate with each other. They experience "hot" sex, but not *passionate* sex. There is a profound difference between the two. Two people who are highly aroused, whether from testosterone or titillation, can have intense, toe-curling sex. But in order to experience *passion,* they have to be emotionally close to each other as well.

This is not to say that hot sex is bad sex. Many couples from time to time have hot lovemaking sessions that are totally devoid of intimacy. These lusty encounters can keep them grinning for days. But if lust is *all* they experience, they are missing the soul connection. I recall a conversation with a woman who was attending one of my couples' workshops in New York. "I thought I had a perfect marriage," she told me. "My husband and I had the greatest sex you could ever imagine. We still do. We have experienced every known form of erotic activity." She had no idea that her husband was desperately unhappy with the relationship until he took her to dinner one evening and announced: "I want a divorce. I don't like the way you live your life. We don't have any common interests. I don't really know what you think or feel. I don't even know who you are." It took her three days to realize he meant every word he said. Hot sex had been satisfying enough for her but not for him. He longed for more emotional connection.

A woman I know had a similar reaction to her sexy but emotionally distant lover. Her lover prided himself in his ability to bring her to orgasm four or five times a night, but he never told her he loved her or looked in her eyes. One night after an hour of steamy sex he crowed, "Now tell me, have you ever had it better than that?" She didn't know how to respond. She said to me later, "How could I tell him that sex without closeness barely registers on my scale?"

A FEAR OF PASSION

In my fifteen years of experience as a marital therapist, I have encountered very few couples in long-term relationships who have created the magic formula S_2I. What is it that keeps more couples from experiencing passion? The answer is this: *On the deepest levels of passion and intimacy, we are all fearful pilgrims.* We stand on separate plateaus from our partners, divided by a canyon of fear, afraid to reach out and form a bridge. A fear of intimacy or a fear of sexuality keeps us cowering away from the edge.

I realize that most people don't view their lovemaking difficulties this way. They imagine they would enjoy spectacular sex if only:

"There wasn't so much stress in my life."
"We had more time for sex."
"My partner was more loving."
"My partner was more sexy."
"I lost fifteen pounds."
"My partner was more attractive."
"My partner was more sensitive."
"My partner was more emotional."
"My partner was more romantic."

They blame the partner or life circumstances for the lack of passion. They fail to realize that they are held back by fear.

In my work with couples I have learned that some fears are especially widespread. Here are ten of the ones I see most often. As you read them, try to determine which ones (if any) apply to you or your partner.

1. THE FEAR OF GETTING WHAT YOU LONG FOR: Paradoxically, one of the most common reasons that people fear passion is that they long for it so deeply. If you've ever had a leg "go to sleep" from a lack of circulation, you can recall the pins-and-needles sensation of having the blood flow back into the limb. As long as the circulation was blocked, you didn't feel any sensation. When the

circulation was restored, you had to go through an uncomfortable period as the blood flowed through constricted veins.

An analogous reaction takes place when you've been deprived of passion for a long period of time. As time goes on, you do your best to numb yourself to the emotional pain. Your psyche can tolerate only a certain amount of discomfort before your defense mechanisms take over. When you finally get involved in a loving, intimate relationship, you have a powerful, complex response. First, you experience a surge of joy—there are few human experiences as deeply gratifying as passionate intimacy—but then you begin to feel the pent-up pain of having been unloved for so long. Your heart begins to ache. It's as if the circulation to your heart had been cut off and now was being restored. Along with the joy of getting what you want, you experience the pain you've been repressing for so long. This is one of the reasons that some people sob deeply after a peak sexual experience.

This reaction is most pronounced in people who have been deprived of love for much of their lives. If you didn't feel loved and cared for as a child and had a series of disappointing love relationships as an adult, you will come face-to-face with decades of deprivation when you finally experience sexual passion. Understandably many people are afraid to experience these feelings. They approach the boundaries of passion but then pull back in order to keep themselves emotionally insulated. They choose to remain numb rather than expose themselves to the pleasure/pain of release.

2. A FEAR OF ENGULFMENT: Some people are afraid that if they remove all the emotional and physical boundaries between themselves and their partners, they will lose a sense of self. They believe that the only way to remain psychically safe is to keep up the emotional barriers. The nature of this fear differs from person to person. One person might be afraid of being manipulated or controlled by a more dominant partner. Another might be afraid of being overwhelmed by the responsibility of caring for a needy partner. Yet another might be afraid of merging with the partner and losing a sense of identity.

A fear of engulfment almost always originates in childhood.

Being intimate with a partner brings back primal memories of a strained relationship with a caretaker. Unwittingly people tend to use the same protective maneuvers with their partners that they used with their parents. Unfortunately it is not possible to experience passion and remain emotionally defended. Passion demands vulnerability.

3. A FEAR OF TRIGGERING PAIN FROM THE PAST: If sexual or physical abuse is in your background, letting down your defenses may trigger a flood of unpleasant memories. People often need therapy to cope with the intrusive nature of past abuse.

But even those people who weren't sexually abused can find that deep levels of passion and intimacy bring to mind histories they'd just as soon forget. Who has not had an embarrassing or humiliating experience connected with his or her sexuality? These experiences may be buried deep in the past, and you can ignore them as long as you remain aloof. However, as you move toward greater intimacy, the discomfort begins to surface. Being in a safe, loving, intimate relationship is the final step in the healing process, but at first it may feel like a new injury.

4. A FEAR OF BEING REJECTED: Each of us has a dark side, a part of our personality that we try to deny. We live with the illusion that we can keep it hidden from our partners by revealing only a portion of our inner world. We are afraid that "if you really knew me, you wouldn't like me."

But when we censor our thoughts and feelings, we can't fully connect with our partners. There is too much of us being held in reserve. Before we can experience passionate sexuality, we have to reveal ourselves to our partners in our entirety.

5. A FEAR OF RELINQUISHING CONTROL: Sex and intimacy are two of the most powerful chips in any relationship struggle. Withholding one or both of them is a time-honored way to control your partner. In many relationships, one partner withholds the intimacy chip and the other partner withholds the sexuality chip. Their arguments can be reduced to the following sentences:

Partner A: "I won't be intimate with you unless you put out sexually."

Partner B: "I won't be sexual with you unless you are more intimate."

Neither partner will experience passion unless both partners relinquish their chips.

6. THE FEAR THAT THE PARTNER'S NEEDS ARE INSATIABLE: Some of us live with the fear that "If I give an inch, my partner will take a mile." People who are wary of the *emotional* side of passion worry that their partners will want to talk and be intimate all the time. They will have no private space or time to themselves. They will be consumed by their partners' need to connect. People who are wary of the *sexual* side of passion worry that there will be no end to their partners' sexual demands. One concession will lead to another and another. Before long there will be no limits to their sexual activities.

What people don't realize is that an unwillingness to satisfy a partner's basic needs and desires creates an exaggerated sense of neediness in the partner. He or she only *appears* to be insatiable. Once the partner's needs have been satisfied for a long enough period of time, the demands will gradually diminish. Couples have to have the trust and courage to weather the transition period.

7. THE FEAR OF CHALLENGING GENDER ROLES: Because of social conditioning, it is not uncommon for women in this culture to associate intense sexuality with wantonness or immorality and for men to associate emotional intimacy with femininity or weakness. "Nice" girls aren't supposed to be sexual. "Real" men aren't supposed to be vulnerable. To break out of these stereotypes, people have to challenge their gender conditioning. They have to find some way to resurrect those parts of the core self that have been cut off by our overly restrictive view of masculinity and femininity.

8. THE FEAR OF BEING SEXUAL WITH PEOPLE OUTSIDE THE RELATIONSHIP: Muting your sexuality is one way to protect yourself from temptation. As long as you remain sexually blocked, you don't

have to worry that other people will be sexually attracted to you or that you will be strongly attracted to others. When you free up your sexuality, you no longer have this protection. You may fear that you won't be able to resist sexual advances or control your own desires.

Learning how to set and maintain appropriate sexual boundaries is a necessary precondition for Hot Monogamy. It's a myth that sex is an overwhelming force over which you have no control. When you free up your sexuality, you may indeed experience attraction to and from other people. However, you can develop the discipline not to act on it. Mature people make the choice all the time not to follow up on their sexual responses to others. As you deepen the level of passion and intimacy with your partner, this will become easier and easier to do because the satisfaction you experience within your relationship will far surpass the momentary pleasure you might find with others.

9. THE FEAR OF LOSING CONTROL: Some people are worried about how they might act or look if they were to experience intense sexual arousal. They're afraid they will look unattractive or act in some inappropriate manner.

In essence what they're afraid of is losing control. The sex act is an instinctual process. Your body responds in ways you can't predict. Your hips gyrate. You make spontaneous sounds. Your face contorts. Your muscles convulse. Words come unbidden out of your mouth. If you feel that you have to maintain control in order to be attractive, safe, or acceptable, then passion will remain out of reach. To experience passion you have to relinquish bodily control.

10. THE FEAR OF LOSING THE PARTNER: There is no guarantee that your partner will always be with you. Death or divorce or life circumstances may leave you alone and bereaved. As soon as you risk being completely open and committed to your partner, you are confronted with the possibility of losing that love.

People who have experienced a great deal of loss in their lives may be especially reluctant to experience passion. Unwittingly they erect emotional barriers to protect themselves from future pain.

FACING YOUR FEAR OF PASSION

If you and your partner are no longer held back by any of these fears, you have cause for celebration. You are among those fortunate individuals who are capable of experiencing intense levels of sexual passion. Your task is to continue to nurture all nine areas of your relationship so you can scale new heights of intimacy and sexuality. There is no upper limit to passion.

If you find that your lovemaking is still inhibited by one or more of these fears, there is much you can do to overcome them. First and foremost, it will help a great deal simply to acknowledge your fear. When you identify a specific anxiety—"I'm afraid of losing control" or "I'm afraid of losing you"—then you no longer have to deny your role in the impasse. This alone is a giant step forward because denial takes up a tremendous amount of energy.

Once you have acknowledged your role in preventing passion, you will have less of a tendency to project your difficulties onto your partner. It is human nature to take what we're afraid of and cast it out of ourselves, to project it onto others. For example, people who are sexually blocked have a tendency to project their fear of sexuality onto their partners, criticizing them for being insatiable, oversexed, immoral, or perverted. This way they can comfort themselves that they are "normal" and their partners "abnormal." Similarly, people who are afraid of their feelings have a tendency to accuse their partners of being overly emotional: "You should be more rational." "Think things through!" "You're always overreacting."

Projection may ease your mind in the short term, but it creates long-lasting relationship difficulties. You cannot create a more passionate sexual relationship if you blame your partner for your part in the struggle.

Ideally, once you have acknowledged your fears to yourself, you will have the courage to reveal them to your partner. This can be a gift of the highest order. After years of denial, you find a way to lower your defenses and admit your frailty: "I've never said this in words, but I'm afraid of being close when we have sex. I don't know why. It makes me anxious to be intimate and sexual at the same time." Or "I've always been afraid of losing control when we have sex. I keep holding back. I don't know what I'm afraid of. I approach orgasm; then I pull back." Or "Somewhere inside me it feels wrong to be openly sexual. It's something that comes from way back in my childhood." Or "I think I've been withholding sex because I don't want to give you what you want. It would feel like too big a concession."

As in these examples, you don't have to have it all figured out before you share your fears. What's important is that you give your partner a glimpse of your inner struggle. I have the privilege of witnessing this gut-level honesty in my work with couples, and I have yet to see a partner who was not deeply touched by the experience. Self-revelation has the opposite effect from criticism. When you reveal your weaknesses to your partner, your partner is more likely to share his or her own weaknesses, causing the trust level to zoom upward. *As a general rule, criticism and projection create distance; self-revelation invites intimacy.*

HOW TO EXPERIENCE MORE PASSION

In addition to acknowledging your overall fears of sexuality and intimacy, you need to overcome the specific difficulties that stand in your way, such as low desire, sexual inhibitions, a lack of romance, or a lack of emotional intimacy. That's exactly what the Hot Monogamy program is designed to do. Let's review all that you've accomplished so far. By taking the Sexual Style Survey, you've highlighted your strengths and weaknesses in the nine key areas of your love relationship. By reading each of the chapters that focus on those areas, you've answered some questions, and I hope that you have acquired new insights. Then, by tackling the exercises at the end of the chapters, you've been gradually transforming your insights into new behavior patterns. I encourage you to retake the survey when you've finished a majority of the exercises so you can see the extent of your progress.

Remember, you won't always be able to predict the most fruitful areas of your relationship to explore. It could be that your greatest breakthroughs will come in precisely those areas you've been avoiding. Look back over the chapters or review your survey results, and identify those categories that still represent the greatest challenge for you. (If you're in doubt, ask your partner where he or she would like you to concentrate your efforts.) Like many people I've worked with, you are likely to make the greatest progress in areas you are most reluctant to explore.

To summarize, I list below some of the ideas that I hope have become clear to you as you've read this book and gone through the exercises:

KEY IDEAS

- The intense biological attraction you feel for your partner tends to decrease after the first few months or years of a relationship. This is normal.
- Sexual desire is a complex phenomenon that has both biological and emotional components.
- Most of the time one partner will be more interested in making love than the other.
- Most men have a higher sex drive than most women.
- When a woman has a higher sex drive than her male partner, the difference in desire may be especially troubling.
- Men and women tend to have different conversation styles.
- In most love relationships, both partners display intimacy-blocking behaviors.
- Men are predisposed toward autonomy and women toward relationship. Each is capable of both.
- Human anatomy favors the male orgasm.
- A majority of women need clitoral or G spot stimulation in addition to intercourse to reach orgasm.
- Women who have the most enjoyable sex lives take the most responsibility for their own arousal.
- Every body is unique. There is no one lovemaking position or technique that works for all men or all women.
- Many couples are too restrictive in their lovemaking practices.
- As a relationship matures and as people mature, men as well as

women need more physical stimulation to become fully
aroused.
- Romantic love is a delightful, short-lived phenomenon.
- To create ongoing romance, you need to discover what says "I
love you" to your partner and do it.
- Improving your body image allows you to relax and enjoy your
sexuality fully.
- Sensuality is an untapped resource in most relationships.
- Most couples need to make their sexual relationship a higher
priority in their lives.
- Most people have some fear of intense levels of intimacy and
passion.

Acquiring new insights about human sexuality is a key part of this
program. But I want to emphasize again how important it is for you
to complete the exercises at the end of each chapter. They are
designed to lead you to new and deeper levels of intimacy. They
will inspire you to add more variety to your lovemaking and to
become more sophisticated, talented lovers. They will help you let
go of any lingering inhibitions and experience more intense levels
of sexual desire. A lifetime of physical pleasure and renewed emotional closeness awaits you.

CARA AND THOMAS: AMONG THE FORTUNATE FEW

To give you a better idea of what lies ahead of you, I want to give
you an intimate look at one of those fortunate couples who have
mastered the art of creating and sustaining sexual passion.

Cara and Thomas, both in their mid-forties, have been married
for sixteen years. This is the second marriage for both of them.
Thomas is an administrator in a social service agency, and Cara is
a graphic artist. I interviewed them early in the process of gathering
information for this book. As I reviewed my notes in preparation
for writing this chapter, I was struck anew by how well they illustrated most of the key elements of this program.

I began the interview by asking Cara and Thomas to fill out
the Sexual Style Survey, the same one featured in this book. When

they completed the survey, I had them compare scores. From their comments it was evident that both of them had difficulty separating sexuality from intimacy. Thomas said, "I had trouble responding to the statements in the sexual desire category. I can't separate sexual desire from romance or intimacy. If you focus just on sex, then you tend to focus on the bedroom or wherever it is that you make love. You miss the broader dimension."

Cara added, "The broader dimension is everything. The touching, for example. For me, all physical contact between us is part of the sex act. Washing dishes together. Sitting next to each other on the sofa. I don't separate it out at all. If the affection is there during the day, I'm more sexual in bed." For them, the nine categories of the survey blended together seamlessly.

Several times in the interview I noticed that both of them referred to lovemaking as "being connected." For example, Thomas began one sentence by saying, "If I've been connected to Cara recently . . ." It took me a moment to realize he was talking about having made love to her. They view sex as a way to connect with each other on a number of important levels.

Something that is unique to their relationship is the way that they deliberately use sex as a way to *create* intimacy. Typically, it works the other way around. Most couples establish a level of emotional intimacy that then leads spontaneously to lovemaking. Cara explained their opposite approach: "If we're not communicating, in a major way, if we're at odds about money, for example, which can be a major issue, then this chasm grows. We've found that we can use intercourse to forge a connection. For us, sex can be the truest form of communication."

Thomas added, "To make love this way, you have to get rid of the mental idea that you have to feel a certain way, be turned on, feel close, in order to have sex. You don't. You can just decide to do it. For us, closeness can come as a *result* of having sex."

"We've invented a name for this kind of lovemaking," said Cara. "We call it a marital. It doesn't require that we have orgasm, and it's not necessarily very romantic. It can be almost mechanical. But it reestablishes that physical, sexual connection between us, which makes all our other problems seem more manageable."

Later in the interview Cara said that one of the most enjoyable aspects of lovemaking to her was simply the extended period of physical contact. "Physical contact is incredibly important to me. It can be anything, a pat on the leg. Some physical reassurance can totally change my mood. And for me sex is the ultimate form of physical contact."

"Cara just touched on a word that I would use," said Thomas, "and that is 'reassurance.' When my life is difficult, I feel like I have blinders stuck on my face. My focus seems about three inches in front of my eyes."

"He gets so strained-looking," commented Cara.

"At those times it's easy to feel that I'm all alone, that nobody else knows what I'm going through. It's hard to articulate those feelings. When Cara and I are connected physically, it's not necessary to put them into words. My blinders are removed, and I feel more relaxed, safer, more accessible. This carries over into my work life as well."

Despite their busy schedules, Cara and Thomas manage to make sex a high priority in their lives. "There was a time early in our relationship when we would spend hours in bed," recalled Cara with a smile. "We might spend half a day in bed touching, talking. We were aware that spending time in this way could lead to a deep level of intimacy, but we weren't prepared for the level it took us to."

"Of course, spending this much time in bed isn't always possible anymore," Thomas said, laughing.

"But even now," said Cara, "if we've been out of touch, I need a long time to make love. Like hours. To touch, talk, feel warm, supported. For me sex is a time to relax. I always thought I was supposed to go fast. Catch up. Catch up. You can't do that with sex. Or act as if you're feeling sexy when you're not."

Midway through our conversation I asked Thomas and Cara if they had always been sexually compatible or if they'd had to work at it.

"It all evolved over time," said Thomas. "It wasn't there at first."

One thing that evolved during the course of their relationship was a greater degree of body acceptance. "About the fourth or fifth time we were together," said Thomas, "I had a sudden insight. It wasn't a flashing neon sign insight, but it came close. I still remember the words that came to me: 'This person will help me get to know my body.' This has proved true. I would not have scored high on the body image category of the survey before living with Cara. That's not the way I thought of myself."

Cara echoed his thought: "I haven't always had a strong or positive body image either. The fact that I now feel so comfortable with my body is a reflection of Thomas's acceptance of me. It's a gift of this relationship."

Many of the couples who have the most fulfilling sexual relationships have found some way to merge their religious or spiritual beliefs with their lovemaking. This is true for both Cara and Thomas. Thomas comes from a Catholic background, and he is aware that some aspects of Catholicism have restricted his sexuality, but he focuses on the positives. "There's a lot about the Catholic religion that I respect," he said. "There's a great deal of emphasis on self-restraint, and I think that's crucial. I don't think you can have great sex without self-restraint. That probably sounds contradictory."

Cara asked him, "You mean, like waiting for me to have orgasm first?"

"That's one example," Thomas replied.

"He's really good at that."

Thomas laughed.

"That's a real nice feature of our sexuality," said Cara. "The technicalities. We've resolved all the technical issues. It wasn't all that difficult. If you love someone, if you trust him, you can simply tell him what you like. It's a matter of trust and communication."

"Another aspect of self-restraint that's important to me is taking the focus off my own needs," added Thomas. "I'm usually pretty aware of what I want on a moment-to-moment basis. If I weren't also aware of what Cara wants, I think I would be pretty hard to live with. I try to listen to her in the broadest sense, picking up on feelings and body language as well as words. This keeps me from being so self-centered." Here was that concept of teamwork and accommodation that is so essential for a lasting love relationship. Thomas has learned to balance his own needs with an awareness of Cara's needs. There is no holding back, none of the "me first" mentality that is so destructive of intimacy.

Every couple has unique areas of strength and weakness in their sexual relationship. A plus for Cara and Thomas is that they have similar levels of sexual desire. Said Cara: "Sometimes I wait around for Thomas to get turned on because I don't want to do the initiating. But if it doesn't happen, then I'll initiate. It always seems that he's ready. It's not like he's saying, 'Not tonight, dear.' It's fairly mutual."

Another advantage is that Cara is easily orgasmic. But this is not just a biological gift: Cara has found a way to relax into a positive mental state that helps her experience more fulfilling orgasms. "I try not to struggle for orgasm," she said. "Sometimes I might have this picture in my mind of an orgasm that I'm trying to make happen, and then I'll deliberately think certain thoughts that I know will bring me to orgasm. But this creates an instant-gratification kind of orgasm that isn't entirely fulfilling. It's as if I experience two kinds of orgasm. In the other kind my whole body responds. To get there, I can't think certain thoughts. The thoughts have to think me. It's a more profound experience. It takes longer, but I feel more ready to face the world after one of those."

The main struggle for Cara and Thomas has been in the realm of emotional intimacy. Cara had a painful childhood. Her father was an alcoholic, and her mother suffered from manic depression. An only child, Cara spent many years of her childhood feeling alone and unloved. These feelings surfaced early in her relationship with Thomas. "When we first started making love, all he'd have to do was rub my head and I'd cry. There was this tremendous amount of grief stored up in my body that I had never released. I would cry gallons of tears."

Cara was experiencing that pleasure/pain phenomenon I talked about earlier that can happen when people finally receive the love they've been longing for. Many people would not have had the courage to weather feelings that intense; they would have blocked the feelings or backed away from the relationship rather than feel the pain. Cara believes that Thomas's calm response to her emotional outbursts was a primary reason she was able to work through them. "The wonderful thing about Thomas is that he didn't get carried away with the sadness," she said. "He wasn't going, 'Oh, my God. This person has had a hell of a time.' He just allowed me to experience my feelings. The touching and the lovemaking and the crying were the beginning of a tremendous healing for me. I still am aware of some grief, but it's almost like a residue. I can see so much more clearly that I was meant to be on this planet, which was not something I felt very often growing up."

I asked Thomas why he was able to be so nurturing and accepting of Cara. "We're kind of like a mortise and tenon," he explained. "I grew up with an unfulfilled need to nurture. I wanted to comfort my parents so much, and there were no takers. My mother was convinced she had to do it all. She wouldn't accept any help. My father was emotionally bruised. I never knew why. Out of some grace, I was able to look at Cara and see that she was in pain but not feel threatened by that or feel that I had to rescue her. I sensed that just standing by her was what was required of me." Cara and Thomas are living proof that one of the best ways to create sexual passion is with a healthy measure of *com*passion.

Several times during this interview I was so touched by the love between Cara and Thomas that I was moved to tears. So much of my time as a marital therapist is spent with couples who are mired in conflict that it was a privilege to talk with a couple who had managed to surmount most of their difficulties. Their depth of knowledge of each other, their high level of acceptance, and their ability to revel in their sensuality were an inspiration to me.

Sex can be a brief, incendiary encounter between relative strangers; it can be a desultory, mechanical act between partners who have grown weary of each other; or it can be a glowing, lasting, healing experience between people who have become spiritual soul mates. Cara and Thomas are two of those people who experience passion on a regular basis. As I witnessed the love they have created together, I realized they were walking on sacred ground. They have truly achieved the Hot Monogamy that this book is all about.

To get information about Pat Love's upcoming workshops, lectures, and resources, send a stamped, self-addressed envelope to:

PAT LOVE
The Austin Family Institute
2404 Rio Grande
Austin, TX 78705

Or call 1-512-478-1175

RECOMMENDED READING

I have grouped the following recommended books according to the nine areas of this program so you can focus on areas of greatest interest to you.

TALKING ABOUT SEX

D'EMILIO, JOHN, AND ESTELLE B. FREEDMAN. *Intimate Matters: A History of Sexuality in America.* New York: Harper & Row, 1989. A comprehensive, readable survey of sexual attitudes in the United States. Knowing our history, we can better understand why it's so difficult to talk freely about sex.

REISS, IRA, WITH HARRIET M. REISS. *An End to Shame: Shaping Our Next Sexual Revolution.* Buffalo, N.Y.: Prometheus, 1990. Reiss, a well-known sociologist, makes you think about how and what you were taught about sex.

SEXUAL DESIRE

BASS, ELLEN, AND LAURA DAVIS. *The Courage to Heal: A Guide for Women Survivors of Child Sexual Abuse.* New York: Harper & Row, 1988. A book that will prove helpful to women who experience sexual desire disorders because of prior sexual abuse.

CARNES, PATRICK. *Don't Call It Love: Recovering from Sexual Addiction.* New York: Bantam, 1991. A comprehensive book describing sexual compulsion and obsession that provides methods for dealing with the associated problems. Carnes is the recognized expert in this area and uses the twelve-step recovery program of Alcoholics Anonymous in his approach.

————. *Out of the Shadows: Understanding Sexual Addiction*. Minneapolis: CompCare, 1983. One of the first books to explore the problem of compulsive sexual behavior.

CUTLER, WINNIFRED B. *Love Cycles*. New York: Villard, 1991. One of my favorite books explaining the biological components of love and attraction. It's well worth the trek through scientific studies.

KNOPF, JENNIFER, AND MICHAEL SEILER. *Inhibited Sexual Desire*. New York: Warner, 1990. A practical book for couples with low or differing levels of sexual desire.

LEW, MIKE. *Abused Boys: The Neglected Victims of Sexual Abuse*. Lexington, Mass.: Lexington, 1990. A book for men who were victims of sexual abuse.

MALTZ, WENDY. *The Sexual Healing Journey: A Guide for Survivors of Sexual Abuse*. New York: HarperPerennial, 1992. Maltz's book features a series of exercises called "relearning touch" that help abuse survivors feel comfortable with physical intimacy.

INTIMACY

ALLEN, MARVIN. *In the Company of Men: A New Approach to Healing for Husbands, Fathers and Friends*. New York: Random House, 1993. Allen describes an innovative, gender-specific therapy that helps men express their emotions and create lasting, intimate love relationships.

HENDRIX, HARVILLE. *Getting the Love You Want*. New York: Harper & Row, 1990. Hendrix explains the psychological roots of romantic attraction, why you get into conflict, and, best of all, how you and your partner can work together to further your emotional healing and growth. Highly recommended

LERNER, HARRIET GOLDHOR. *The Dance of Intimacy: A Woman's Guide to Changing the Patterns of Intimate Relationships*. New York: Harper & Row, 1989. Lerner has a knack for speaking intimately to the reader. A classic.

LOVE, PATRICIA. *The Emotional Incest Syndrome.* New York: Bantam, 1990. In this earlier book I help people who grew up with an invasive or overinvolved parent become more available for intimate, adult relationships.

MOIR, A., AND D. JESSEL. *Brain Sex: The Real Difference Between Men and Women.* New York: Lyle Stuart, 1989. A fascinating book describing brain physiology and gender differences in men and women.

TANNEN, DEBORAH. *You Just Don't Understand.* New York: Ballantine, 1991. A linguist looks at the way men and women use language and shows how these gender differences complicate our ability to understand each other.

TECHNIQUE

BARBACH, LONNIE GARFIELD. *For Each Other: Sharing Sexual Intimacy.* New York: Signet, 1984. A book often recommended by sex and marital therapists. Filled with exercises and practical advice.

BLANK, JOANI. *The Playbook for Men About Sex.* San Francisco: Down There Press, 1981. Joani Blank, a sex therapist/educator and founder of the Good Vibrations organization, has written a book to "enhance sexual self-awareness and pleasure in men of all ages and sexual lifestyles."

CASTLEMAN, MICHAEL. *Sexual Solutions: A Guide for Men and the Women Who Love Them,* rev. ed. New York: Touchstone, 1989. A down-to-earth, readable book that addresses the common sexual problems men face, such as erection difficulties, early ejaculation, and what to do about them. Good information for both men and women.

GOLDSTEIN, IRWIN, AND LARRY ROTHSTEIN. *The Potent Male: Facts, Fiction, Future.* Los Angeles: Body, 1990. This book addresses the number-one male fear: impotency.

HEIMAN, JULIA, AND JOSEPH LoPICCOLO. *Becoming Orgasmic: A Sexual and Personal Growth Program for Women.* Englewood Cliffs, N.J.: Prentice-Hall, 1988. Another self-help book widely recommended by sex therapists.

KAPLAN, HELEN SINGER. *PE: How to Overcome Premature Ejaculation.* New York: Brunner/Mazel, 1989. This practical book gives men explicit instructions for gaining control over the ejaculatory response.

ZILBERGELD, BERNIE. *The New Male Sexuality: The Truth About Men, Sex, and Pleasure.* New York: Bantam, 1992. Zilbergeld explores the common myths that interfere with men's enjoyment of sex and provides numerous exercises and suggestions. This is a book you'll turn to again and again.

SEXUAL VARIETY

BARBACH, LONNIE, ED. *Women Write Erotica.* Garden City, N.Y.: Doubleday, 1986. This book and the one that follows present a female version of erotica—intimate, sensual, and languid.

————. *Erotic Interludes: Tales Told by Women.* Garden City, N.Y.: Doubleday, 1986.

CHESTER, LAURA. *The Unmade Bed: Sensual Writing on Married Love.* New York: HarperCollins, 1992. This anthology of contemporary American writers celebrates the intimacy and sensuality of married love from courtship to later years. Bedside reading for couples practicing Hot Monogamy.

FISHER, HELEN E. *Anatomy of Love: The Natural History of Monogamy, Adultery, and Divorce.* New York: W.W. Norton, 1992. Fisher, an anthropologist, examines the evolution of human sexual behaviors in enlightening, entertaining terms.

FRIDAY, NANCY. *My Secret Garden: Women's Sexual Fantasies.* New York: Trident, 1973. The book that destroyed the myth that only men fantasize about sex.

PITTMAN, F. *Private Lies.* New York: W.W. Norton, 1989. The best book I know of concerning affairs. Who has them. Why. What to do about them.

ROMANCE

HENDRIX, HARVILLE. *Getting the Love You Want: A Guide for Couples.* New York: Harper & Row, 1990. Hendrix delineates the differences between the romantic love stage and what he calls the Conscious Marriage, a mature, sustainable love that heals the soul and the psyche.

RUSH, ANNE KENT. *A Romantic Massage: Ten Unforgettable Massages for Special Occasions.* New York: Avon, 1991. This book will inspire you to be more sensual and romantic. Tastefully illustrated.

BODY IMAGE

STUART, RICHARD B., AND BARBARA JACOBSON. *Weight, Sex, & Marriage.* New York: Simon & Schuster, 1987. The authors examine the complex roles that weight and body image play in marital happiness, sexual satisfaction, and self-esteem.

WOLFF, NAOMI. *The Beauty Myth.* New York: William Morrow, 1991. A provocative look at the way our society's obsession with female beauty diminishes women's lives.

SENSUALITY

KENNEDY, ADELE P., AND SUSAN DEAN. *Touching for Pleasure: A 12 Step Program for Sexual Enhancement.* Chatsworth, Calif.: Chatsworth Press, 1988. A very practical guidebook to deriving more sensual satisfaction from lovemaking.

LIDELL, L. *The Sensual Body: The Ultimate Guide to Body Awareness and Self-Fulfillment.* New York: Fireside, 1987. A similar book with an emphasis on self-discovery.

PASSION

ANAND, MARGO. *The Art of Sexual Ecstasy: The Path of Sacred Sexuality for Western Lovers.* Los Angeles: Jeremy Tarcher, 1989. This book is a good introduction to the more spiritual, Eastern approach to human sexuality.

SCHNARCH, DAVID M. *Constructing the Sexual Crucible: An Integration of Sexual and Marital Therapy.* New York: W.W. Norton, 1991. This book is written in a rigorous, academic style, but it has valuable insights for those who are up to the challenge.

PRODUCTS AND SOURCES

ASTROGLIDE: Astroglide is a water-based, Ph-adjusted, superslippery personal lubricant, the best of its kind. It is currently available from some Planned Parenthood organizations as well as the following pharmacies: Payless Drugstores, Osco/Sav-On, CVS/People's.

If Astroglide is not available in your area, your pharmacist can order it from a major drug wholesaler. For more information, write BioFilm, Inc., 3121 Scott Street, Vista, CA 92083, or call 800-325-5695. (In California, 800-848-5900.)

BETTER SEX VIDEOS: The Better Sex Videos is a widely advertised series of videotapes on sexual technique and sexual variety that are designed to be both educational and erotic. The following tapes are available:

Volume 1: *Better Sexual Techniques*
Volume 2: *Advanced Sexual Techniques*
Volume 3: *Making Sex Fun*
Volume 4: *Exploring Sexual Fantasies*
Volume 5: *Sharing Sexual Fantasies*
Volume 6: *Acting Out Your Sexual Fantasies*

The videos are $29.95 each plus shipping and handling. Sets are available at a discount. (There is also a condensed version for those who prefer less explicit illustrations.) For more information or to order call: 800-888-1900.

EVE'S GARDEN: Eve's Garden is a retail store and mail-order business located on the fourth floor of a midtown New York City office building (no sleazy storefront). Its goal is to "offer women the space to enjoy, expand and celebrate their own sexuality." One customer referred to it as "the only politically and emotionally correct erotica boutique in New York. And tasteful, too." The store offers erotica, books on intimacy and sexual technique, massage oils, candles, vibrators, finger cots, and other assorted sex toys, all displayed within a wholesome, female-friendly environment. (Men who wish to visit the store must be accompanied by a female companion.)

Address: 119 West 57th Street, Suite 420, New York, NY 10019. You can also write to this address for mail-order catalogs (cost $3). Your confidentiality is assured.

FEMME DISTRIBUTIONS: Producer Candida Royalle has created a line of erotic videos featuring sexual scenes between caring people. Fans call them "spice without raunch." These R-X videos are available in major video outlets and through mail order. Current titles include: *Femme, Christine's Secret, Urban Heat, Three Daughters, A Taste of Ambrosia, Rites of Passion,* and *Sexual Escape.*

For a mail-order catalog or more information write to Femme Distributions, Inc., 588 Broadway, Suite 1110, New York, NY 10012, or call 212-226-9330.

THE HEALTHY SEX NIGHTSHIRT: This is a cotton nightshirt designed by sex therapist Wendy Maltz to reinforce positive attitudes about sex. Multicolored design with thirty-three positive affirmations such as: "Healthy sex is . . . having choice, nurturing, built on trust, playful, loving myself, respectful, being honest, and physically safe." Cost: $22 plus $3 shipping and handling. All orders must be prepaid by check or money order only, no sales tax. Make checks payable to: Maltz and Associates, P.O. Box 648, Eugene, OR 97440 (503-484-4480). Special rates for groups wishing to sell shirts for fund-raising. A portion of all profits is donated to sexual abuse recovery programs.

GOOD VIBRATIONS: Good Vibrations offers sexual products at its retail outlet in San Francisco, California (1210 Valencia Street) or through mail-order catalogs. The people at Good Vibrations foster better communication about sex and offer quality sex toys and erotic and educational books and videos in a clean, wholesome environment. They do not sell, rent, or give your name to any person, business, or organization. All items and literature are shipped in plain brown packaging with "Open Enterprises, Inc." on the return label.

Two catalogs are available. The first, titled "Good Vibrations," describes sexual paraphernalia such as vibrators and dildos as well as safe sex supplies. Price: $4. The second catalog, "The Sexuality Library," describes books and erotic videos. Also $4. (You can order both catalogs for $5.) Send a check or money order to 1210 Valencia Street, San Francisco, CA 94110. You can also order the catalogs with your credit card by calling 415-974-8990.

IT'S MY PLEASURE: It's My Pleasure is a small retail store in Portland, Oregon, which, like Good Vibrations and Eve's Garden, offers a wholesome approach to sexuality and sexual variety. Its range of products includes personal lubricants, educational and erotic books, sex toys, and erotic videos. The owners are helpful, informative women who make you feel comfortable about your sexuality. They will come to your house for a "home show" if you desire. Write: 4526 SE Hawthorne, Portland, OR 97215 (503-236-0505).

THE RUBBER TREE: The Rubber Tree is a nonprofit mail-order source of safe sex products, including a wide variety of condoms, dental dams, lubricants, and spermicides. (Item 12 contains sixty different condoms so you can try a wide variety.) Bulk order discounts. Free catalog available upon request. Write: 4426 Burke Avenue North, Seattle, WA 98103 (206-633-4750).

UNDERCOVER WEAR: For information about attending or hosting a home lingerie party, contact Undercover Wear at their world headquarters. Undercover Wear caters to all tastes from the ultraconservative to the barely there. Write: UnderCover Wear, Inc., 007 Undercover Wear Way, Wilmington, MA 01887 (617-938-0007).

RELATIONSHIP
AND SEX COUNSELING

This book presents a comprehensive program designed to help you and your partner create an intimate, romantic, sexually satisfying love relationship. It should provide all the information and support most couples need. However, those couples with more serious difficulties will benefit from working directly with either a relationship or sex therapist. Here are some indications that you and your partner might need additional *relationship* therapy:

- One of you is compulsive about drugs or alcohol, spending, dieting, eating, exercise, entertainment, gambling, or risk taking.
- You continue to engage in verbal abuse, name-calling, backbiting, yelling, the "silent treatment," sarcasm, and/or frequent criticism.
- You take your anger out on your children.
- One or both of you turn to a child for emotional support, as a confidant, best friend, playmate, sexual partner, or scapegoat for emotional problems.
- A parent or in-law is overly involved in your relationship.
- There is a frequent threat of divorce or separation.
- There is physical abuse or the threat of physical abuse.
- One partner exerts excessive control over the other person's life.
- There is unresolved conflict surrounding an affair.
- You are unable to talk about your unmet needs.
- You argue over and over again with no progress or change.
- There are important subjects you are still unable to discuss.

- You routinely "keep score" and stack up points against each other.

Here are some indications that you may benefit from additional *sex* therapy:

- You have completed the program yet continue to be sexually frustrated.
- There is a wide sexual desire discrepancy with no negotiated settlement in sight.
- You have difficulty maintaining an erection or reaching orgasm.
- You ejaculate much sooner than you would like.
- You have an unresolved history of sex abuse.
- You or your partner has a dislike or aversion to sex.
- You or your partner engage in compulsive sexual activities that bring you embarrassment, shame, or anxiety or make you feel out of control.
- Sex is the only way you communicate love and closeness.
- You use sex to control, punish, or shame each other.
- Sex is the primary way that you deal with emotional pain.

If any of the above descriptions pertain to you, you owe it to yourself to get competent help. The wisest people know when to seek guidance; they practice prevention, not crisis management.

Choosing a therapist may be one of the most important decisions you will ever make, so make your selection carefully. Not all counselors are trained to address relationship or sexual issues, and some that are competent in these areas may not be compatible with you.

One of the best ways to find a counselor is to get a referral from a friend or acquaintance who has had a satisfying relationship with a therapist. Lacking such a referral, ask your family doctor or minister. You can also ask for a referral from a nearby university hospital with a human sexuality program.

If you are looking specifically for a sex therapist, send $4 to the American Association of Sex Educators, Counselors, and Therapists (AASECT) for a list of counselors, psychologists, clinical social workers, and physicians who are certified sex therapists in your area. (AASECT address: 435 North Michigan Avenue, Suite 1717, Chicago, IL 60611-4067 [312-644-0828].)

As a last resort, turn to the phone directory. The yellow pages list therapists under a wide variety of headings, including: Counselors, Psychotherapists, Psychiatrists, Physicians and Surgeons (Psychiatrists), Psychologists, Psychologists' Referral and Information Services, and Mental Health Services.

I recommend that you interview more than one therapist before you begin a course of therapy. Here are some questions you might ask during your initial interview:

Are you licensed?
Do you specialize in relationship or sex therapy?
Do you have an ongoing practice with couples?
What are your fees?
Will my insurance company cover any of my bills?
What professional organization(s) do you belong to?

Note: A counselor/therapist may belong to one or more of the following organizations:

American Counseling Association (ACA)
American Association for Marriage and Family Therapy (AAMFT)
International Association for Marriage and Family Counselors (IAMFC)
National Association of Social Workers (NASW)
American Psychological Association (APA)
American Medical Association (AMA)
American Association of Sex Educators, Counselors, and Trainers (AASECT)

In addition to receiving a satisfactory answer to these questions, trust your own judgment. Both you and your partner should feel comfortable and safe with the therapist and be convinced of his or her professionalism and competence. Fees, insurance, length of vis-

its, and probable duration of treatment all should be discussed on
or before the first appointment.

NATIONAL ORGANIZATIONS

Many of the following national organizations will provide you with
information and referrals to therapists or support groups in your
area:

American Association of Sex Educators and Therapists (AASECT),
435 North Michigan Avenue, Suite 1717, Chicago, IL 60611-4067
(312-644-0828). AASECT is a national certifying organization. It will
provide you with a list of sex therapists in your area.

National AIDS Hotline (800-342-2437). Information, support, and
referrals for testing and treatment.

National Self-Help Clearing House, Graduate School, City University of New York, 33 West 42nd Street, Room 1222, New York, NY
10036 (212-840-1259). This clearinghouse provides listings of a wide
variety of self-help groups throughout the country.

S-Anon, P.O. Box 5117, Sherman Oaks, CA 91413 (818-990-6910).
An organization for those who are involved with sexual addicts.

Sex Addicts Anonymous (SAA), P.O. Box 3038, Minneapolis, MN
55403 (612-339-0217). This national headquarters will provide you
with information on compulsive sexual behavior and a list of self-
help groups in your area.

Sex and Love Addicts Anonymous (SLAA), Augustine Fellowship,
P.O. Box 119, New Town Branch, Boston, MA 02258. Support and
information about self-help groups for people with compulsive sexual problems.

SOURCE NOTES

CHAPTER 1: THE LONGING FOR HOT MONOGAMY

Page 6. I want to credit sex therapist Helen Singer Kaplan for coining the term "Hot Monogamy" to refer to the desire to experience sexual passion in a monogamous, long-term relationship.

Pages 13–14. Dr. Cutler elaborated on the synchronicity between men and women in monogamous relationships in her book *Love Cycles* (New York: Villard, 1991). I recommend this book for anyone wanting to know more about the biochemistry of love relationships.

CHAPTER 3: WHY DON'T WE TALK ABOUT SEX?

Page 40. The study about the greater sexual satisfaction of women who could talk freely about sex was conducted by David J. Hurlbert and published in the *Journal of Sex and Marital Therapy*, 17, 3 (Fall 1991), p. 183.

The *Redbook* magazine study on female sexuality was discussed at length in a book titled *The Redbook Report on Female Sexuality*, written by Carol Tavris and Susan Sadd (New York: Delacorte, 1975).

Page 56. Exercise 2, "Transforming Criticisms into Requests," is based on an exercise that my colleague Harville Hendrix developed to use in his Imago Relationship Therapy.

CHAPTER 4: WHEN I'M HOT AND YOU'RE NOT

Page 67. In a recent survey of 289 sex therapists conducted by Peter Kilmann et al., a difference in desire was judged to be the most common presenting problem. This finding was discussed in an article titled "Perspectives of Sex Therapy Outcome: A Survey of AASECT Providers," which appeared in the *Journal of Sex and Marital Therapy*, 12 (1986), pp. 116–38.

Helen Singer Kaplan was the first to divide a sexual encounter into these three particular stages. She was also one of the first therapists to draw attention to the problems that many people have with desire. Her book *Disorders of Sexual Desire and Other New Concepts and Techniques in Sex Therapy* (New York: Brunner/Mazel, 1979) is considered an essential text for sex therapists.

Page 69. For an interesting academic study on whether the higher level of male desire is caused by hormones or social conditioning, see Russel Knoth, Kelly Boyd, and Barry Singer, "Empirical Tests of Sexual Selection Theory: Predictions of Sex Differences in Onset, Intensity, and Time Course of Sexual Arousal," *Journal of Sex Research*, 24 (1988), pp. 73–89.

This comment by Helen Singer Kaplan on the greater strength of the male sex drive appeared in an article titled "Sex on the Brain," written by Michael Hutchison and published in *Playboy* magazine (April 1990).

Page 72. The study by Knoth, Boyd, and Singer above determined that the modal boy in their study experienced sexual arousal several times a day. The modal teen girl was aroused only once or twice a week. Furthermore, twice as many boys as girls reported a very intense level of sexual arousal.

The normal range of testosterone for men is between 300 and 1,200 nanograms per deciliter of blood. The range for women is between 20 and 120. For a comprehensive overview of the role that androgens play in male and female sexual behavior, see Barbara Sherwin's article "A Comparative Analysis of the Role of Androgen in Human Male and Female Sexual Behavior: Behavioral Specificity, Critical Thresholds, and Sensitivity," *Psychobiology*, 16 (1988), pp. 416–25. Sherwin points out that women appear to react more strongly to testosterone than men. Thus, the fact that men have from ten to twenty times more androgen than women does not mean that they are ten to twenty times more desirous of sex. From various research I would give a rough estimate that the typical man experiences sexual desire from two to three times as often as a typical woman. Furthermore, his desire appears to be more intense. Nevertheless, there are those exceptions to the rule in which the woman is more desirous of sex than the man.

Barbara Sherwin's classic study of testosterone and sexual desire in women was presented in an article titled "The Role of Androgen in the Maintenance of Sexual Functioning in Oophorectomized Women," which appeared in the journal *Psychosomatic Medicine*, 49 (1987), pp. 397–409. The graphs on page 74 appeared in that article as well.

Page 73. The reaction the women had to the testosterone study was also reported by Winifred Gallagher in an excellent article titled "Sex and Hormones," *Atlantic Monthly* (March 1988), pp. 77–82. I first got interested in the role of testosterone in female sexual desire by reading this.

Patricia Schreiner-Engel's study was reported in the article "Sexual Arousability and the Menstrual Cycle," *Psychosomatic Medicine*, 43 (1981), pp. 199–212. Schreiner-Engel's comments are from the *Atlantic Monthly* article just mentioned.

Page 76. The study about the lower level of sexual desire of women in their menopausal years, conducted by N. L. McCoy and J. M. Davidson, is titled "A Longitudinal Study of the Effects of Menopause on Sexuality." It appeared in the journal *Maturitas*, 7 (1985), pp. 203–10. Another related study contrasted the sexual behavior of two groups of women. The average age in the first group was twenty-four. The average age in the second group was fifty-four. The androgen levels in the women in the first group were "very much higher." The younger women also experienced "significantly higher levels of sexual gratification." This study, conducted by Harold Persky et al., is "The Relation of Plasma Androgen Levels to Sexual Behaviors and Attitudes of Women," *Psychosomatic Medicine*, 44 (1982), pp. 305–19.

Page 77. The study about the relationship between testosterone levels and male sexuality was conducted by P. D. Tsitouras et al. See "Testosterone, HL, FSH, Prolactin and Sperm in Healthy Aging Men," *Abstracts, 7th International Congress on Endocrinology* (1951). Refer to Winnifred Cutler's book *Love Cycles* for a more detailed look at the cycles of a man's desire.

Page 78. The amount of testosterone being administered in Barbara Sherwin's study was 1 ml of an estrogen-androgen preparation in a monthly injection. One milliliter of this drug contained 150 mg T enanthate, 7.5 mg E_2 dienanthate, and 1 mg E_2 benzoate. The injection increased the women's plasma T levels to between 1.2–2.5 ng/l during the first three weeks; this exceeds the normal female range. In later studies Sherwin occasionally cut this dosage in half.

Page 79. Dr. T. Taylor Segraves made this remark at the Menninger Sexual Desire Disorders Conference, October 24–26, 1991. For a copy of the complete set of tapes from this conference, you can call the Division of Continuing Education at 1-800-288-7377.

Page 91. The list of ten indicators of sexual addiction is from Patrick Carnes' book, *Don't Call It Love: Recovering from Sexual Addiction* (New York: Bantam, 1991).

Page 92. You will find Wendy Maltz's list of top ten symptoms of sexual abuse on page 3 of her book *The Sexual Healing Journey: A Guide for Survivors of Sexual Abuse* (New York: HarperPerennial, 1992). A longer "Sexual Effects Inventory" appears on pages 62–69.

CHAPTER 5: INTIMACY

Page 96. For a fascinating discussion of the difference in communication styles between men and women, I recommend that you read Deborah Tannen's book *You Just Don't Understand* (New York: William Morrow, 1991).

CHAPTER 6: SEXUAL TECHNIQUE

Page 123. The survey of forty thousand women was conducted by *Ladies' Home Journal*. The results were reported in the article "The Love Life of the American Wife," which appeared in February 1993, p. 128.

William Acton made this pronouncement about the asexual nature of women in his book *The Functions and Disorders of the Reproductive Organs*, the third American edition of which appeared in 1871.

Page 124. The marriage manual written by Dr. Joseph H. Greer is titled *The Great Book of Life*. It was published in 1931 by the Stein Company.

Page 127. For more information about Sylvester Graham and his health crusade and the restriction of male and female sexuality, refer to John S. Haller and Robin M. Haller, *The Physician and Sexuality in Victorian America* (New York: W.W. Norton, 1977). The letter to the physician from the young man suffering from "spermatorrhoea" appears in this book on page 221.

Page 129. For a detailed look at why assertive women experience greater sexual satisfaction, see David Farley Hurlbert, "The Role of Assertiveness in Female Sexuality: A Comparative Study Between Sexually Assertive and Sexually Nonassertive Women," *Journal of Sex & Marital Therapy*, 17 (1991), pp. 183–90.

The study that concluded that anorgasmic women have more difficulty asking their partners for the kind of stimulation they require to reach orgasm is titled "Attitudinal and Experiential Correlates of Anorgasmia." It was written by Mary Pat Kelly et al. and appeared in the *Archives of Sexual Behavior*, 19 (1990), pp. 165–81.

CHAPTER 7: VARIETY

Page 148. The study on the erotic effects of new sexual techniques in sexually explicit movies is titled "Repeated Exposure to Sexually Explicit Stimuli: Novelty, Sex, and Sexual Attitudes." Written by Kathryn Kelley and Donna Musialowski, it appeared in the *Archives of Sexual Behavior*, 15 (1986), pp. 487–97.

Page 154. More detailed instructions for creating an extended sexual orgasm can be found in the book *ESO: Extended Sexual Orgasm*, by Alan Brauer, M.D., and Donna Brauer (New York: Warner, 1983).

Page 157. The survey on men's preference for fellatio is mentioned in Susan Crain Bakos, *Dear Superlady of Sex* (New York: St. Martin's, 1990), p. 107.

Page 158. Madelyn Renee Messe and James H. Greer studied the hypothesis that Kegel's exercise intensified sexual arousal in their article "Voluntary Vaginal Musculature Contractions as an Enhancer of Sexual Arousal," *Archives of Sexual Behavior*, 14 (1985), pp. 13–27.

Page 160. The fact that a majority of men are interested in sexy lingerie also appeared in Bakos's *Dear Superlady of Sex*, p. 221.

Page 162. The statistics on romance novels come from an article titled "I'm Hungry. But Not for Food," which appeared in the July 6, 1992, edition of *Forbes* magazine, pp. 70–74.

For more information about the kind of women who read romance novels, see Claire Coles and M. Johanna Shamp, "Some Sexual, Personality, and Demographic Characteristics of Women Readers of Erotic Romances," *Archives of Sexual Behavior*, 13 (1984), pp. 187–209.

Page 163. The survey documenting the growing use of sex aids by women is in the February 1993 issue of *Ladies' Home Journal*.

For a thorough discussion of the use of vibrators, see Joani Blank, *Good Vibrations* (San Francisco: Down There Press, 1989). To order, see Appendix B.

Page 166. Hillel Rubinsky et al. described the similarity between male and female response to visual erotica in their study "Early-Phase Physiological Response Patterns to Psychosexual Stimuli: Comparison of Male and Female Patterns," *Archives of Sexual Behavior*, 16 (1987), pp. 45–56.

CHAPTER 8: CREATING LIFELONG ROMANCE

Page 176. The interest that many women have in romance was revealed in the study "Female Sexual Response and Timing of Partner Orgasm," written by Carol Anderson Darling, J. Kenneth Davidson, and Ruth P. Cox. It appeared in the *Journal of Sex and Marital Therapy*, 17 (1991), pp. 3–20.

Page 184. The study about the relationship between anxiety and passion was described by Elaine Hatfield and Richard L. Rapson, "Passionate Love/Sexual Desire: Can the Same Paradigm Explain Both?," *Archives of Sexual Behavior*, 16 (1987), pp. 259–79. (The quotation on this page is from this article.)

Page 186. Robin Monique conducted the study on how often women touch their baby girls and boys. Her research article is titled "Neonate-Mother Interaction—Tactile Contacts in the Days Following Birth," *Early Child Development and Care*, 9 (1982), pp. 221–36.

CHAPTER 9: SEX AND BODY IMAGE

Page 212. More than thirty thousand people responded to the *Psychology Today* survey on body image, which appeared in September 1986.

Page 214. The quotations from Kathleen E. Woodiwiss's novel *Shanna* appear on pages 20 and 41 (New York: Avon, 1977).

The description of Janet Dailey's ageless heroine appears in *The Glory Game* (New York: Pocket Books, 1989), p. 4.

Page 218. The relationship between body image and sexual functioning was studied in the research article "Body Image for Women: Conceptualization, Assessment, and a Test of Its Importance to Sexual Dysfunction and Mental Illness," by Barbara Anderson and Joseph LeGrand in the *Journal of Sex Research*, 28 (1991), pp. 457–77.

Page 219. These references to mythical male penises are from Zilbergeld's book *The New Male Sexuality* (New York: Bantam, 1992), p. 50.

Page 226. The article by Terri Sutton appeared in *City Pages* on February 19, 1992.

CHAPTER 10: BECOMING A MORE SENSUOUS LOVER

Page 239. Helen Fisher goes into detail about the role that our senses play in our sexuality in her delightful book *The Anatomy of Love* (New York: W.W. Norton, 1992). For quote, see p. 42.

Page 248. The way people respond to sexual fantasies was studied by S. Cado and H. Leitenberg in their research article "Guilt Reactions to Sexual Fantasies During Intercourse," *Archives of Sexual Behavior*, 19 (1990), p. 49.

INDEX